FIRST EDITION

Teaching Literacy
in Early and Middle Childhood

Dr. Karen Loman, Dr. Angela Danley, and Dr. Natalie Tye
UNIVERSITY OF CENTRAL MISSOURI

cognella® ACADEMIC PUBLISHING

Bassim Hamadeh, CEO and Publisher
Kassie Graves, Director of Acquisitions
Jamie Giganti, Senior Managing Editor
Jess Estrella, Graphic Designer
Annie Petersen, Specialist Acquisitions Editor
Gem Rabanera, Project Editor
Elizabeth Rowe, Licensing Coordinator
Allie Kiekhofer, Associate Editor
Rachel Singer, Interior Designer

Cover image copyright © Depositphotos/alenkasm

Printed in the United States of America

ISBN: 978-1-5165-0166-3 (pbk) / 978-1-5165-0167-0 (br)

Contents

CH. 6: Vocabulary   182

CH. 7: Writing 212

Introduction

Over the years the three of us have read many wonderful books on teaching literacy. We are always excited to share them with our students and colleagues. When the opportunity to write our own book became available, we decided to focus on instructional strategies that support literacy in early and middle childhood. Our intent with this endeavor is to support and enhance the wonderful resources available and provide teachers and teacher candidates with strategies and activities they can implement with their own students. The articles selected as part of this anthology focus on specific instructional strategies for the components of literacy.

Each of the chapters included strive to provide deeper understanding into specific literacy content. Readers will find the layout to be similar in each chapter, beginning with a short introduction, followed by learning activities for the reader designed to assist with content comprehension. Follow the suggested before, during, and after reading activities for a complete immersion into the text. These will guide you through the content and allow for greater understanding and application of content.

We are excited to share the strategies and content knowledge in this book with teachers and teacher candidates. This text provides a unique combination of learning activities for educators with practical and theoretically sound instructional strategies focused on literacy. Enjoy the learning experience!

Chapter One

Introduction by Natalie Tye

INTRODUCTION TO READING 1.1:

PRINT CONCEPTS

☐ *READING 1.1*
**FUNCTION BEFORE FORM: BUILDING CONCEPTS
ABOUT PRINT**
By Mary Shea

Concepts About Print

INTRODUCTION TO READING 1.1
Print Concepts

Early reading and writing begin with the introduction of print and modeled reading from adults (Morrow, 1999). Further, print-rich environments foster early literacy development in children through authentic experiences. The introduction and understanding of early reading and writing cannot solely be through the teacher or from the environment. In order to foster a desire to read and write, teachers must immerse reading and writing strategies in the classroom and through the curriculum (McKie, Butty, & Green, 2011).

Teachers entice children with a love for reading through read-alouds, finger plays, and rhymes, to name a few. By the same token, teachers encourage early writing by modeling writing in the classroom (McKie, Butty, & Green, 2011). Examples include writing during calendar time, class topic brainstorm sessions, morning messages and providing sentence starters to complete together in class.

Regardless of what activities are implemented to encourage early literacy development, there are three key strategies for creating a classroom of confident early readers and writers: variety, confidence, and authentic experiences. This chapter highlights the importance of these three strategies through a learning progression for young children in the classroom.

Variety. I know what you are thinking—variety in what? The answer to this question is variety in everything related to print. The classroom teacher needs to consider that children are not the same and are not intrigued by the same experiences or materials. In order to stimulate an interest in reading, provide variety in book types (McKie, Butty, & Green, 2011; Morrow, 1999; Strickland & Abbott, 2010). There should be big books, small books, short books, thick books, picture books, books with text, board books, and those with paper pages. There should be fiction and non-fiction; fantasy and fact; books about dinosaurs, families, pets, and more. The classroom teacher also encourages writing through a variety of materials in the classroom. Children love to draw and practice writing using a variety of media. Classrooms encouraging early writing provide crayons, colored pencils, markers, glitter pens, pencils, chalk, dry erase markers, highlighters, and charcoal, to name a few. Variety in print allows a teacher to draw children's attention to the task of reading and writing through exciting opportunities.

Confidence. Confidence is easy, right? Children need confidence to learn how to read and write. But how does this happen? Confidence begins with an adult acknowledging the attempt of reading or writing. *Good job* and *that's great* are not enough to instill confidence in young hesitant children. Teachers rely on encouraging words to show children support in the learning process. Such words as *I know you can do it* and *I see how hard you worked to write your name* acknowledge a belief in the child's ability to learn and be successful.

Authentic practice. What could this possibly mean? Children need to see and practice print through experiences that are real and relevant to their life and world (McKie, Butty, & Green, 2011; Morrow, 1999). Classrooms with environmental print on building blocks, menus, coupons, newspapers in dramatic play, and sheet music with words to favorite songs in music provide children opportunities to experience reading and writing through authentic practice.

BEFORE READING

What do you see? Before reading the following article, reflect on the environment around you. Just stop and look around. Take a mental note of what you see with print. When you look around, are you surrounded by print? Now, think about a classroom. You can imagine a university classroom, a classroom you were in as a child, or a classroom you are in now. Write down all the ways print is modeled and experienced in the classroom.

DURING READING

Keep your classroom in mind and begin transferring your experiences to those of young learners. As you read the chapter, consider what makes a print-rich environment. What motivates the children to learn?

AFTER READING

Go back to your list from before the reading. Is there meaning in the print you saw in your environment? Reflecting back on that list, how can you add print to your classroom for the purpose of motivating others to learn? On the back of your paper, create a chart with three columns. Put each of the key strategies mentioned at the beginning of the chapter in a separate column. Now, generate a list under each column of ideas to encourage early reading and writing in the classroom.

Function Before Form
Building Concepts About Print

BY MARY SHEA

Research in Emergent Literacy

A body of research from close to 50 years of studies reveals how literacy develops, the factors that motivate children's explorations with language, and the concepts children have constructed about language and print. Many researchers conclude that preschool experiences play a significant role in children's literacy development (Durkin, 1966; Heath, 1983; Holdaway, 1979; Martens, 1998; McNaughton, Parr, & Smith, 1996; Morrow, 1983; Neuman, 1997; Paratore, 2003; Schickedanz, 1990; Schulze, 2006; Smith & Elley, 1997a; Soderman & Farrell, 2007; Taylor, 1983; Taylor & Dorsey-Gaines, 1988; Teale, 1982, 1984; Weinberger, 1998). As previously mentioned, Durkin's (1966) seminal research on children who came to school reading, or learned to read with ease, set the stage for research in emergent literacy (IRA, 1998).

DURKIN'S STUDY AND FINDINGS

Durkin's (1966) study identified several common factors in early readers. Notably, IQ or socioeconomic statuses (SESs) (i.e. professional, working class) were not among them.

Early readers
- were highly *motivated* to engage in literate activities. This motivation wasn't innate; it germinated during positive, supported, and engaging literacy experiences;

- were broadly exposed to print and print forms, including an array of real world genres from books to newspapers, magazines, and environmental print;
- had engaged in meaningful interactions with others focused on print;
- had witnessed numerous demonstrations of purpose-driven literate activities;
- had their queries about print and how it works answered with enough, but not too much, information;
- had opportunities to create print messages; they were writers.

Writing was a gateway into reading for these children. In the process of encoding their own messages, they learned how print works. Durkin's (1966) findings outlined the stages of young children's evolution as writers. Other research supports her findings, concluding that concepts about print develop in stages as a result of children's supported exploration in writing and reading (Cecil, 2007; Clay, 1993; McGill-Franzen, 2006; Schulze, 2006; Sulzby, 1990; Vukelich, Christie, & Enz, 2002). Stages offer a lens through which to understand children's writing rather than rigid benchmarks for measuring achievement. Children's work often reflects elements of multiple stage levels.

DURKIN'S STAGES OF EARLY WRITING DEVELOPMENT

Durkin's (1966) research concluded that young writers progressed through developmental stages that could be broadly described. Children moved through them at their own pace and in their own way.

Stage 1—Drawing and Scribbling

Children draw and scribble. Sometimes they do one or the other; sometimes they use both forms to create messages. Iredell (1898) stated, "scribbling is to writing what [as] babbling is to talking." Platt (1977) reiterated the analogy, explaining that controlled scribbling initiates the representational use of print for ideas.

The next two stages are very closely related. They can be considered separately or combined as a beginning and later phase of the same stage when tracking children's progress.

Stage 2—Letter-like Forms

Children begin to create letter-like forms. These include all kinds of distinct shapes, lines, and angles. The child has learned that message making with print is different from drawing and scribbling; it has distinct and repeated marks with lines and curves that form letters and words (Kempton, 2007; Meek, 1991).

FIGURE 1-1. Madison Draws and Writes.

Stage 3—Copying Objects and Letters

Children copy print found in the environment; they use letters they've learned to form when constructing messages.

Stage 4—Asking Questions About Spelling

Children continue to use logic and experiences to compose messages, but they're beginning to recognize constancy in print representations. When that understanding causes dissonance, they seek help for particular forms. Durkin (1966) suggested that in *ask the expert* stage, children might query, How do you make ... (meaning spell)?

FIGURE 1-2. Emily Draws and Writes Hearts.

FIGURE 1-3. Skylar Copies from Book.

Children's efforts to write at this stage reflect growing appreciation for conventional print forms, but their message making remains genuinely self-directed. Meek (1991) states "in the case of writing, composing [constructing personal messages] counts for more than copying."

Stage 5—Reading One's Writing

Children read their own messages and gradually the messages written by other authors. Their reading informs their writing; continued writing stimulates growth in reading.

Durkin's (1966) findings have been thoroughly examined over time. After reviewing several studies replicating her seminal work, Anderson, Hiebert, Scott, and Wilkinson (1984) confirmed Durkin's findings. Their conclusions were reported in *Becoming a Nation of Readers*. More recently, Dickenson and Tabors (2001) identified multiple correlations between early literacy opportunities at home and children's success in kindergarten.

Yet, too often, these findings from research are not the driving force in early childhood classrooms. The full body of research referenced throughout this text—which includes both quantitative and qualitative studies on young children's emergence into literacy—provides evidence of a significant positive effect for young children's engagement in authentic literacy activities. The study described next demonstrates young children's early concept building— constructions made from the fabric of experiences and observations in their family life and community.

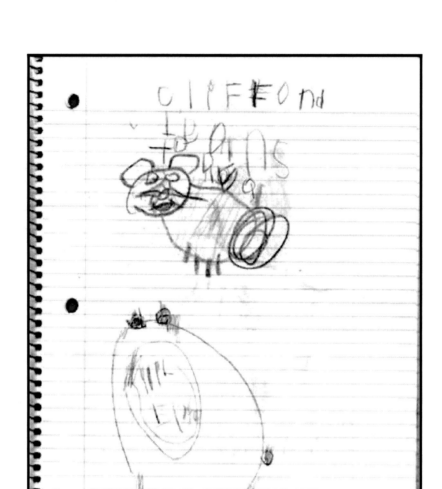

FIGURE 1-4. Emma Writes About Clifford and Mouse.

A Study of Preschool Children's Concepts About Print

In a research project focused on pre-kindergartners' concepts about print, four- and five-year-olds engaged in a series of literacy related tasks (Shea, 1992). Children observed and participated in tasks involving reading and writing behaviors.

THE STUDY

The sample included pre-K classes at schools representing diverse populations. The study was designed to reveal pre-school children's working hypotheses about written language, to identify universal patterns across their theories, and to examine the results obtained against findings from other research. Children's responses on a series of tasks demonstrate the concepts they hold about reading and writing. Data from the study reveal that all children construct an intricate web of theories about print as they go about the business of life in the company and care of adults who respect, accept, and support their approximations as novices. For example, they learn that:

- writing is different from drawing;
- writing stands for ideas and messages—writing can be read;
- print is mapped onto the page from left to right with a return sweep;
- written words are constructed with letters;
- there's a limited set of letters to use for writing;
- words have a variety of letters—a string of the same letter isn't a word;
- words have different sequences of letters (generative principle).

Data from this study also reinforce findings from the body of research on emergent literacy. Literacy learning, like other learning, is a social event. Children respond to "an explosive force from within ... to express themselves" (Goodman, Smith, Meredith, & Goodman, 1987). They "do not wait for formal instruction before they read and write" (Whitmore et al., 2005). Children jump right in, explore, and use print. Demonstrations and invitations to participate in daily literacy occasions (e.g. writing grocery lists, reading coupons) provide opportunities for explaining how and why tasks are done. Frequently interjected, "I know you can do this" statements from adults build children's confidence and persistence with literate activities (Shea, 1992).

Two separate tasks in the study clearly demonstrate children's concept-building in reading and writing. The nature of communication throughout the researcher–subject interactions in the study led to unexpected findings, which validate the power of high expectations and positive affirmation for increasing children's confidence and motivation to engage in literate activities.

READING TASK

This task reveals what children know about reading. Children were asked to identify and *read* photographs with environmental print; each enlarged photograph had additional contextual surroundings.

They were asked, "Is there something to read in this picture?" and "Can you point to where it is?" Then, they were asked what it said. If a child responded, "I don't know; I can't read yet" it was suggested that he pretend to be Mommy or Daddy. What would that person say if asked to read it? Without fail, gentle coaching for pretend reading allowed the few hesitant ones to respond with what they imagined the adult would say. Sometimes, it took a pregnant

FIGURE 1-5. No Parking.

pause of silence followed by a smile of encouragement before a slow start with "Hmmmm ... " produced a response similar to ones that follow. Patience and complimentary nudges from the adult were always rewarded with an answer, even though some responses were more logical than others as predictions.

When asked how they (or Mommy or Daddy when they were reading) knew what it said, children's answers reflected the use of *historical context* (Shea, 1992) in some cases. They connected objects in the picture with familiar ones and events. An example of historical context is: "It says *Don't Park Here* because I saw that sign at my Grandma's house." Children also used *immediate context* to assign meaning to print or situations in the photograph.

An example of immediate context: "It says *Broken Road Be Careful Where You Go You May Fall In* because the road is broken right there [in the picture]."

FIGURE 1-6. Bridge Closed.

Although not conventionally correct, these children systematically used contextual clues to read embedded print messages. They demonstrated awareness of print around them and an assumption that meaning is associated with the situation in which print is found.

WRITING TASK

Children reveal their knowledge about the functions and forms of writing in this task. When asked to write, a few children played it safe; they'd fill the paper with huge letters, spelling their name or writing it repeatedly.

These children would typically say, "I don't know how to write; I'll learn that when I go to school." Sadly, they had fully internalized an idea, probably transmitted in their environment by well-meaning adults; writing must be correct and the mechanics would be introduced formally in school. Concern about correctness becomes a gatekeeper to early exploration with print—experimentation that builds interest, motivation, concepts, and confidence as a language user. Any loss of opportunity to play with language is regrettable.

Similarly, Heath (1983) found that Roadville (a white working-class textile mill community in the Piedmont Carolinas) mothers typically allowed children to use pencils and crayons under supervision; they didn't encourage scribbling. Roadville children were encouraged to

Example 15

FIGURE 1–7. Filling the Page.

follow a system when coloring or labeling—with the same expectations of correctness and neatness they'd meet when filling in workbooks in school.

Contrary to rigid "up tight, gotta be right" behaviors, other children— the literacy explorers in the study—responded differently. Identified across cultural and SES groups, these adventurers had been allowed to experiment with reading and writing in their own way; they showed no trepidation.

Literacy explorers dove into the materials available (including colorful smelly markers), creating drawings and print messages. The literacy explorers composed; their writing was a communication. Ray and Glover (2008) discuss children's composing as a process of creating—representing *their* feelings, thoughts, or ideas. Composing can be done in different sign systems (i.e. written language, art, music, dance); it's a matter of choice—and talents. People compose when they encode (represent thinking and feeling) in art, music, dance, or in print. Young children compose in all of these sign systems too. Supporting composition developmentally—across sign systems—expands several horizons.

When children have access to an array of attractive supplies, they explore and experiment playfully with each (Coles & Goodman, 1980; Klenk, 2001). If children said they didn't know what they had written when asked to read it, a suggestion to describe what they were thinking about while writing was offered. The adult responded to the child's description with, "Well, I'd guess it says what you just told me." Children usually agreed with this logic.

The concept conveyed was that writing represents ideas; what you think can be spoken, what you say can be written down with marks and what you write can be read. The children's writing also represented a wide variety of forms from scribble to initial letters and some correctly spelled personally important words (such as Mom, Dad, names, love).

Sometimes, there was ambivalence about the difference between drawing and writing, but this was expected. Young children typically move freely from one expressive process to the other (Mayer, 2007). The children would frequently say, "I'm writing a house. I'm writing the flowers" when they were actually drawing a house with flowers.

But, drawing was often the path into marking. Eventually, the child added marks and expressed what his *writing* said. Messages were often a compilation of ideographic (picture writing) and graphic (scribble, marks, letter-like forms, and letters) symbols (Temple, Nathan, Temple, & Burris, 1993). Graves (1994) defines writing as a process of composing that connects covert ideas with the marks, letters, and/or words used to make them readable.

Some children worked with intentionality, knowing from the beginning what they wanted to say; they harnessed the power of the print, making it work for them. Others began making marks and decided what the writing said as they wrote or when they were *reading* it. But, whenever children used marks to communicate, it was acknowledged as writing (Calkins, 1994; Graves, 1994; Harste, Burke, & Woodward, 1983; Schulze, 2006). Children's efforts were encouraged; their compositions received praise. Remarks of encouragement and affirmation were spontaneous—unplanned and unscripted; the outcomes attributed to them were unexpected.

UNEXPECTED FINDINGS: THE POWER OF EXPECTATION AND POSITIVE AFFIRMATION

A strong expectation for success was communicated to children when introducing each task in the preschool study. It began with, "I know you're going to like this activity. I can tell that you're clever." The intention was simply to establish rapport and support risk-taking by making it clear that the request was based on a belief that they would like to read or write and *could do it.*

For example, in the writing task, children were invited to create a personal message using their own version of *kid writing.* They could be in charge of how the writing would go, but they would need to read it back when they finished. The request was, "Since I'm used to grown-up writing, I might get stuck on some of the words in kid writing. I'll need your help to read it." Cambourne (1988) states that expectation is the most critical condition for learning; the other conditions are moot without first communicating a vision of the child as a natural born learner. The young writers and readers who *gave it a go* had learned (directly or indirectly) that they are capable; they were willing to explore and expand their thinking. Parents and family members had nurtured their interest and efforts, inviting them to join the literacy club (Smith, 1988). Once children are empowered with a *can do* attitude, amazing things happened.

Several parents of children at one of the sites attended a session where the study was described. Before the meeting, a parent whose daughter had been involved in the study had a story to share. She explained that her daughter had not shown the same interest in literacy activities that an older brother had demonstrated when he was the same age. This had caused the parent some concern until a recent episode occurred. It seems that she and the child were driving in the car when an 18-wheeler passed them. The child calmly proclaimed, "Mommy, I know what it says on that truck." Assuming that this was impossible since there were no pictures accompanying the print, but wishing to encourage interest in reading, the mother asked the child what it said. The child responded confidently, "It says 'mushrooms', Mommy." Indeed, the word "mushrooms" was boldly printed on the truck along with other smaller print. The mother said she almost drove off the road in her astonishment. Upon collecting her composure, she asked, "How did you know?" The child nonchalantly replied, "Because Mrs. Shea said I'm a clever girl" (Shea, 1997).

We can't know with certainty how this child learned the word "mushrooms", but her attribution for knowing the word is important. Simple words expressing genuine expectations of capability are powerful and have far-reaching effects. Confidence to inquire and experiment lays the foundation for learning. When a child believes she can make sense of print, she is motivated to notice it. Perhaps this child queried options on a pizza menu to be sure mushrooms were either included or excluded as an ingredient. With that examination, she may have learned the word. Although not verified, one can reasonably suggest that self-confidence sparked the attention that led to word recognition.

It's during the process of attending to and mucking around with print that essential conceptual understandings are constructed. Sinclair (1989 in Ferreiro & Teberosky) points out that

> skills are quite secondary when it comes to understanding the nature and function of writing [and] ... learning to read and write cannot be reduced to a set of perceptual-motor skills, or to willingness or motivation, but must grow from a deeper layer of conceptual development.

In supportive environments, young children build deep layers of understanding about literacy. Knowing what works in these settings can inform curricular mapping for literacy instruction in early childhood classrooms, transforming practice and reducing the achievement gap (Taylor, 1993). The key is to provide ample time, lots of choice, and an environment that supports learning exploration. These ingredients nurture language seeds within the child.

Children Experiment With the Functions and Forms of Print

Young children in any culture and community are surrounded with print and significant others using it in all kinds of ways; they are naturally curious about everything they observe. This leads them to explore the *functions* (uses) that they notice print serving. Young children label, list, make notes, and write stories with a focus on using print. Attention to its *forms* (e.g. letters and other conventions) is secondary, growing from experimentation as young writers attempt to refine their constructions (Owocki, 1999).

Newkirk (1989) suggests that list writing is the first sign of exposition when it is used to document what is known. Such play with the functions of print draws children's attention to conventions, including how print is placed on the page, letter-sound relationships, spelling, and other conventions (Owocki, 1999; Whitmore et al., 2005).

This playful writing is the child's work; it's focused, consuming, and joyful. "Nobody needs to teach a child to play, but good teachers move play into new areas of learning ... and relinquish control" (Kempton, 2007, p. 63). In their literacy play, children mimic how significant others in their world act, self-directing literacy learning. Vygotsky (1978) noted that in "play

FIGURE 1-8. Emma's Santa Letter.

a child always behaves beyond his average age, above his daily behavior" (p. 102). Children's play as learning and learning through play is socially, emotionally, and cognitively fulfilling.

Young children typically scribble aesthetically when first presented with a marking tool. When they realize that others perceive a communicative intent in their playful marking, children begin to report messages for displays of marks (Goodman, 1989). They also become more aware of environmental and other print around them; they ask questions about it. Soon previously discussed stages (Durkin, 1966) can be identified in the child's progressive forays into composing.

These children are theory builders, following the logic of their observations, experimentation, and feedback from others (Gentry, 2005). "Children do not follow a learning path that goes from 'true position' to another, more advanced 'true position' ... [They] hold false theories as a necessary part of the process of learning to think" (Papert, 1980). This method is not deficient; it's one that allows children to flex cognitive muscles as they process experiential input on their way to conventional knowledge. But, too often, "our educational system rejects the 'false theories' of children, thereby rejecting the way children really learn." Young children learn most effectively when the environment complements natural learning paths—when they lead, but have the security of a sensitive guide at their side.

From Experimenting to Concept Building

Sometimes, there are false starts in children's concept building; their ideas about print can be a bit off target—even amusing—but the logic behind them is often quite sophisticated (Ferreiro & Teberosky, 1989; Goodman, 1996; Harste et al., 1984; McGee & Richgels, 1996; Owocki, 1999; Taylor, 1983). For example, Kristina's spelling reflects an ability to thoughtfully separate and represent sounds even though the results are not in standard form.

When blinded by a sense of *gotta be right* (conventional), it's easy to miss the significance of young children's early writing and dismiss it as inconsequential play. Mayer (2007) concludes that emergent writing (writing that intends to communicate) begins when children are around three to five years old. The preschool and primary grade years lay the foundation for refined aspects of writing expected in later years. The young child who has had opportunities for joyful concept building about print has a huge head start in knowledge, attitude, and interest; he's predisposed for success with formal literacy instruction.

Bissex (1980) clearly shows an accelerated learning curve in the documentation of her son Paul's writing development—knowledge that benefits early reading. "Learning to write at the same time as one learns to read adds much to the knowledge one needs to become a fluent reader" (Smith & Elley, 1997a). Clay (1991) points out that the writing-child must break down ideas into their smallest parts (sounds and letters) and then synthesize these into words and sentences; gradually, the child writer begins to match symbols with sounds. When complete, the child reads the construction to confirm his meaning was represented. Clay (2001b) suggested that the classroom that "emphasizes early creative writing and succeeds will [also] produce ... good readers." The pattern of this growth becomes evident when observing children's writing over time and across purposes that are playful, authentic, gently supported, and highly self-directed.

FIGURE 1–9. Kristina's Thank-you.

ENGAGING ON THEIR OWN TERMS

Children intently observe the actions of significant others in their environment; they act scientifically. They're trying to make sense of the world they live in and become part of it. Children mimic and try on the behav-iors they notice. We see this in their fantasy play with dolls or trucks; likewise, we see it with their drawing, marking, and writing. Children want to write when the conditions are right (Turbill, 1983). "Wanting to write motivates children to learn how print works. Learning to write often precedes learning to read" (McGill-Franzen, 2006).

In their writing as play, children organize their responses and the way they behave according to the pretend situations they've constructed; they're in control. But, beyond the immediate activity, abstract thinking and metacognition are evolving (Dyson, 2003; Owocki, 1999; Whitmore et al., 2005). Most children—in a risk-free, supportive environment—take to writing like ducklings to water. Just drop them in, encourage and model, and away they go—competent and proud!

FROM JOURNALING TO JOURNALISM

Rachel spent two years in preschool because she just missed the cut-off date for beginning kindergarten in the local school district. The preschool she attended has writing time every day—with both the three-year-old and four-year-old class. Paper used for writing has the alphabet—with upper and lower case letters—written across the top of the page. There's a space for drawing and the area for writing is delineated with bars and lines. Rachel writes on the line rather than using it to determine a height for lower case letters. In Figure 1-10 Rachel explains what she has represented in the picture. "Mom AnD DAD AnD I Ane KechinG BuDerflis" (Mom and Dad and I are catching butterflies). Rachel draws less in Figure 1-11, but documents something she's just learned in different lessons; the form is exposition. She proudly states what she knows about the heart. Newkirk (1989) argues that "as long as chil-dren have access to a variety of non-narrative forms, they will adopt them."

NOVICE NOVELIST

After numerous explorations into composing using kid writing, Mathew decided he wanted to write a book. On his own, Matthew (five years old) authors and illustrates a Pooh adventure (this can be found on the companion website). Pooh and his friends go to a local ice cream shop after getting together to play. Matthew follows story format, beginning "One day, Pooh was walking to his house." He introduces the setting (time and place) and main character, continues with events ("then ... "), and concludes with a simple resolution ("So they went to Anderson's to get ice cream."). His spelling reveals an ability to hear and record sounds with letters and use a repertoire of automatic writing words (known spellings). Both skills grow with this kind of meaningful practice.

In their uses of literacy, these children controlled the situations; they made decisions, experimented, and assessed the outcomes. Their early literacy experiences were risk-free, enjoyable, and personally meaningful, causing them to consistently engage and learn. It was just play in their minds—play with enormous potential for learning literacy.

FIGURE 1-10. Catching Butterflies.

FIGURE 1-11. Heart.

PLAY WITH A CONSEQUENCE

The children described are building a conceptual framework of literacy knowledge—the big picture or *macro* knowledge. Cole (2004) explains that the macro is "the substance from which global understandings are constructed." Rachel and Matthew understand how print fits into their world and needs; they show interest in using it for personal reasons. When these children are exposed to formal instruction and the micro skills—whatever the program or methodology—they're able to tune into the teacher's frequency. They assimilate and accommodate the *micro content* of text. The *micro content* of text includes situational grapho-phonic (letter/sound), syntactic, and semantic cues and the integration of these (Cole, 2004). Formal literacy instruction makes sense to them because they know how they'll use the information. They're the lucky ones; they'll easily meet and exceed expectations established by schools. They already use print to encode ideas; they use reading to decode written messages.

Literacy Curriculum That Works: Start Where They Are

Children's use of random letters indicates a budding awareness of the alphabet principle; letters are used to encode words. Young writers' phonetic spellings demonstrate the isolation and ordering of separate sounds (phonemic awareness) and matching of each to the letter or letters for spelling words. Children's word choice indicates the breadth of background knowledge and vocabulary they have amassed. Young writers soon acquire an automatic writing vocabulary; with frequent use, they remember how to spell words previously requested. When the child can independently write a word, he can most often read it. Thus, the young writer acquires a bank of sight words (sight vocabulary) that can be used in reading and as a basis for analyzing other words with similar sounds and patterns. As mentioned, formal literacy instruction makes sense to these children; they attach new knowledge to prior knowledge, expanding existing schema.

What these children have learned through family literacy experiences can be accelerated in children who come to school without a rich literacy schema. When children write—right from the start—in school, the process becomes a vehicle for establishing and strengthening macro literacy concepts; it also provides authentic practice of micro skills that are too often taught separately. There will always be a natural range of developmental levels in early childhood classrooms, but our curriculum and methodologies can lessen the gaps created by experiential differences. Transferring learning in isolation to personally meaningful applications also generates motivation to participate because children view the work as relevant. Persistent and prolonged engagement in meaningful literacy practice also increases children's performance on formal assessment measures.

Johnson (1999) reported that end-of-the-year reading tests given to her kindergarten students, who wrote throughout the year, documented their extensive phonetic knowledge. She hypothesizes that the "writing experience [in her classroom] gave the letters and sounds deeper meaning." Clark's (1987) research concluded that being encouraged to write and use temporary spelling (sound spelling) led to greater achievement gains for all children, including those who came to school with literacy experiences that do "not fit mainstream expectations in school, but achieve functionality and intellectual purpose in families' daily lives" (Whitmore et al., 2005).

The writing samples in this text come from homes and classrooms that support children's writing right from the start; they document the range of literacy knowledge and specific skills (e.g. phonics) children acquired. Their writing provided a readiness curriculum for reading.

Setting up such conditions—ones that foster literacy exploration and build *can do* attitudes—establishes a conceptual framework for filling in specific literacy knowledge. "Children who are encouraged to write early and inventively perform better in reading, especially in word recognition, than children who do not have this practice" (Temple et al.,

1993). Ray (2004) suggests that the way to start is "no matter what, let them write every day." Concept construction begins at home when children have a purpose (e.g. making a note, writing a book, creating a list) for assimilating and filing literacy insights. It continues seamlessly in classrooms that reflect the same conditions. These classrooms significantly reduce achievement differences, allowing all children to thrive.

Ensuring a Solid Foundation for Literacy Learning

McGill-Franzen (2006) points out that

> if we are to improve literacy in our nation, we all have to embrace the belief that teaching reading [and writing] to 5-year olds can be a school [or family] experience that's every bit as playful, imaginative, inquiry-driven, and developmentally appropriate as anything John Dewey or Jean Piaget might have dreamed up.

Collaboratively, teachers can apply research findings to design such a curriculum and environment at their school.

This book describes classroom communities that make children's journey into literacy joyful—places that stimulate excitement for learning no matter how old you are! Schulze (2006) emphasizes that such classrooms are especially critical for the many children who have not had the empowering, concept-building preschool literacy experiences their peers have enjoyed. Knowing that the quality of children's literacy experiences from birth through age five has a profound effect on their success in school (Dickenson & Tabors, 2001; Strickland & Barnett, 2003), early childhood teachers fill any gaps that exist as soon as possible.

Meaningful early childhood curriculum includes instruction in specific literacy skills that's imbedded in authentic reading, writing, and discussion. Quality literature is central to learning activities. Children respond to story or information through conversation and writing. Writing is incorporated across the curriculum; children write to learn and show what they know. Specific skills are tools for the real job of literacy—not standalone goals.

Assessment of literacy development is focused on how children apply skills functionally; their writing verifies acquisition of separate skills and much, much more. The young writer's ability to accurately use the labyrinth of writing forms (structures and conventions) grows developmentally when adults provide patience, effective instruction, scaffolded practice, sensitive feedback, appreciation of effort, and audience for his message. The same ingredients led to Shaun White's competence in snowboarding and David Beckham's agility with a soccer ball.

When children write right from the start they understand right from the start that knowledge in isolation is not enough; one must be able to use skills—just as literate people use them in the world. "It is not surprising, therefore, that a major research finding in emergent literacy is that writing—if much experimentation is encouraged—can play a pivotal role in children's learning to read" (Cecil, 2007, p. 162). And grand conversations about life, literature, and the world around them get young writers started. Talk generates subject matter children know about, care about, and can write about; it sustains their composing.

The next chapter discusses the importance of frontloading children's background knowledge about the world, language structures, and meaning vocabulary through adult-guided immersion in quality literature and meaningful real or vicarious learning experiences. But, these adult-guided opportunities must include talking *with* (not just *to*) the child, respecting him as a partner. Such grand conversations produce learning. What's the connection to writing you might wonder? It's simple. One cannot write without something to say or without knowing how to map ideas onto the page. And, one cannot express thoughts interestingly, coherently, and persuasively without expanded word knowledge.

Chapter References

McKie, B. K., Butty, J. M., & Green, R. D. (2011). Reading, reasoning, and literacy: Strategies for early child-hood education from the analysis of classroom observations. *Early Childhood Education Journal,* 40, 55–61.

Morrow, L. M. (1999). Where do we go from here in early literacy research and practice. *Issues in Education,* 5(*1*), 117.

Strickland, M. & Abbott, L. (2010). Experience: Books, strategies, and concepts. *Reading Teacher,* 64(*1*), 66–68.

Chapter Two

Introductions by Natalie Tye

Phonemic Awareness

INTRODUCTION TO READING 2.1
Phonemic Awareness

Phonemic awareness is one of the best predictors for later reading success (Chapman, 2003; Nichols et al., 2004). Phonemic awareness is the ability to recognize the individual units of sound embedded in words and in turn be able to understand how the combination of sounds creates words (Chapman, 2003; Nichols et al., 2004). Phonemes are these individual units of sound. It is the combination of phonemes that creates words (Chapman, 2003). Once this process is understood, it becomes easier to create new words by replacing one sound with different sound (Nichols et al., 2004). For example, the word *bat* has three phonemes /b/a/t/. The combined units of sound create the word *bat*. Once this is recognized and understood, it becomes easy to remove the /b/ sound and replace it with the /m/ sound to create a new word, *mat*. To be clear, phonemic awareness is the focus on sound rather than print. This chapter will focus on the role phonemic awareness plays in learning to read as well as strategies and activities to support phonemic awareness development.

Strategies to foster phonemic awareness include both explicit and implicit instruction techniques (Deavers, Solity, & Kerfoot, 2000). Explicit phonemic awareness is the process of building instruction from parts of the word to the whole word. This process starts with phonemes and moves to blending of sounds into words (Deavers, Solity, & Kerfoot, 2000). A different approach to phonemic awareness is implicit instruction, where instruction begins with the whole and graduates to the parts, learning to separate and identify the phonemes that make up the word (Deavers, Solity, & Kerfoot, 2000). Both techniques will be discussed throughout the chapter, including benefits and strategies for each.

Before determining what is needed for children learning to grasp phonemic awareness, it is necessary to understand the pieces and parts brought together in the reading process. What exactly is phonemic awareness and how does research support the idea that phonemic awareness is crucial for later reading success? Kirby, Desrochers, and Roth (2008) focus attention on what has been identified as the six causal constructs that contribute to reading success.

BEFORE READING

Before reading the following article, Begin thinking about the reading process. Break down the process for learning to read. What constructs are needed to form an understanding of reading at an early age?

DURING READING

While reading, consider how the six individual constructs are taught in the classroom. How do they work together?

AFTER READING

Upon completion of reading this article, reflect on your own understanding of phonemic awareness. What resonated with you from the article? Take a moment and journal about the reading and how the information can be applied in the classroom setting. Which activities stood out to you and seemed possible for you to use in your classroom?

Teaching Phonemic Awareness

BY TIMOTHY R. BLAIR

What it is and What Research Can Tell Us

Phonemic awareness is the understanding that words in our language are made up of a sequence of individual, connected sounds or phonemes. A phoneme is a speech sound. Students with this understanding can identify sounds and manipulate them. Heilman (2006) lists the following understandings a child can exhibit when this ability is achieved:

- Words have small sounds that can be pulled apart and put back together.
- Sounds in words have a specific order (first, middle, and final).
- Sounds in words can be counted.
- Sounds in words can be moved, removed, or replaced to make new words.
- Several sounds can be represented by different letters.

Phonemic awareness is a major predictor of becoming a successful reader in not only first grade but beyond (National Institute of Child Health and Human Development, 2000). This ability to hear individual sounds, discriminate among them, and manipulate them is the foundation for learning the sound/symbol relationships of English.

Many students have little difficulty with phonemic awareness. Being read to and informally playing with words in the home and in preschools teaches students about sounds and letters. However, first-graders lacking phonemic awareness have extreme difficulty with traditional phonics instruction and need a blend of implicit/indirect instruction and explicit/direct instruction to promote its development.

Teacher Behaviors

- Provide both implicit/indirect instruction and explicit/direct instruction to teach specific aspects of phonemic awareness.
- Provide an abundance of meaningful practice to promote student awareness and mastery.
- Monitor student progress.

Teaching Strategies

1. *Engage in implicit/indirect instruction,* and informally play with sounds by singing songs, playing rhyming games, and reading tongue twisters and books that rhyme or feature alliteration (i.e., contain words that begin with the same sound). Discuss the sounds in the rhyming books, songs, tongue twisters, and games, and have students say them. Play around with sounds with students by asking questions such as, "What words rhyme?" "What is the first sound of all the words in our song or book?" "Can you give me another word with the same sound?" Ask students to match sounds to various objects and words in sentences and stories.
2. *Employ explicit/direct instruction,* and practice with sounds and their components in the following areas:
   - *Phoneme substitution.* Examples: Ask students to say the word *TIN* and to then indicate what the word would say if the sound of /t/ is replaced with the sound of /p/. Do the same with the word *BOOK,* where the beginning sound of /b/ is replaced with /t/.
   - *Phoneme isolation.* Examples: Ask students to listen to the word *TOP* and to tell you where in the word they hear the sound of /t/. Or in the word *BLOSSOM,* where do they hear the sound of /s/? Or in the word *RADIO,* where do they hear the sound of /o/?
   - *Phoneme deletion.* Examples: Ask students to say the word *AIRPLANE* and to then say the word without saying *PLANE.* Then ask students to say the word *FARM* and then to say the word without saying /f/, or to say the word *BOLD* and then to say the word without the /b/.
   - *Phoneme segmentation.* Examples: Ask students to say a word one sound at a time, as in the word *NO* (n-oh) or *HOT* (h-o-t).
   - *Blending words.* Examples: Pronounce words in small parts, such as *s-un* and *can-dee,* and ask students to put the parts together and pronounce the whole word.

Activities

- ***Recognizing words with the same sound.*** Give students a set of words—for example, *cat, dog,* and *cake.* Ask students to say the words aloud. Then have students say the words that have the same beginning sound. You may want to ask students to tell/say what the beginning sound is. Do this several different times.

- Isolating sounds. Show students a list of words. Focus on one word at a time. For example, show the word *dog,* and ask students to say the beginning sound of the word. You can do this with the first and last sounds in a word. Be sure you do this several times with other words.

- *Phoneme segmentation.* In this activity, you want students to break a word into its separate sounds, saying each sound as they tap out or count it. Then they will write and read the word. For example, ask students how many sounds are in the word *dog*? Students then tap out or count out each sound in *dog.* Then ask students to write the sounds in *dog.* After students write the sounds out, have them say the word again.

- *Phoneme blending.* In this activity, you want students to listen to a sequence of separately spoken phonemes and to then combine the phonemes to form a word. Students then write and read the word. For example, ask students, "What word is /d/ /o/ /g/? Students should sound each phoneme out and then blend the phonemes to say *dog.* Then ask students to write the sounds in *dog.* After they write the word, they should say the word aloud.

- *Identifying sounds in a story.* This activity allows students to integrate literature with phonemic awareness. Read a story with students. After you are finished reading the story, select a sound that appears throughout the story. Initially, you may want to choose a sound that appears at the beginning of words because this is the easiest. Then ask students to find this sound at the end of a word and even in the middle. You can go through the whole story identifying the chosen sound.

- *Identification of rhyming words.* This can be taught through the repetition of songs, poems, nursery rhymes, and chants. Choose an appropriate piece of text to repeat several times; usually, it is best if it is repeated several times initially and then revisited on a regular basis over time. Read the piece of text to students once. Ask them if they notice anything. Make sure to point out the rhyming at the end of the line. Read the passage a second time, but this time around, have students raise their hands every time they hear a rhyming word.

- *Inventing rhyming words.* Read a passage full of rhyming words to students several times. After students are familiar with a passage that has a recognizable rhyming pattern, cover up random rhyming words throughout the story and allow students to make up their own rhyming words that may fit into the text.

- *Find your match.* Give each student a card with a word written on it. Ask students to find the word that "matches" theirs. This can mean that students need to find the person who has a word that rhymes with theirs, has the same initial sound, or has the same ending sound. This can be repeated as many times as you can keep students' attention. For students who are still having difficulties reading, as many students will be at this stage, it may be more helpful to put a picture instead of a word on these cards.

- *Sound guessing.* In a bag, have simple objects that relate to the story being read to students. You may want to begin with objects that only have three sounds. This simplifies the process. Put your hand in the bag and grab an object. Give students clues as to what you are holding in your hand. Then pronounce the phonemes of the object you are holding. For example: "I have an object in my hand that you write with */p/ /e/ /n/.*" Make sure to emphasize the distinct phonemes. Have students repeat the phonemes to you and then blend the phonemes together. If students become very good at this, you may want to add more difficult words with more sounds.

- *Categorizing sounds.* Show students a set of three or four words. Once you have chosen the words, you need to make sure that one of the words has an "odd" sound. For example, ask students which of the following words doesn't belong: *hat, hot, rat.* Students should say that the word *rat* does not belong because it does not begin with */h/.* You can do this with ending sounds as well.

Teaching Struggling Students

When children meet phonemic awareness standards teachers feel accomplished knowing instructional methods and strategies were effective. It is only when children do not meet standards and exhibit frustration during phonemic awareness activities that teachers question instructional strategies and activities in the classroom. Blair (2013) offers a clear understanding of phonemic awareness by focusing on mastery level child behaviors and then providing teacher guidance for those children still lacking phonemic awareness in first grade. Once struggling children are identified in the classroom, intervention strategies and activities are necessary to assist children with this crucial step in learning to read. Teachers may find it challenging to know where to start or how to teach to these lower performing students. The following article guides the teacher by identifying the main goals for working with children struggling to grasp phonemic awareness. Further, Blair (2013) provides specific strategies and activities to apply in the real-world classroom.

BEFORE READING

Before reading this article, think about a classroom of children learning to read. What behaviors are evident in those children finding success with early reading? How can you identify children having difficulty with phonemic awareness? Keep these ideas in mind as you read through the article, "Teaching Phonemic Awareness." The teacher must first know which children are struggling to be able to implement specific strategies and activities to assist with mastery.

DURING READING

While reading the article, place yourself in the situation of working with struggling readers. What strategies resonate with you? Begin thinking about the activities and how you could implement them in your own classroom.

AFTER READING

After reading the article, create a list of ways to implement the activities provided. How can you reach those students who most need assistance with phonemic awareness?

Longitudinal Predictors of Word Reading Development

BY JOHN R. KIRBY, ALAIN DESROCHERS,
LEAH ROTH, AND SANDY S. V. LAI

[...]

Six Causal Constructs

Let us now turn to more specific evidence regarding the six causal constructs. We pay particular attention to their theoretical definition, how they are measured, and the evidence for their causal contribution to reading. The last of these is considered in terms of two criteria, the ability of the construct to predict reading performance after controlling other plausible causal and background factors, and the effects of instruction in the skill underlying each construct.

PHONOLOGICAL AWARENESS

Phonological awareness refers to the oral language ability to perceive and deliberately manipulate the sound components of words, such as the basic speech units of phonemes, rimes, and syllables (Adams, 1990). In particular, the ability to perceive phonemes as individual and separable speech sounds is strongly associated with reading success. Poor phonological awareness hinders the acquisition of the *alphabetic principle,* the understanding of the relationship between letters and sounds (Stanovich. 1986). Moreover. Adams (1990) argued that phonological awareness development requires explicit instruction because mere exposure does not enable the acquisition of phonological awareness at the phonemic level.

Phonological awareness has been measured with a host of tasks varying in target content, process, and explicitness. Target content ranges from syllable awareness (least difficult), through onset-rime awareness, to phoneme awareness (most difficult). The processes involved include both synthesis (blending provided sounds into a word) and analysis (taking a provided word apart): analysis tasks include identification (specifying the sound located in a particular position in the given word), segmentation (separating word phonemes or counting them), and deletion (pronouncing a word after removing a given sound). More complex tasks include repeating a word in pig latin (placing the first sound at the end of the word) and spoonerisms (reversing the first sounds of successive words). These tasks vary in the degree of explicit awareness required; whereas only implicit awareness is required to indicate which of three words has a different final sound, more explicit awareness is required to identify or reverse the order of given phonemes. All of these tasks correlate well with reading, the easier ones being more appropriate for and showing more variability in younger children, the more difficult ones for older children (see Anthony & Lonigan, 2004).

Phonological awareness has been shown to be one of the most powerful factors in reading development. It is moderately correlated with current reading performance; for example, Swanson. Trainin, Necoechea, and Hammill (2003) calculated a correlation between it and real word reading of .43. based on 194 correlations in 35 independent samples of readers. Phonological awareness is predictive of subsequent reading ability, even after controlling the effects of variables such as IQ and SES (Bradley & Bryant, 1983; Wagner, Torgesen, & Rashotte, 1994). Bus and van IJzendoorn (1999) concluded from their meta-analysis that phonological awareness training improved not only children's phonological awareness skills but also their reading ability. Specifically, they found that the standardised difference between groups who received phonological awareness training and control groups was Cohen's $d = 0.70$. indicating a medium-to-strong effect of phonological awareness on reading skills. Moreover, they found that experimentally manipulated phonological awareness accounted for approximately 12% of the variance in reading skills.

PHONOLOGICAL DECODING

Closely related to phonological awareness, phonological decoding refers to the ability to convert written letters into sounds through grapheme-phoneme conversion (GPC). In other words, phonological decoding is the phonic analysis of print. Because GPC requires phoneme differentiation, phonological decoding is necessarily dependent upon phonological awareness skills. However. phonological decoding involves more than merely manipulating sounds. For example, being able to segment the $Ik/$ sound in "cat" is not equivalent to being able to translate the c grapheme into the /k/ phoneme. In addition to phonemic knowledge, phonological decoding requires insight into the alphabetic principle and understanding that the writing system represents sound (Bowey, 1996); it also requires other skills, for instance to generate alternative pronunciations and choose amongst them. Thus, phonological aware-ness is a necessary but insufficient prerequisite for phonological decoding. Both are especially important in beginning readers, as the high frequency of unfamiliar words requires frequent phonological processing of print. Share (1995) argued that phonological decoding was the self-learning mechanism through which a beginning reader develops both word-specific and general orthographic knowledge, subsequently leading to efficient visual word recognition. Moreover, phonological decoding remains a necessary skill for reading unfamiliar words, even in the most proficient readers (see Rastle & Coltheart, 1998; Rey, Ziegler, & Jacobs, 2000).

The most common measure of phonological decoding involves asking the child to read pseudowords, which are nonwords that conform to the phonological and orthographic struc-tures of the language. Nonwords prevent holistic recognition of the stimuli as they are not part of the reader's lexicon; thus, the only means of pronouncing them is through phonologi-cal decoding.

There is considerable evidence that phonological decoding, as represented by pseudoword reading, is correlated with real word reading. Correlations in the early elementary grades gen-erally exceed .70. indicating that phonological decoding accounts for a majority of the variance in word recognition (Share, 1995). Swanson et al.'s (2003) meta-analysis found a correlation of .61 between pseudoword and real word reading, based on 24 correlations in 12 independent samples. Other estimates are even higher (e.g. in Share, 1995). An example of a pseudoword reading task is the Word Attack subtest of the Woodcock Reading Mastery Tests—Revised (Woodcock, 1998); the Woodcock manual shows correlations between Word Attack and word reading at the Grade I, 3, and 5 levels of 0.79, 0.72, and 0.70, respectively (Woodcock, 1998).

Instruction in phonological decoding usually consists of phonics instruction. Recent meta-analysis results (Ehri, Nunes, Stahl, & Willows, 2001; National Reading Panel, 2000) show moderate effects of phonics instruction on reading achievement, effect sizes generally ranging from .4 to .7. Ehri et al. further demonstrated that phonics instruction was effective across age and SES ranges.

Although the literature has consistently supported the predictive role of phonological skills (phonological awareness and phonological decoding) in reading development in chil-dren, phonological skills alone do not account for all of the variance in reading. For example. Bus and van IJzendoom's (1999) meta-analysis showed phonological awareness training to account for only 12% of the variance in reading. Even the highest estimates of the correla-tion between phonological decoding and word recognition (Share, 1995) leave considerable variance to be explained. Further evidence comes from the literature on reading disabili-ties, which describes some individuals, known as surface dyslexics, who have adequate phonological skills but nevertheless are impaired in reading (e.g., Castles & Coltheart, 1993; McDougall. Borowsky. MacKinnon, & Hymel, 2005). Consequently, researchers have been seeking other factors that also predict reading development. Two of the leading candidates in the literature thus far are naming speed and orthographic processing, which the following sections describe.

NAMING SPEED

Naming speed, also known as Rapid Automatized Naming (RAN) or speed of lexical access, refers to the speed at which children can name sets of stimuli (Wolf, O'Rourke, Gidney, Lovett, Cirino, & Morris, 2002). In brief, the process of rapid naming involves attention to the stimuli, integration of visual information with stored visual or orthographic representations, retrieval of phonological labels, and activation of articulation (Wolf & Bowers, 1999). Because these processes are analogous to the task of reading in that they involve similar fluency and integration skills, naming speed tasks represent a microcosm of reading in their requirement of rapid visual-verbal connexions. Although some researchers have argued that naming speed's predictive power in reading is because of its ability to measure the speed of access to phonological codes and is thus not independent of phonological awareness (e.g., Share, 1995), research has found naming speed to consistently account for variance in reading after controlling for the effects of phonological awareness (for a review, see Wolf, Bowers, & Biddle, 2000).

There is considerable debate over what naming speed is and why it correlates with reading. Wolf and Bowers (1999) suggested that naming speed may be a precursor of orthographic processing abilities in children. They argued that naming speed may affect the rate at which children can learn orthographic patterns as a result of exposure to print. They indicated that slow naming speed could do this by "impeding the appropriate amalgamation of connexions between phonemes and orthographic patterns," by reducing the "quality of orthographic codes," and by increasing the number of repetitions required to unitize codes. Specifically, readers with poor naming speed do not register letter sequences quickly enough to "chunk" them into orthographic units and instead process the letters independently for an extended period of time (Bowers & Newby-Clark, 2002). In other words, poor naming speed may hinder the ability to acquire good orthographic processing skills. This also suggests that slow naming speed would lead to slow or inefficient phonological decoding.

Kail, Hall, and Caskey (1999) argued that general processing speed, as measured by the speed with which children can complete a series of simple cognitive tasks, underlies the association between naming speed and reading. However, Bowey, Storey, and Ferguson (2004) found that naming speed accounted for unique variance in word reading after controlling for the effects of age and general processing speed. Thus, it appears that naming speed's contribution is independent of phonological abilities and pure processing speed.

The standard measures of naming speed are the RAN Tests of Denckla and Rudel, 1976, and the more recent variants in the Comprehensive Test of Phonological Processing (CTOPP; Wagner, Torgesen, & Rashotte, 1999). All of these measures involve presenting a visual array of approximately 50 stimuli, usually consisting of four or five high-frequency digits, letters, colours, or objects, repeated in random order. The naming speed is the speed at which a child serially or continuously names the array, making as few errors as possible.

Swanson et al. (2003) found that the correlation between naming speed and real word reading was .41, based on 107 correlations in 33 independent samples. There is a great deal of evidence that naming speed predicts reading development, after controlling key variables. For example, in a study examining 85 Grade 2 children, Manis, Doi, and Bhadha (2000) found that RAN-Digits significantly predicted 4.3 to 19.6% and RAN-Letters significantly predicted 7.1 to 27.7% of the variance in various reading tasks, after controlling for vocabulary and phonological awareness. In a longitudinal study of 79 children, Kirby, Parrila, and Pfeiffer (2003) found that naming speed (measured in kindergarten with Colour and Picture Naming) was a unique predictor of reading measures from Grades 3 to 5, after controlling for kindergarten letter recognition and intelligence. Thus, naming speed measured before formal reading instruction significantly predicted reading ability five years later. Several authors have shown that the naming speed-reading relationship is stronger in less able readers (McBride-Chang & Manis, 1996; Johnston & Kirby, 2006).

To our knowledge, there have been no successful attempts to improve naming speed and therefore reading. What has been attempted instead is the improvement of one of the presumed consequences of naming speed, orthographic processing.

ORTHOGRAPHIC PROCESSING

Writing systems have specific conventions and rules concerning the visual and orthographic aspects of print, and thus reading benefits from knowledge of such orthographic constraints and regularities (Levy, Gong, Hessels, Evans, & Jared, 2006). Orthographic processing refers to the use of that knowledge, to abilities that concern the more visual and holistic aspects of reading, such as memory for letters, letter patterns, and words (Barker, Torgesen, & Wagner, 1992). Orthographic processing allows reading to be fast, through the automatic recognition of larger units, especially those that do not correspond to GPC rules (irregular words). Orthographic processing has several sources, the most apparent being print exposure, as repeated exposure to print leads to a stable visual representation of an orthographic unit, which may be a word or a subunit of a word (Barker et al., 1992; Stanovich & West, 1989). Levy et al. (2006) have shown that orthographic knowledge can be measured before formal reading instruction begins, for instance in the discrimination between letters and scribbles; presumably this knowledge comes from exposure to print. Share (1995) has emphasised that readers acquire orthographic knowledge through repeated successful experiences of decoding words. Thus, the orthographic lexicon expands, in part, through the successful application of phonological decoding. In this sense, orthographic processing is partially dependent on phonological skills, in that the accurate decoding of words leads to the development of links between the phonological and the orthographic lexicons (as described in the Dual Route theory, Coltheart et al., 2001). It is perhaps more accurate to say that orthographic processing is enhanced by successful reading. It has also been argued to depend upon naming speed (Wolf & Bowers, 1999).

Orthographic processing has been measured with a variety of techniques, all based on the premise that the measure cannot be performed well with only phonological decoding. Amongst the measures used have been irregular word reading (Castles & Coltheart, 1993), pseudohomophone discrimination (i.e., selecting the correct spelling of irregular words from pairs such as RAIN- RANE; Olson, Forsberg, Wise, & Rack, 1994), and word likeness judgment (which is more like a word, FILK or FILV; Cunningham, Perry, & Stanovich, 2001).

Despite the theoretical dependence of orthographic processing on phonological skills and print exposure, it has been shown to contribute to reading after controlling phonological skills and print exposure (Barker et al., 1992; Cunningham, Perry, & Stanovich, 2001; Cunningham & Stanovich, 1990; Stanovich & West, 1989). With respect to naming speed, we know of only two studies that have assessed the effects of naming speed and orthographic processing in the same analysis. Roth, Lai. White and Kirby (2006) found that orthographic processing and naming speed each made a significant contribution to a range of reading variables after controlling each other in a sample of Grade 3 children, though adding orthographic processing to the model weakened the effect of naming speed. In a sample of Grade 4, 6, and 8 children, Roman, Kirby, Parrila, Wade-Woolley, and Deacon (in press) found that orthographic processing survived the control of naming speed, but naming speed did not survive the control of orthographic processing in predicting word reading. Both of these results are consistent with the theory that naming speed contributes to orthographic processing and thus to reading; it is not yet clear whether naming speed has an independent effect, perhaps at an earlier age level or amongst less able readers.

Furthermore, there is some evidence that orthographic processing's contribution to reading seems to increase with age. After controlling for earlier reading level, preschool age, verbal IQ, and verbal memory, Badian (2001) found that preschool orthographic processing developed from being a nonsignificant predictor of reading comprehension in Grade 1, to significantly predicting 3% of the variance in Grade 3, and finally accounting significantly for 5% of the variance in Grade 7. Roman et al. (in press), however, found that the effect of orthographic processing was constant across Grades 4, 6. and 8, so it may be that orthographic processing's effect increases to Grade 3 and then levels out. This is consistent with Share's (1995) self-learning hypothesis in that beginner readers heavily rely on phonological skills to decode words but later rely more on orthographic knowledge as they become more skilled in reading.

Because orthographic processing is largely seen as the consequence of reading experience and print exposure, most interventions have attempted to increase exposure to certain words or parts of words (e.g., the rimes of words). Some interventions are framed as attempts to increase fluency, that is, word reading speed, which is also related to orthographic processing. For example, Lemoine, Levy, and Hutchinson (1993) found that the time taken to name words decreased after repeated presentations of those words, but this did not generalise to new words. Levy, Bourassa, and Horn (1999) found that children with slow naming speed (and thus at risk for poor orthographic processing) did not benefit from whole- word presentation (presumably designed to increase orthographic knowledge), and instead benefited more from phonological segmentation or from rime training. Colasante, Kirby, Parrila, and

Wade-Woolley (2006) found that children with slow naming speed benefited more from a phonologically oriented than from an orthographically oriented programme.

MORPHOLOGICAL AWARENESS

A fifth, and relatively less explored, contributor to reading ability is morphological awareness, which refers to children's "conscious awareness of the morphemic structure of words and their ability to reflect on and manipulate that structure" (Carlisle, 1995, p. 194). Morphemes are the smallest units of meaning within words, and are of several types. Some *are free* morphemes that can exist as free-standing words (e.g., *visit* in *revisited*) and others are *hound* morphemes that have no independent lexical status (e.g., the prefix *re-* in *revisited)*. The meaning of a word is represented through a melding of individual units of meaning. The base of a word provides the primary root of meaning that is then modified by any accompanying affixes. Some multimorphemic words are inflexions, formed when grammatical affixes are added to make a word that is a member of the same grammatical class as the base (e.g., hat + s = hats); others are derivations, in which the result is a member of a different grammatical class (e.g., con + dense = condense). A further group of multimorphemic words are composed of two or more bases (dead + line = deadline).

Morphologically complex words are words that contain more than one morpheme, which can be reduced to smaller units, providing cues for pronunciation, spelling, and meaning (Carlisle, 2003). Over half of the words in English are morphologically complex (Nagy, Beminger, & Abbott, 2006). Morphological complexity increases as word frequency decreases. As such, children encounter increasing numbers of these complex words with each grade as text exposure expands. Understanding morphemic suffixing patterns that determine any spelling shifts that may occur when adding suffixes to a base or stem (e.g., *carry/i + age = carriage*) may aid a reader in deconstructing morphologically complex words to determine the constituent morphemes, thereby enhancing word meaning. By parsing words for meanings of component parts, a reader may be able to understand the meaning of new, morphologically complex words (Carlisle & Fleming, 2003; Nagy et al., 2006). Readers with the ability to parse words should similarly be able to both deconstruct and reconstruct morphologically complex words.

Morphological awareness has been measured with a variety of tasks (for a preliminary taxonomy, see Deacon, Parrila, & Kirby, 2007). Some require only implicit awareness of morphology, for instance in selecting which word best completes a sentence (e.g., The children enjoyed the *perform/performance*); whereas in others the knowledge must be more explicit (identifying the base within a word). The words used within a morphological awareness task can vary in the transparency of the relation between two words; this transparency can be in terms of phonology (is there a pronunciation shift, as from *sign* to *signature*?), orthography (is there a spelling change, as from *carry* to *carriage*?), or semantics (is the meaning relation clear, as it is from *walk* to *walked,* but as it is not between *vacate* and *vacuum*). Some of the tasks that have been used include distinguishing morphologically related pairs (*pot—potting*) from those that are not (*corn—corner*), identifying the bases of multimorphemic words (e.g., what is the base of *business*?), and making morphological analogies (*walk* is to *walked* as *kiss* is to___?; for further examples, see Deacon et al., 2007).

There is considerable evidence that morphological awareness makes a unique contribution to various reading abilities, after controlling factors such as IQ, working memory, vocabulary and phonological awareness (e.g., Bryant, Nunes, & Bindman, 1998; Carlisle, 1995, 2003; Carlisle & Stone, 2003; Deacon & Kirby, 2004). Roth et al. (2006) showed that morphological awareness predicted various reading measures in Grade 3 children after controlling IQ, phonological awareness, naming speed, and orthographic processing. Roman et al. (in press) found the same effect on word reading, after controlling age, phonological awareness, naming speed, and orthographic processing in a sample of Grade 4, 6, and 8 children. There are relatively few instructional studies, but those that exist show positive effects of morphological awareness instruction on reading outcomes (Ambak & Elbro, 2000; Bowers & Kirby, 2006; Nunes & Bryant, 2006; Nunes, Bryant, & Olsson, 2003).

VOCABULARY

The final causal factor is vocabulary. As mentioned earlier, there are various ways in which vocabulary can influence reading: through text-specific words, through recognition of less familiar words when sounded out, and through verbal ability. Thus, vocabulary can contribute to both word recognition and to comprehension. The sources of vocabulary knowledge include home experience, general mental and verbal ability, and education (for reviews, see Beck et al., 2002; Biemiller, 2007). Vocabulary may also be influenced by morphological awareness. We should note that vocabulary has been studied extensively, in many different ways; our review is necessarily cursory.

Vocabulary is measured with oral and written tests. Although the written tests (e.g., select the option that is closest in meaning to the presented word) are common and convenient, they often confound a predictor of reading with reading itself. Furthermore, written and oral vocabularies may be different; some words may be understood when heard but not when seen, and other words may be more familiar in writing than when heard. Many intellectual assessment batteries include oral vocabulary measures (e.g., Wechsler, 1999); some reading tests include vocabulary subtests (e.g., MacGinitie & MacGinitie. 1992), and there are many standalone measures (e.g., Peabody Picture Vocabulary Test; Dunn & Dunn, 1981). Text- or context-specific measures are necessarily constructed informally. We suggest that each type of test (oral or written, generic or text-specific) has a purpose, but it is incorrect to assume they are the same or that the same inferences should be drawn from each.

There is ample evidence that vocabulary knowledge is correlated with reading achievement (e.g., Biemiller, 2007; Biemiller & Boote, 2006; National Reading Panel, 2000). Perhaps because many investigators see vocabulary as a trait related to intelligence, it is often treated as a covariate in predictive analyses. There is much less evidence that increasing vocabulary increases reading ability (Biemiller, 2007). Not surprisingly, teaching the specific words to be encountered in a given text does improve comprehension of that text (Beck et al., 2002); but that is not a generalizable finding. Attempts to teach vocabulary in a broader sense have been less numerous and less clearly successful in affecting reading (Biemiller, 2007). To some extent, the lack of positive results may stem from the ways in which vocabulary is taught: for example, memorizing definitions of certain words is unlikely to generalise to understanding the meanings of other words, and may not even generalise to understanding the original words in context. Beck et al. (2002) and Biemiller (2007) both make the point that the meanings of many words will be learned in any case, and those of others will never be used; the key is to teach the words that are needed. The solution to the instructional dilemma may lie in teaching morphology in the context of a broader programme devoted to word study.

Summary and Conclusions

This review demonstrates support for the importance of the phonological awareness, naming speed, phonological decoding, orthographic processing, morphological awareness, and vocabulary in influencing reading development. Although we have described them and their effects separately, it is important to recognise that they covary with each other and contribute to each other in various ways. As we indicated at the outset, our focus on these causal, cognitive constructs in word reading does not indicate that other variables are not involved, especially in reading comprehension. On the other hand, the six on which we have focussed are precise enough that their roles in reading development can be understood. Further, there is clear evidence that teaching several of these constructs contributes to improvements in reading achievement.

The evidence reviewed in this paper has implications for assessment and instruction. The predictive relationships between these constructs and reading demonstrate the importance of early and regular assessment of these constructs. There are established, published measures of some of these constructs, but not of all. Further instrument development is required. There is also clear support for both regular-class and remedial instruction in several of the constructs. It is clear that phonological awareness and phonological decoding can be instructed and are effective in improving reading. Naming speed is clearly predictive of reading, but there have not been demonstrations yet that it can be taught. Orthographic processing and vocabulary are both related to reading success, but it is not yet clear that they can be taught as generic skills and that they successfully generalise to reading. Morphological awareness has some support as a target of instruction, and may help integrate the effects of orthographic processing and vocabulary. Both curriculum development and teacher education are required to apply this knowledge effectively in education.

References

Adams, M. J. (1990). *Beginning to read: Thinking and learning about print*. Cambridge, MA: MIT Press.

Anthony, J. L., & Lonigan, C. J. (2004). The nature of phonological awareness: Converging evidence from four studies of preschool and early grade school children. *Journal of Educational Psychology, 96*, 43–55.

Arnbak, E., & Elbro, C. (2000). The effects of morphological awareness training on the reading and spelling skills of young dyslexics. *Scandinavian Journal of Educational Research, 44*, 229–251.

Badian, N. A. (2001). Phonological and orthographic processing: Their roles in reading prediction. *Annals of Dyslexia, 51*, 179–202.

Barker, T. A., Torgesen. J. K., & Wagner. R. K. (1992). The role of orthographic processing skills on five different reading skills. *Reading Research Quarterly, 27*, 334–345.

Beck, I. L., McKeown. M. G., & Kucan, L. (2002). *Bringing words to life: Robust vocabulary instruction*. New York: Guilford Press.

Biemiller, A. (2007). *The influence of vocabulary instruction on reading. In the Encyclopedia of Language and Literacy Development*. Canadian Language and Literacy Research Network. http://www.literacyencyclo-pedia.ca/.

Biemiller, A., & Boote, C. (2006). An effective method for building meaning vocabulary in primary grades. *Journal of Educational Psychology, 98*. 44—62.

Bowers, P. G., & Newby-Clark, E. (2002). The role of naming speed within a model of reading acquisition. *Reading and Writing: An Interdisciplinary Journal, 15*, 109–126.

Bowers, P. N., & Kirby. J. R. (2006). *Morpho-phonological word structure: Can instruction add transparency to opaque words?* Paper presented at the annual meeting of the Society for the Scientific Study of Reading, Vancouver, BC.

Bowey. J. A., Storey, T., & Ferguson, A. N. (2004). The association between continuous naming speed and word reading skill in fourth- to sixth-grade children. *Australian Journal of Psychology, 56*. 155–163.

Bradley, L., & Bryant, P. E. (1983). Categorizing sounds and learning to read: A causal connection. *Nature. 301*, 419–421.

Bryant, P., Nunes, T., & Bindman, M. (1998). Awareness of language in children who have reading difficulties: Historical comparisons in a longitudinal study. *Journal of Child Psychology and Psychiatry, 39*, 501–510.

Bus, A. G., & van IJzendoorn, M. H. (1999). Phonological awareness and early reading: A meta-analysis of experimental training studies. *Journal of Educational Psychology, 91*. 403–414.

Carlisle, J. F. (1995). Morphological awareness and early reading achievement. In Feldman, L. B. (Ed.), *Morphological aspects of language processing* (pp. 189–209). Erlbaum, Publishers: Hillsdale. NJ.

Carlisle, J. F., & Fleming, J. (2003). Lexical processing of morphologically complex words in the elementary years. *Scientific Studies in Reading. 7*, 239–254.

Carlisle. J. F., Stone. C. A., & Katz. L. A. (2001). The effect of phonological transparency on reading derived words. *Annals of Dyslexia, 51*, 249–274.

Carlisle, J. F. (2003). Morphology matters in learning to read: A commentary. *Reading Psychology, 24*, 291–332.

Castles, A. (2006). The dual route model and the developmental dyslexias. *London Review of Education. 4.* 49-61.

Castles, A., & Coltheart, M. (1993). Varieties of developmental dyslexia. *Cognition, 47.* 149-180.

Colasante, C., Kirby. J. R., Parrila, R., & Wade-Woolley, L. (2006). *Remediating naming speed and phonological deficits in reading disabled children: An evaluation of two intervention programs.* Paper presented at the annual meeting of the Canadian Language and Literacy Research Network. Charlottetown. PEI.

Coltheart, M., Rastle, K., Perry, C., Langdon, R., & Ziegler. J. (2001). DRC: A dual route cascaded model of visual word recognition and reading aloud. *Psychological Review, 108,* 204-256.

Cunningham, A. E., Perry, K. E., & Stanovich, K. E. (2001). Converging evidence for the concept of orthographic processing. *Reading and Writing: An Interdisciplinary Journal, 14,* 549-568.

Cunningham. A. E., & Stanovich. K. E. (1990). Assessing print exposure and orthographic processing skill in children: A quick measure of reading experience. *Journal of Educational Psychology. 82,* 733-740.

Deacon, S. D., Parrila, R., & Kirby, J. R. (2007). A review of the evidence on morphological processing in dyslexics and poor readers: A strength or weakness? In F. Manis, A. Fawcett, G. Reid. & L. Siegel (Eds.), *Dyslexia handbook.* Thousand Oaks. CA: Sage.

Deacon. S. H., & Kirby, J. R. (2004). Morphological: Is it more than phonological? Evaluating the roles of morphological and phonological awareness in reading development. *Applied Psycholinguistics. 25,* 223-238.

Denckla, M. B., & Rudel, R. G. (1976). Rapid "automatized" naming (R. A. N.): Dyslexia differentiated from other learning disabilities. *Neitropsyciologia, 14,* 471-479.

Dunn, L. M., & Dunn, L. M. (1981). *Peabody Picture Vocabulary Test—Revised.* Circle Pines, MN: American Guidance.

Ehri, L. C., Nunes, S. R., Stahl, S. A., & Willows. D. M. (2001). Systematic phonics instruction helps students learn to read: Evidence from the National Reading Panel's meta-analysis. *Review of Educational Research, 71,* 393-447.

Goswami, U., & Bryant, P. E. (1990). *Phonological skills and learning to read.* Hove, East Sussex, United Kingdom: Erlbaum.

Gough. P. B., & Tunmer. W. E. (1986). Decoding, reading, and reading disability. *Remedial and Special Education, 7,* 6-10.

Johnston. T. C., & Kirby, J. R. (2006). The contribution of naming speed to the simple view of reading. *Reading and Writing. 19,* 339-361.

Kail, R., Hall, L. K., & Caskey, B. J. (1999). Processing speed, exposure to print, and naming speed. *Applied Psycholinguistics, 20,* 303-314.

Kirby, J. R., Parrila, R., & Pfeiffer, S. (2003). Naming speed and phonological processing as predictors of reading development. *Journal of Educational Psychology. 95.* 453-464.

Lemoine, H. E., Levy. B. A., & Hutchinson, A. (1993). Increasing the naming speed of poor reader: Representations formed across repetitions. *Journal of Experimental Psychology, 55,* 297-328.

Levy, B. A., Bourassa, D. C., & Horn, C. (1999). Fast and slow namers: Benefits of segmentation and whole word training. *Journal of Experimental Child Psychology, 73.* 115-138.

Levy, B. A., Gong, Z., Hessels, S., Evans, M. A., & Jared. D. (2006). Understanding print: Early reading development and the contributions of home literacy experiences. *Journal of Experimental Child Psychology, 93.* 63-93.

MacGinitie, W. H., & MacGinitie, R. K. (1992). *Gates—MacGinitie Reading Tests* (2nd Canadian ed.). Toronto, Ontario. Canada: Nelson.

Manis, F. R., Doi, L. M., & Bhadha. B. (2000). Naming speed, phonological awareness, and orthographic knowledge in second graders. *Journal of Learning Disabilities, 33,* 325-333.

McBride-Chang. C., & Manis, F. R. (1996). Structural invariance in the associations of naming speed, phonological awareness, and verbal reasoning in good and poor readers: A test of the double deficit hypothesis. *Reading and Writing: An Interdisciplinary Journal, 8,* 323-339.

McDougall. P., Borowsky, R., MacKinnon. G. E., & Hymel. S. (2005). Process dissociation of sight vocabulary and phonetic decoding in reading: A new perspective on surface and phonological dyslexias. *Brain and Language, 92,* 185-203.

Nagy, W., Berninger, V., & Abbott, R. (2006). Contributions of morphology beyond phonology to literacy outcomes of upper elementary and middle-school students. *Journal of Educational Psychology, 98,* 134-147.

National Reading Panel. (2000). *Teaching children to read: An evidence based assessment of the scientific literature on reading and its implications for reading instruction.* Bethesda, MD: National Institute of Child Health and Human Development.

Nunes. T., & Bryant. P. (Eds.) (2006). *Improving literacy by teaching morphemes.* London: Routledge.

Nunes. T., Bryant, P., & Olsson, J. (2003). Learning morphological and phonological spelling rules: An intervention study. *Scientific Studies of Reading. 7.* 289-307.

Olson, R., Forsberg, H., Wise. B., & Rack, J. (1994). Measurement of word recognition, orthographic, and phonological skills. In G. R. Lyon (Ed.), *Frames of reference for the assessment of learning disabilities: New views on measurement issues* (pp. 243-278). Baltimore: Brookes

Plaut. D. C. (2005). Connectionist approaches to reading. In M. J. Snowl- ing & C. Hulme (Eds.). *The science of reading: A handbook* (pp. 24-38). Oxford: Blackwell publishing.

Rastle, K., & Coltheart, M. (1998). Whammies and double whammies: The effect of length on nonword reading. *Psychonomic Bulletin Review, 5,* 277-282.

Rastle, K., & Coltheart, M. (1999). Serial and strategic effects in reading aloud. *Journal of Experimental Psychology: Human Perception and Performance, 25.* 482-503.

Rey, A., Ziegler. J., & Jacobs. A. (2000). Graphemes are perceptual reading units. *Cognition, 75.* BI-B12.

Roman, A. R., Kirby. J. R., Parrila. R., Wade-Woolley. L. & Deacon, S. D. (in press). Towards a comprehensive view of the skills involved in word reading in Grades 4. 6, and 8. *Journal of Experimental Child Psychology.*

Roth, L., Lai, S., White, B., & Kirby, J. R. (2006). *Orthographic and morphological processing as predictors of reading achievement.* Paper presented at the annual meeting of the Society for the Scientific Study of Reading, Vancouver, BC.

Share, D. L. (1995). Phonological recoding and self-teaching: *sine qua non* of reading acquisition. *Cognition. 55.* 151–218.

Stanovich. K. E. (1986). Matthew effects in reading: Some consequences of individual differences in the acquisition of literacy. *Reading Research Quarterly, 21.* 360–407.

Stanovich, K. E., & West, R. F. (1989). Exposure to print and orthographic processing. *Reading Research Quarterly, 24,* 402–433.

Sunseth, K., & Bowers, P. G. (2002). Rapid naming and phonemic awareness: Contributions to reading, spelling, and orthographic knowledge. *Scientific Studies of Reading, 6.* 401–429.

Swanson. H. L., Trainin, G., Necoechea, D. M., & Hammill. D. D. (2003). Rapid naming, phonological awareness, and reading: A meta-analysis of the correlation evidence. *Review of Educational Research. 73,* 407–440.

Wagner, R. K., Torgesen, J. K., & Rashotte, C. A. (1994). Development of reading-related phonological processing abilities: New evidence of bidirectional causality from a latent variable longitudinal study. *Developmental Psychology, 30,* 73–87.

Wagner, R. K., Torgesen, J. K., & Rashotte, C. A. (1999). *Comprehensive Test of Phonological Processes (CTOPP).* Austin. TX: Pro-Ed.

Wechsler, D. (1999). *Weclisler abbreviated scale of intelligence.* San Antonio. TX: The Psychological Corporation.

Wolf, M., & Bowers. P. G. (1999). The double-deficit hypothesis for the developmental dyslexias. *Journal of Educational Psychology. 9!,* 415–438.

Wolf, M., Bowers, P. G., & Biddle, K. (2000). Naming-speed processes, timing, and reading: A conceptual review. *Journal of Learning Disabilities. 33.* 387–407.

Wolf. M., O'Rourke. A. G., Gidney. C., Lovett. M., Cirino. P., & Morris. R. (2002). The second deficit: An investigation of the independence of phonological and naming-speed deficits in developmental dyslexia. *Reading and Writing: An Interdisciplinary Journal, 15,* 43–72.

Woodcock. R. W. (1998). *Woodcock Reading Mastery Tests-Revised (WRMT-R): Forms G & H.* USA: American Guidance Service.

Teaching Phonemic Awareness in Preschool

Reading readiness begins much earlier than formal school experiences. Early introductions to reading can encourage an excitement to want to read, as well as provide a foundation for later reading success. With that being said, what does an early introduction to phonemic awareness look like? Formal school phonemic awareness strategies and activities are typically guided by teachers and reinforced in the home through practice. In the instance of preschool learning, children are not developmentally ready for this type of instruction. Learning experiences for this young age group need to be purposeful and relevant to personal understanding, with meaningful implementation. If young children do not find personal meaning and cannot apply learned knowledge in their own life, they will not be as engaged or excited about the activity. Therefore, teachers must provide meaningful experiences for children to gain phonemic understanding at an early age. The following article will provide an understanding of how early learning experiences focused around reading readiness can affect children's ability to grasp phonemic awareness.

BEFORE READING:

Before reading the following article, consider what phonemic awareness activities might look like in a preschool classroom. How can early reading activities be incorporated in the preschool classroom? Before reading, create a chart with three columns. Label the first as "strategies," the second as "activities," and the third as "comments."

DURING READING:

During the reading, keep your chart close by. When you encounter a strategy related to phonemic awareness, add it to the strategy column. If you think of strategies not mentioned in the article, go ahead and feel free to add them to your list.

AFTER READING:

Upon completion of the article reading, review your list of strategies. Now, go back and identify the activities mentioned throughout the article. When you find specific activities related to strategies listed in your chart, add them to the "activity" column of the chart in line with the appropriate strategy. As with the "during reading" activity, feel free to add other activities not mentioned in the article as well. Upon completion, what strategies and activities stood out to you and seemed possible for you to use in your classroom? Add your thoughts to the comments column.

Literacy Instruction in Canadian Child Care Centers

BY MICHAL PERLMAN AND BROOKE A. FLETCHER

The preschool period is critical in determining children's developmental trajectories (National Research Council & Institute of Medicine, 2000; NICHD, 2005). With the significant rise in maternal employment rates over the past few decades, there has been a dramatic increase in the number of preschool-age children enrolled in child care centers (Lamb, 1998; Scarr, 1998). As children spend more time in center-based child care, caregivers need to provide not only custodial care but also early educational instruction in order to support the acquisition of the social and early academic skills that children will need upon formal school entry.

There is growing consensus among educators and parents that children need enriching educational experiences that support their development of literacy abilities from an early age (Bowman, Donovan, & Burns, 2001). The long-term links between children's literacy skills at formal school entry and positive academic outcomes in subsequent years of schooling have been well documented (Barnett, Lamy, & Jung, 2005; Cunningham & Stanovich, 1997). Children who begin school with poor literacy skills typically remain poor readers (Adams, 1990; Dickinson, McCabe, & Essex, 2006). In addition, the number of children in public schools who have been diagnosed with learning disabilities has steadily increased over the past several years, with the vast majority of these diagnoses stemming from difficulties in learning how to read (Snow, Burns, & Griffin, 1998). As a result of these findings, the importance of high-quality early literacy instruction prior to kindergarten has become a major focus of concern for researchers, educators, and policymakers (Rueda & Yaden, 2006; Saracho &

Spodek, 2003). Yet, surprisingly, we know very little about the types of literacy instruction that take place in child care centers, what drives such instruction, and what such instruction predicts. This study will begin to fill some of the gaps in our knowledge.

Emergent Literacy Skills

The acquisition of literacy related skills is a dynamic, ongoing process that begins very early in a child's life (Teale & Sulzby, 1986) and includes skills related to phonological and print awareness (Hill & Nichols, 2006). The term "emergent literacy" encompasses skills, knowledge, and attitudes that are developmental precursors to conventional forms of reading and writing. The skills subsumed under emergent literacy are the basic building blocks of more advanced forms of literacy (Connor, Morrison, & Slominski, 2006) and can be thought of as occurring on a developmental continuum of literacy that begins prior to formal school entry.

Phonological, phonemic, and print awareness are examples of emergent literacy skills (Senechal, LeFevre, Smith-Chant, & Colton, 2001). Phonological awareness refers to a sensitivity to any size unit of sound (Yopp & Yopp, 2000) and is essential to the attainment of early decoding skills (Pullen & Justice, 2003). Phonemic awareness, on the other hand, is a type of phonological awareness, defined as the knowledge that speech consists of a sequence of sounds (i.e., phonemes) (Yopp & Yopp, 2000). Print awareness includes alphabet knowledge and print concepts. Children in early child care settings who have well-developed print knowledge may know that text is read from left to right and top to bottom, that the story continues on the following page when one page of text has been read, and that the white spaces between groups of letters represent breaks in spoken words (Pullen & Justice, 2003).

Emergent literacy skill building within early childhood education includes exposing children to print-rich environments, including instructional activities requiring risk- taking, and the manipulation of print (Hill & Nichols, 2006). Examples of evidenced-based strategies that have been shown to improve emergent literacy skills include exposing preschool-age children to activities involving segmentation of sentences into words, clapping or dancing to individual syllables within words, having children identify letters, shared storybook reading, and rhyming activities (Adams, 1990; Anderson, Moffat, & Shapiro, 2006; Justice & Kaderavek, 2002; Lonigan, Burgess, Anthony, & Barker, 1998; Seifert, 2006). In this study, we focus on the following early literacy instructional strategies: reading aloud, word instruction, letter identification, letter-word sounds, symbol recognition, and word segmentation.

The development of emergent literacy skills is critical for later success in reading (Adams, 1990; Adams, Treiman, & Pressley, 1998) and writing (Seifert, 2006). The child care center can play a pivotal role in facilitating the acquisition of literacy skills. The developmental framework of a large component of children's reading skills in early elementary school has been found to be rooted in the preschool period (Lonigan, Burgess, & Anthony, 2000). Furthermore, the ordering or spacing of children's performance in phonological sensitivity from preschool to kindergarten and 1st grade has been reported not to change despite growth in these skills (Lonigan et al., 2000). Thus, providing opportunities for children to develop their emergent literacy skills in child care centers is crucial. The potential benefits of literacy instruction in child care classrooms is promising, especially for children who come from home environments that do not provide plentiful opportunities for such instruction. For example, it has been estimated that children from families of low socioeconomic status enter 1st grade with an average of 25 hours of one-to-one book reading experiences, whereas middle-class children enter with upwards of 1,000 hours of such experience (Adams, 1990, p. 85). Thus, for some children whose parents do not have the resources, time, or motivation to provide a literacy-rich environment, the child care center may be the main source of literacy exposure.

Literacy Instruction in Practice

Although there is considerable research pertaining to emergent literacy skills and what early literacy instruction *should* look like, surprisingly little is known about the type of literacy instruction that children in child care classrooms *actually* receive. This is not to say that educators and policymakers have not recognized the important role that child care centers have in facilitating children's literacy development. For instance, the *Head Start Child Outcomes Framework* (Head Start, 2000), a guideline for Head Start staff to use in assessing critical skills pertaining to school readiness among 3- to 5-year-old children, focuses on emerging literacy skills. Furthermore, researchers generally agree that upon formal school entry, children should: 1) have acquired basic phonological awareness skills, such as identifying initial sounds in words, segmenting words into syllables, and rhyming; 2) have mastered print awareness skills; and 3) be able to identify a minimum of 10 letters (see Hawken, Johnston, & McDonnell, 2005, for a review).

When surveyed, child care staff report that they agree or strongly agree that some daily classroom time should be devoted for emerging literacy skill instruction (Hawken et al., 2005). But in fact, it seems that explicit instruction that targets emergent literacy skills is limited. For example, Dickinson, McCabe, and Anastasopoulos (2002) observed 100 preschool classrooms in New England for at least one full day and found that storybook reading did not occur in approximately 40% of the total number of observations; when it did, it typically lasted for less than 10 minutes. Also of concern was the finding that half of the classrooms observed did not have a separate area for books or where children can read. Connor et al. (2006) videotaped 34 preschool classrooms in a major midwestern city in the United States and found that, at a classroom level of instruction, staff spent an average of only 4 minutes per day reading aloud with students. Approximately one additional minute of daily classroom instruction was divided among vocabulary, comprehension, concepts of print, and other language arts activities. Thus, while researchers, policymakers, and perhaps even caregivers may acknowledge the importance of literacy instruction and report that they engage in such instruction, the limited available empirical evidence suggests that, in reality, the amount of such instruction is minimal. The small amount of teacher-led instruction focusing on increasing phonological awareness and other emergent literacy skills may be due to the pedagogical beliefs of preschool teachers that the goal of early childhood education should be to promote children's social, emotional, and physical well-being, and not focus heavily on academic learning (Lee, 2006). However, consistent with the approach adopted in the current study, it is important to note that activities that support emergent literacy skills do not have to involve drilling of skills, but instead can be student-focused and embedded in play and other social situations, such as in songs and craft activities.

Predictors of Literacy Instruction in Child Care

Most of the research that has examined predictors of child care literacy instruction and subsequent acquisition of related skills focuses on structural and process components of child care that predict children's oral language skills. Structural characteristics of child care centers include such indices as child-to-staff ratios, the size of the group in which a child receives care, and staff education and experience. Process quality refers to the experiences that children have with caregivers, peers, and materials in child care, and thus includes measures of caregiver/child interactions and environment rating scales, such as the Early Childhood Environment Rating Scale-Revised (EC- ERS-R; Harms, Clifford, & Cryer, 1998).

With respect to structural features of child care centers, it has been reported that better child-to-staff ratios tend to allow for more opportunities for children to engage in discussion with their caregivers that support children's language development (Dickinson, 2001) and to predict better receptive and expressive language skills among young children (Burchinal, Roberts, Nabors, & Bryant, 1996). A host of positive outcomes for young children have been found to be related to teachers' educational background, including whether or not they have obtained a bachelor's degree in early childhood education (ECE) (Barnett, 2004; Howes & Brown, 2000). Specific to literacy acquisition, children in child care classrooms with staff who have at least an associate's degree in ECE have been found to have higher standardized receptive language scores than those children in classrooms with staff who had lower levels of education (Burchinal, Cryer, Clifford, & Howes, 2002; Howes, 1997). However, based on large samples, more recent research has reported conflicting findings with respect to level of teacher education and child outcomes. Early et al. (2006) report that level of teacher education does not predict gains in children's vocabulary, rhyming, or identification of letters.

The materials in the classroom also are associated with children's engagement in literacy instruction (see Farran, Aydogan, Kang, & Lipsey, 2006 for a review of classroom environmental effects on children's literacy acquistion). For example, the number of books, the amount of different recording materials (e.g., paper), and the number of recording instruments (e.g., pencils) have been reported to be closely related to the frequency of children's reading and writing. Access to books has been repeatedly linked to literacy acquisition.

Furthermore, classrooms that emphasize literacy through materials and instruction are positively correlated with children's use of these materials.

The Present Study

The present study had three research objectives. The first was to document the different types of literacy instruction that take place in child care classrooms, in order to provide empirical information about how centers prepare children for success in literacy acquisition. This is important, given how little is known about the amount and content of literacy instruction in child care centers. This goal was achieved through detailed observations of staff, as well as from measures examining aspects of the physical classroom environment (e.g., quantity and quality of instructional materials). As research has indicated that large variations exist across child care classrooms with regard to the quality of literacy environments (Connor et al., 2006; Stone & Twardosz, 2001), the authors also explored the prevalence of the different types of literacy instruction across classrooms and providers. Based on the results of previous research (Hawken et al., 2005), it is expected that at least some class time will be devoted to literacy instruction, such as reading aloud, vocabulary building, and letter-word sounds.

The second objective was to examine factors that may predict literacy instruction in child care centers. Specifically, such structural quality characteristics as child- to-staff ratios, group size, and caregiver credentials were used as independent variables in the prediction of several components of literacy instruction as outcomes. It is expected that the amount and complexity of literacy instruction will be predicted by better child-to-staff ratios, smaller group sizes, and higher levels of staff education, as these characteristics may create opportunities for more structured teacher-led activities.

The final research objective was to conduct preliminary analyses of the impact of literacy instruction on children's concurrent pre-academic functioning. This analysis was constrained by the availability of appropriate child outcomes described in the methods section. It is expected that receiving greater amounts of literacy instruction will predict children's more successful concurrent pre-academic functioning.

As Canadian policymakers currently rely heavily on studies that use U.S. samples to inform decisions, the current study will provide greatly needed Canadian data for Eruidine decision-making.

Including Parents in Phonemic Awareness Instruction

When preparing reading readiness curriculum teachers generally do not consider including parents in planning or implementation. Most often, learning is considered a result of instruction and activities in the classroom with teachers and peers. However, the learning and activities implemented at home play an important role in a child's ability to learn to read at an early age. By extending the learning from the classroom and into the home, teachers are able to include parents in the learning process. The home-school partnership enhances student learning through reading practice opportunities. The following article shares a research-based perspective of how parental involvement can affect children's ability to learn to read.

BEFORE READING

Before reading this article, think about the typical role parents play in the classroom. Are parents involved in the curriculum? What are some ways parents become involved in the learning process?

DURING READING

While reading, starting thinking about how the teachers in the article involve parents in the curriculum. What do you think were the obstacles in involving parents in the curriculum? How could parents be encouraged to participate in the learning process through extending learning into the home?

AFTER READING

After reading the article, identify the benefits to involving parents in the learning process. Now consider the typical role parents play in the classroom? How can you change the home-school learning mindset? What are some purposeful learning activities to be implemented at home?

Home Grown for Reading

Parental Contributions to Young Children's Emergent Literacy and Word Recognition

BY MARY ANN EVANS AND DEBORAH SHAW

About a half a century ago—a phrase that conveys just how much our conception has changed—children were given "reading readiness tests" at school entrance to assess whether they were "ready" for the new initiative of learning to read. About 20 years ago, in concert with views of child development as a constructivist process, this conception began to change toward an understanding of learning to read as a process that starts much earlier in life and that is based upon a variety of foundational skills acquired before children enter formal schooling. The term emergent literacy, launched by Teale and Sulzby (1986) in their edited volume, and brought to life in Clay's (1993) observational studies of young children, was introduced to refer to this conception. More recently, it has come to refer to the skills and reading-like behaviours that are developmental precursors to their conventional and more advanced counterparts.

The view that the home environment in which children grow plays a substantial role in their literacy development is nicely illustrated by a large-scale study of twins completed by Petrill, Deater-Deckard. Schatschneider, and Davis (2005). Here, family environment characteristics were associated with children's reading outcome beyond what could be explained by genes shared by parents and children. The purpose of this review article is to detail key activities of the home environment provided by parents to young children that are predictive of reading development in general and. more specifically, of aspects of emergent literacy skills contributing to word recognition skill—phonological ability, alphabetic knowledge, concepts of print, and vocabulary. Given the salience of shared book reading as a home activity, a separate section is devoted to its different facets, changing nature, and potential effects. To provide a background for why these specific topics have been selected, a brief outline follows directly below of what is meant by emergent literacy and of the transition from emergent literacy to conventional word recognition.

Emergent Literacy and Word Recognition

In explicating the term emergent literacy, Whitehurst and Lonigan (1998) distinguished between "inside-out" and "outside-in" knowledge. The first refers to information relied on within the printed word to translate print into phonological representations or spoken words (i.e., to decode), and conversely to translate spoken words into print. This includes alphabetic knowledge (letters and the sounds they represent) and phonological awareness (awareness and ability to reflect on the sounds in spoken words). The second—outside-in—entails information from outside the printed word to help the reader derive meaning from it, and includes domains such as semantic and syntactic knowledge, knowledge of narrative structure, and broader conceptual understanding. Similarly, Scarborough (2001) conceptualised skilled reading to be comprised of two strands of underlying skills. The first consists of word recognition skills that include phonological awareness, decoding, and sight recognition of words. The second consists of language comprehension skills entailing vocabulary, syntax, background knowledge of facts and concepts; knowledge about print concepts and genres; and verbal reasoning skills. The distinction in both articles parallels a "simple view" of reading put forth by Gough and Tumner (1986) in which reading is conceptualised as the product of decoding and comprehension, decoding being the act of translating print to sound and in doing so recognising spoken words in print and their associated meanings and usages.

Several stage theories have been put forward for the development of word recognition, many of which are consistent to some degree with that of Ehri (1999). In the first stage called prealphabetic, logographic, selective-cue, or paired-associate, children identify words based on their overall shape, context, or the background on which they appear. During the second partial alphabetic stage, also referred to as the visual recognition, or rudimentary alphabetic phase, children use some letters—often the first and/or last in words—in combination with their limited knowledge of letters to guess at words. In the third full alphabetic stage, named by others as the spelling-sound, or cipher reading stage, a more complete knowledge of letter—sound correspondences allows children to more accurately decode words and store sight words to help them read new words by analogy. Finally, in the fourth phase, the consolidated alphabetic phase, children consolidate their knowledge of recurring letter patterns and words through repeated exposure and experience to read more efficiently. In fact. Share (1999) has proposed that once a certain level of skill in phonolog- ically recoding words has been reached, it becomes a self-teaching mechanism in which children are able to create at least an approximation of how words are pronounced, recognise those word as a part of their vocabulary, and develop the word-specific orthographic representations neces- sary for skilled reading. Accordingly, attention is rightly directed at phonological awareness, alphabetic knowledge (letter name knowledge and letter sound knowledge), concepts of print and printed words, and vocabulary in the development of reading skill. Each of these areas and research supporting a linkage between home activities and their development is presented below.

Phonological Awareness

Phonological awareness, the conscious awareness of linguistic units (syllables, rhymes, phonemes) of spoken language, is widely accepted to play an important role in learning to read (see reviews by Adams, 1990; Castles & Coltheart, 2004; National Reading Panel, 2000; Scarborough, 2001). As outlined in these reviews, longitudinal and correlational studies have indicated that phonological awareness is concurrently and predictively related to reading performance after controlling for confounding variables, such as intelligence, socioeconomic status, and general language ability, and children with reading difficulties perform less well on phonological awareness tasks than normal age-matched or reading level-matched peers.

Phonological awareness appears to develop from larger to smaller sound units, with con- scious awareness of syllables and rhymes preceding that of single phonemes, and from initial to ending to medial positions in spoken words. Controversy exists regarding which aspects of phonological awareness are more important (see Castles & Coltheart, 2004; Goswami, 2002), with some suggesting that rhyming is less critical than phonemic awareness (i.e., awareness of individual phonemes; Blaiklock, 2004; Hatcher & Hulme, 1999; Muter et al., 1998; Wagner et al., 1997). Bryant (2002) has argued that rhyme awareness nonetheless may be an important developmental precursor. If so, parents who tell nursery rhymes to, read rhyming poetry to, and sing songs with their children, encouraging them to fill in the rhyming words, may facili- tate the beginnings of this skill. Some support for this notion is provided by Bryant, Bradley, McLean, and Crossland (1989 who found that children who knew more nursery rhymes were better at rhyming tasks and later more successful in reading. In addition, Evans, Shaw, Bell, Moretti. and Fox (2002) found that the earlier parents began reading books to their children, the better children were on phonemic awareness tests after controlling for cognitive abilities.

A possible explanation is that books for young children are often written in rhyming stanzas with strong rhythmic structure in the syllables.

Alphabetic Knowledge

The predictive relationship between phonemic awareness and reading is not simple, however, in that some letter knowledge may be necessary for phonemic awareness (e.g., Blaiklock, 2004; Wagner et al., 1997; Wimmer, Landerl, Linortner, & Hummer, 1991). In addition, its relationship to subsequent word recognition is sizeably reduced after controlling for letter knowledge (e.g., Castles & Coltheart, 2004; Evans. Bell, Shaw, Moretti, & Page, 2006; MacMillan, 2002). In fact, the meta-analyses by the National Reading Panel (2000) of the effectiveness of phonological awareness training programmes led to the conclusion that although phonological awareness is important for learning to read, it alone it is not sufficient. Rather letter knowledge must accompany it, with programmes that combine phonological and letter training being more effective.

In addition, young children's letter knowledge, both names and sounds, before school entry and in the early primary grades, is itself predictive of future reading achievement (see reviews by Adams, 1990; Foulin, 2005; Scarborough, 1998). One mechanism for this relationship may be that high letter knowledge, especially letter naming fluency, reflects the thoroughness and confidence with which letter names are known and degree to which letters and other visual stimuli can be labelled automatically and effortlessly (Adams, 1990). A second is that letter names are closely related to their sounds, which may facilitate learning grapheme-phoneme correspondences and decoding (Treiman. Tincoff. Rodriguez, Mouzaki, & Francis, 1998).

During the preschool years, letter knowledge appears to progress from reciting the alphabet, to printing and recognising one's own name, to identifying, labelling and printing letters of the alphabet (Bialystok, 1992; Byrne & Fielding-Barnsley, 1989; Mason, 1980). Many parents report explicitly teaching their children the names and/or sounds of letters and how to print them, and provide their children with alphabet blocks, books, and friezes. For example in Haney and Hill's (2004) study, 71% parents of children ages 3 to 5 reported teaching letter names and 65% reported teaching letter sounds. Similarly Levy, Gong, Hessels, Evans, and Jared (2006) found that parents reported involving their children in printing their names and learning or practising letter names and sounds as frequently as reading them storybooks. The former activities clustered with others entailing practising reading and writing. The extent to which parents involved their children in this cluster of activities was concurrently related to children's understanding of the printed forms of words, even after controlling for children's age and independent pursuit of these same activities. Likewise studies contrasting the frequency of informal print exposure through shared book reading with the frequency of parent- reported teaching about print (Evans, Shaw, & Bell, 2000; Sénéchal, 2006; Sénéchal & LeFevre, 2002; Sénéchal, LeFevre, Thomas, & Daley, 1998) demonstrated that informal print exposure was unrelated to letter knowledge and subsequent reading skill in first grade, but reports of teaching about print were positively predictive. Only later, once children had developed the ability to decode words with relative ease, did informal print exposure (and as will be seen below, vocabulary development associated with it) show any relationship.

Formal and informal print activities need not be mutually exclusive. Justice and Ezell (2002) effectively demonstrated that storybooks can be read to children both for enjoyment and meaning as well as with a print focus, such as asking children to find the letters in their name on the page or with a certain shape, and naming letters. Moreover, they showed that reading to children with such extratextual comments focussed on print resulted in children making greater gains in alphabet knowledge, in print concepts, and in recognising words within picture contexts, than reading books with extratextual comments focussed on the pictures.

In addition, certain kinds of children's books may be viewed as "print salient" via the prominence of the print within the book. The most notable are alphabet books. These often contain an upper and lowercase letter, brief text, and an accompanying illustration of an item or cluster of items whose name begins with the letter and/or letter sound, such as "C is for" for example "chimpanzee," "cat" or "centipede." Also included are books with simple printed signs such as "STOP" or words such as "ZZZZZZ" embedded in the pictures or enlarged in the text.

Alphabet books may be traced back to horn books which appear hanging from children's waists in paintings of the 15th century. Horn books displayed the alphabet in printed or manuscript letters behind a thin transparent covering of horn, hence their name. As printed materials became more widespread in the late 18th century, horn books were replaced by folded sheets with the letters and accompanying illustrations (called battledoors) and still later by alphabet books (Kevill-Davies, 1991). Alphabet books are often the first type of book purchased by parents (Zeece, 1996) and are commonly found in homes. For example, in the study by Levy et al. (2006), parents reported reading alphabet books with their children three times a month and children looking at them on their own an additional three times a month.

Small n observations of parents and their preschool-age children reading a variety of books together by Smolkin and Yaden (1992) and Yaden, Smolkin. and MacGillivray (1993) showed that, whilst parent and child questions and comments about the print were rare, they were more frequent when reading an alphabet book. Similarly. Stadler and McEvoy (2003) found that print-focussed comments were more common with an alphabet book, but only for normally developing and not language-impaired children. Bus and van IJzendoom (1988) also observed that with alphabet books, parent comments were more likely to include naming letters, helping children to recognise sounds in words, and connecting letters to words. Important to note, however, these behaviours were more evident when children had higher levels of emergent literacy. Thus, these studies suggest that parents are more likely to emphasise letters and letter sounds rather than the pictures in alphabet books when they estimate that their children will benefit from these comments.

A limited set of classroom research (Brabham, Murray, & Bowden, 2006; Greenewald & Kulig, 1995; Murray, Stahl, & Ivey, 1996) suggests that alphabet books may foster alphabetic knowledge. Findings from the latter study were also suggestive of gains in phonological awareness. In this study, Murray, Stahl and Ivey assigned three junior kindergarten classroom to one of three conditions over a 3-week period—reading four conventional alphabet books showing letters and corresponding illustrations, versus featuring letter names in the text, versus picture story books. As would be expected with the passage of time and the curriculum, all groups gained in alphabetic, print knowledge, and phonological awareness. Children who read the conventional alphabet books made greater gains in phonological awareness than those who read the letter-name books, but did not differ from those who read the storybooks. Unfortunately, however, there was no control for curriculum to untangle the effects of the different kinds of books from the classrooms in which each was embedded. Similar gains were also observed by Brabham et al. (2006) when contrasting teachers who read alphabet books with an emphasis on phonemes of the letters versus an emphasis on the meanings of the objects associated with the letter sound.

There is also recent evidence from a study by Evans and Saint-Aubin (2008) that the physical layout of some alphabet books may be helpful in drawing children's attention to print. They tracked the eye-movements of preschool age children reading an alphabet book having a simple illustration, a single printed word, and a large letter on each page. Whilst nonreaders attended primarily to the illustrations, they nonetheless fixated the alphabet letter and printed word more than would be expected for nonreaders. Thus, alphabet books, in themselves and in interactions with parents who highlight the names, shapes, and sounds of letters, are likely a valuable resource for developing and consolidating alphabetic knowledge.

Chapter References

Blair, T. R. (2013). *Teaching children to read in diverse communities: A practical guide for reading success.* Academic Media Solutions.

Chapman, M. L. (2003). Phonemic awareness: Clarifying what we know. *Literacy, Teaching and Learning, 7(1)*2, 91–114.

Deavers, R., Solity, J., & Kerfoot, S. (2000). The effect of instruction on early nonword reading strategies. *Journal of Research in Reading,* 23(*3*), 267–286.

Nichols, W. D., Rupley, W. H., Rickelman, R. J., & Algozzine, B. (2004). Examining phonemic awareness and concepts of print patterns of kindergarten students. *Reading Research and Instruction,* 43(*3*), 56–82.

Chapter Three

Introductions by Karen Loman

PHONICS AND SPELLING

Phonics and Word Recognition

INTRODUCTION TO READING 3.1

Phonics and Spelling

Learning to read unfamiliar words is integral to becoming literate. The most effective literacy instruction incorporates a variety of approaches, provides early and explicit instruction, and focuses on strategies learners can use independently. Good phonics instruction develops the alphabetic principle and phonological awareness, provides practice reading and writing words and sentences, develops automatic word recognition and accurate spelling of familiar words, and represents only one part of literacy instruction (Stahl, Duffy-Hester, & Stahl, 1998). Several approaches for teaching phonics and decoding have been identified: analytic (breaks words into component parts), linguistic (uses decodable texts), synthetic (sounds taught in isolation then blended to words), spelling based (study words and word patterns), analogy based (uses known word patterns and parts to read unknown words), and embedded (context). The differences between the approaches are relatively small (Stahl, Duffy-Hester, & Stahl, 1998), thus the best method is a balanced use of multiple approaches. Early and explicit instruction should include letter and sound relationships, common patterns of English spelling and how to use them to decode and spell new words, and strategies for reading and spelling. Strategies should provide students with the means to read and write independently.

Phonics and decoding instruction is critical during the primary grades and still important for older students. Upper grade students need support learning to read, spell, and define multisyllabic (big) words. All students, including upper grade students, need phonics activities that engage them in word manipulation and conversations rather than fill-in-the-blank worksheets/workbooks and premade writing exercises.

BEFORE READING

How does the information you have read so far match your experiences as a student? What approach to phonics do you most often see in classrooms?

DURING READING

Think about how the following strategies and activities are research based and move beyond worksheets and workbooks. Do they represent a variety of approaches? Are they engaging? Would they support early learners and advancing learners?

AFTER READING

Which strategy or strategies did you try? How successful were students? How do you know? Which will you try next?

Teaching Phonics and Word Recognition

BY TIMOTHY R. BLAIR

What it is and What Research Can Tell Us

The ability to pronounce and interpret written symbols—to recognize unknown words—is an integral component of the reading process. Good readers are superior in this ability, while poor readers and beginning readers have trouble with it. However, identifying words is not reading but is a means for developing reading efficiency. Once students have learned ways to automatically decode words (i.e., to identify words quickly with minimal effort), they can devote most of their available attention to processing the text for meaning (Samuels, 1988).

The four major strategies used to recognize or decode unknown words are phonics, structural analysis, contextual analysis, and sight vocabulary. These four strategies together comprise a balanced word recognition program. They are taught concurrently in elementary school because one word recognition or decoding strategy will not be successful in all reading situations. Thus, readers need to develop a flexible, problem-solving approach to identifying unknown words (Durkin, 2004).

Phonics is a compilation of the connections or correspondences that exist between letters and the sounds they record in syllables used to help readers pronounce unknown words. In essence, phonics allows students to use the spelling of a word to get help with its pronunciation. Our language is an alphabetic one in that written words represent a collection of speech sounds, and this fact allows us to use phonics, a method to relate letters to the speech sounds that they represent. Reading programs must teach the content of phonics in the early grades in a direct/explicit fashion (National Institute of Child Health and Human Development, 2000). In addition, phonic instruction must include many opportunities for practice and transfer to new reading situations in everyday reading and writing activities (Armbruster, Lehr, & Osborn, 2001).

For youngsters trying to figure out words not yet in their reading vocabulary, it is an unfortunate reality that a lawful, one-to-one correspondence does not exist between sound and symbol. The English language has many more speech sounds than letters to represent them (26 letters, but anywhere from 42 to 46 speech sounds). Nevertheless, letter-sound generalizations and factors affecting letter-sound correspondences warrant the teaching of phonics to provide one way for students to identify unknown words on their own.

The second strategy for recognizing unknown words—structural analysis—focuses on meaningful structural units. In structural analysis, students identify a word's syllables, root element, prefixes, suffixes, compound elements, contractions, and inflectional endings to decode the word. As with phonics, the use of structural analysis depends on meaningful practice in context.

Contextual analysis is the third strategy for decoding unknown words and involves teaching students to use semantics (the meaning of other words in a sentence and paragraph) to arrive at the pronunciation and meaning of an unknown word, and syntax (the arrangement of word order) to determine the word's part of speech and whether it is singular or plural. Conscious use of context enables readers to arrive at the pronunciation and meaning of many words. Again, as is the case with the other word-decoding strategies, contextual analysis (using both semantic and syntactic clue systems) is rarely used by itself but is best combined with phonics or structural analysis in decoding unknown words.

The fourth and final strategy for recognizing unknown words involves sight vocabulary, which is comprised of the most common words in the English language (sometimes called basic service words), words of interest to students, words that appear regularly in students' first readers, and content-area words. Many sight words in the English language are irregular in nature (do not have a one-to-one sound/symbol relationship) and are taught using the whole-word or sight-word approach. In this approach, students learn a word by looking at it as a whole, not dissecting it. It is assumed that students will learn to identify these words by sight or instantly when presented with them. Words are presented visually to students, pronounced by both teacher and students, discussed and used in sentences, and practiced independently by students. In almost every instance, words learned through the whole-word or sight-word approach need to be practiced in context in a variety of ways.

Teacher Behaviors

- Specify clear instructional goals.
- Do not penalize students for dialectal errors in oral reading as long as reading comprehension is unaffected.
- Use the explicit/direct model of instruction to teach content with an abundance of meaningful practice.
- Monitor student progress.
- Foster a flexible, problem-solving approach in using phonics, structural analysis, contextual analysis, and sight words.
- Provide immediate feedback to students.
- Coach or assist students in the application of skill or strategy in real reading situations.

Teaching Strategies

1. *Analytic phonics.* Begin with a certain number of words that your students know, and have students examine the relationships between the phonic elements. Using the direct/explicit teaching approach, there are two basic ways of teaching a phonics lesson analytically:
   - Inductive—Give examples illustrating a generalization, and guide students to a conclusion.
   - Deductive—Tell students the generalization, and then ask them for examples to verify it.

   The following is an example of the inductive approach: Assume that students know the words *ball, bat,* and *bundle.* Ask students what is alike about the words. Students should discover that the words contain the letter *b,* which represents the /b/ sound. Ask students to tell you other words with the sound of /b/. Have students put the words into sentences and read the sentences aloud. Give students practice exercises for using the words in sentences.

   The following is an example of the deductive approach: List the words *ball, bat,* and *bundle* on the chalkboard (assuming that the words are in students' listening-speaking vocabulary). Tell students that all the words begin with the letter *b* and represent the /b/ sound as in *big.* Ask students to tell you other words with the sound of /b/. Have students put the words into sentences and read the sentences aloud. Give students practice exercises for using the words in sentences.

2. *Synthetic phonics.* Begin immediately with instruction of individual phonics elements. Once students learn the sounds represented by the letters, they blend the parts of the words together to form a known word. In synthetic phonics, there are three variations of sound blending: (1) letter by letter (*b-a-t*); (2) the initial consonant is sounded, and the rest of the word is added as a word family (*b-at*); and (3) the initial consonant with the vowel is sounded together and then the final consonant (*ba-t*).

3. *Word families or phonograms.* Teach your students various clusters of sounds in words—sometimes called word families or phonograms. For example, a common phonogram is *ake,* as in the word *bake.* After teaching students the pronunciation of *ake,* guide them into substituting different beginning sounds with the same cluster of letters and pronounce words such as *rake, sake, take, lake, shake, make,* and *cake.* In this method, there is no need to isolate sounds as students learn to look for known letter clusters in new words. This method is also called "onsets and rimes" with the cluster of letters that rhyme called the "rime" and the preceding letter or letters called the "onset."

4. *Explicit/direct instruction for structural analysis and context.* In addition to teaching the content of phonics in a direct manner, teach the elements of structural analysis and the use of context clues to students in a step-by-step fashion, followed by both guided and independent practice opportunities.

Activities

- *Matching pictures and words.* Show students a picture of an object and follow it by four words, none of which names the picture but one or more of which begin with the same sound as the name of the pictured object. Ask students to draw a circle around the boxes or words that begin with the same sound. You can do this with final consonant sounds as well.
- *Identifying sounds in words.* Show students a series of boxes, each containing three words. Pronounce one of the words, and direct students to underline the word pronounced. Students need not know all of the words as sight words, provided they are familiar with the initial sound of each.

EXAMPLE

1	2	3	4	5
call	tell	hill	may	hat
bank	sell	fill	pay	show
play	fell	bill	say	bat

- *Matching words*: In columns, present words, some of which begin with the same sound and the same letter. Ask students to draw a line from the word in column A to the word in column B that begins with the same sound.

EXAMPLE

A	B
me	be
ball	said
sail	make

- *The final sounds in candy.* Make a list of different names of candies. Begin with the first kind of candy on the list, say the name of the candy, and emphasize the final consonant students hear. Do this for all the candy on the list. You may want to put students into groups to brainstorm other words that end with the final sounds you have been working on. Record students' responses on the chalkboard.
- *Introducing initial consonants.* Print an uppercase letter on the board, and tell students they will learn all about that letter. Next to the uppercase letter, print the lowercase letter (example: Bb). Begin to write words that begin with lowercase *b*. Point to each word, and pronounce it by stressing the initial sound *b* without distorting it. Direct students to look at each word as it is pronounced, and ask if they can give any other words with the sound heard in the words. When a student gives the name of a person that starts with the letter *b*, tell students that we write that name with a capital *B* because it is somebody's name. Make sure you give lots of examples. Note that in no instance are students asked to sound the letter *b* in isolation.
- *Identifying objects.* Show students a picture of an object they will be able to recognize. Then show students a row of pictures, and ask them to mark the objects whose names begin with the same sound as the name of the object in the first picture shown. You can do this with final consonants as well.
- *Vowel patterns.* Select a few easy words that have been used previously and that contain the vowel pattern being taught. Write these words in a column, and pronounce each word with students. Have students note the vowel letter in the middle of the word, and emphasize the sound it represents—for example, the *e* in *met, set,* and *pet.*

- *Single-double vowel patterns.* Prepare lists of words in which column A has a single vowel (e.g., *met*) and column B is identical except for an added vowel (e.g., *meat*). Ask students to read the first word under column A and to listen for the short vowel sound. Then ask them to read the first word under column B, to note the two-vowel pattern, and to listen for the long vowel sound. As a final step, have them read each pair in rapid succession to note the contrasting vowel sound (such as *met-meat* and *led-lead*).

- *The effect of final e.* On the chalkboard, write a column of words that contain the medial vowel *a*. As you pronounce these words, have students tell you which vowel sound they hear in the word *(a)*. Explain that you will change each word by adding the letter *e* at the end. Create a second column with the words from the first column, and add the letter *e*. As you pronounce these words, have students note the *a__e* pattern, and ask them to tell you the vowel sound they hear in each of the words. Be sure to mention that in many short words with two vowels, a final *e* is not sounded, while the first vowel has its long sound. Do many exercises with students, and have them say each word aloud.

- *Long vowel sounds at the end of short words.* Two generalizations cover single vowels at the end of words: (1) If a word has only one vowel that ends the word, the vowel sound usually is long, and (2) if a word has no other vowel and ends with *y*, the letter *y* serves as a vowel and is pronounced as long *i*. These generalizations apply in a limited number of high-frequency words and can be taught at the chalkboard, using columns of words. Utilize activities similar to those previously listed.

- *Short-vowel packages.* Create five packages, and label each package with a different vowel sound. Tape each package to a wall or chalkboard. Ask students to describe the packages and what is on the packages. Once students have noticed that all five packages contain a vowel, review all the sounds each *short* vowel makes. Ask students to give examples of words that contain the short vowel sound. Give each student five index cards. Instruct students to draw and label pictures of words containing the short vowel sound. You may want to do a few as a whole group so students know exactly what to do. Have students take turns reading their short-vowel picture cards and then taping them on the appropriate package.

- *Prefix and suffix strips.* After teaching particular prefixes and suffixes, put them on poster-board strips, and supply several root words as well. Ask students to make as many words as they can from the strips. As a final activity, ask students to put their new words into sentences.

- *Syllable counting.* Provide students with individual cards with the numbers 1, 2, 3, and 4 written on them. Pronounce various words with different numbers of syllables, and ask the students to raise the card indicating the number of syllables they hear in each word.

- **Semantic clues.** Provide students with sentences, leaving out one of the words. Ask the students to supply the correct word, and discuss the reasons why their word makes sense.
- **Word order completion.** Write sentences on the chalkboard, and leave out the verb (or noun, adjective, or adverb). Ask students to supply the appropriate word, and discuss why their choices are correct.

Phonics and Spelling Assessment

Good readers read most words automatically, allowing them to focus on the meaning of the text. Familiar words, high frequency words, often have irregular pronunciations and spellings (for example: one, the, said); because of their frequent usage (Cunningham, 2012), students must learn to automatically recognize and spell them. Phonics assessment should include students' ability to read words fluently in isolation and in text, and to spell high frequency words. Informal reading inventories and running records are written records of a student's oral reading behaviors as observed and recorded by the teacher (Loman, 2002). An informal reading inventory, usually administered only a few times a year, is designed to determine a student's reading level, specific strengths and weaknesses in sight word recognition, decoding, comprehension, fluency, and in some cases vocabulary. Unlike informal reading inventories, ongoing assessments, such as running records, are administered more frequently to determine how well students are progressing. Running records may be used to quickly assess a student's decoding strategies and fluency.

Reading rate, fluency, is another assessment measure teachers may gather from informal reading inventories and running records. Reading rate has a causal effect on comprehension; students who read fluently, with prosody (intonation), understand and engage in text more frequently than do students without fluency.

Spelling words are often grouped by pattern and assessed in a weekly test. Spelling may be best assessed in the context of students' own writing (Weaver, Gillmeister-Krause, & Vento-Zogby, 1996). Many students are capable of spelling words and patterns on a weekly spelling test and are not able to spell the same words or use the pattern correctly in their personal writing. Students learn to spell high frequency words when they are held accountable for always spelling them correctly in their written work once they have been introduced and practiced. Assessment of daily writing, along with word lists, provides a grounded approach to assessing spelling.

BEFORE READING

How often have you told a student to "sound it out"? What made it successful? unsuccessful? How well do the students you work with spell in their personal writing? What is their spelling grade?

DURING READING

How do the assessment strategies in the article inform reading instruction? spelling instruction?

AFTER READING

Why do you think spelling grades don't match students' spelling in their personal writing? How will identifying a child's stage of spelling development inform writing instruction? How can the high frequency word lists be used to assess reading and spelling? How can these assessments help you move beyond telling students to "sound it out" and "memorize the word list" to transferring decoding and spelling strategies to student texts?

Assessment of Word Recognition Knowledge, Spelling, and Fluency

BY ARLEEN S. MARIOTTI AND SUSAN P. HOMAN

Assessing Sight Word Knowledge: The *Fry Instant Word Lists*

Recognition of sight words is a key strategy in word recognition and necessary for fluency. Sight words are those words the reader can rapidly identify without using word-analysis strategies, such as phonics, context clues, or structural analysis. A strong sight word foundation coupled with other efficient word-recognition strategies allows the reader to concentrate on the comprehension of text. If a child is unable to read connected text at grade 3 level, you should examine his/her sight word knowledge.

The *Fry Instant Word Lists* (Fry, 1980) are composed of high-frequency sight words. Fry states that the first 100 Instant Words make up 65% of all written text. Obviously, instant recognition of these words helps the reader in both comprehension and enjoyment. The *Fry Lists* have been adapted here as an informal sight word assessment.

Using The *Fry Instant Word Lists*[2]

This assessment is administered individually.

Directions:
- Provide the child with the student copy of the *Fry Instant Word Lists*.
- Say: "You will read aloud from these lists. I want you to read down each column, starting with list #1. Some of the words you may not know. If that happens, just say 'pass.'" (We recommend that you reveal only one column of words at a time by covering the other columns with a 5 × 8 card.)
- If a child misreads five words consecutively, ask, "Do you know any of the other words on the list?"
- Place a "✓" sign in the second column of your evaluation form if the child reads the word correctly. You should consider a word unfamiliar if the child does not instantly recognize the word, attempts to sound it out, or misreads the word and then correctly identifies it. If the child reads it incorrectly, record the mispronunciation/substitution in the column. If the child passes or does not respond, mark NR (no response) in this space.
- Administer consecutive lists until the child reads less than 75% correct, or less than 18 words on the list.
- Students who score less than 75% correct on any of the four *Instant Lists* should be provided instruction in sight words.

TABLE 3.2-1. The *Fry Instant Word Lists* Student Copy

I	II	III	IV
the	or	will	number
of	one	up	no
and	had	other	way
a	by	about	could
to	word	out	people
in	but	many	my
is	not	then	than
you	what	them	first
that	all	these	water
it	were	so	been
he	we	some	call
was	when	her	who
for	your	would	oil
on	can	make	now
are	said	like	find
as	there	him	long
with	use	into	down
his	an	time	day
they	each	has	did
I	which	look	get
at	she	two	come
be	do	more	made
this	how	write	may
have	their	go	part
from	if	see	over

2 "The new instant word lists." Edward B. Fry, *The Reading Teacher* (December 1980). Reprinted with permission of the International Reading Association.

THE *FRY INSTANT WORD LISTS*
Evaluation Form

Child's Name _____ Grade _____

Date: _____ Date: _____

Word List I	Child's Response ✓ = correct	Word List II	Child's Response ✓ = correct
The		Or	
Of		One	
And		Had	
A		By	
To		Word	
In		But	
Is		Not	
You		What	
That		All	
It		Were	
He		We	
Was		When	
For		Your	
On		Can	
Are		Said	
As		There	
With		Use	
His		An	
They		Each	
I		Which	
At		She	
Be		Do	
This		How	
Have		Their	
From		If	

Total correct ___/25   Total correct ___/25

THE *FRY INSTANT WORD LISTS*
Evaluation Form

Child's Name _____ Grade _____

Date: _____ Date: _____

Word List III	Child's Response ✓ = correct	Word List IV	Child's Response ✓ = correct
Will		Number	
Up		No	
Other		Way	
About		Could	
Out		People	
Many		My	
Then		Than	
Them		First	
These		Water	
So		Been	
Some		Call	
Her		Who	
Would		Oil	
Make		Now	
Like		Find	
Him		Long	
Into		Down	
Time		Day	
Has		Did	
Look		Get	
Two		Come	
More		Made	
Write		May	
Go		Part	
See		Over	

Total correct ___/25   Total correct ___/25

ACTIVITY 3-2.1

Administering a Sight Word Test

Administer the sight word assessment to a child in grades 1–3 and determine his/her proficiency on words in isolation. Based on his/her performance, develop one or two instructional recommendations.

ACTIVITY 3-2.2

Developing a Content Area Sight Word Test

Sight word assessment can also be developed using the words from a content area. Find a text from grades 2–6 in one of the core areas (math, science, social studies) and develop a content sight word assessment. If possible, administer the informal assessment to a child in that grade level and interpret the results.

STRUCTURAL ANALYSIS

Structural analysis, which includes morphology, is the process of interpreting the word parts that make up a word to gain meaning. When the reader uses word parts, it enables him/her to determine not only the pronunciation of the word but also gives insight into the meaning of the word. Structural analysis is especially effective if it is used along with phonic analysis and context clues.

A morpheme is the smallest unit of meaning. To apply morphemic analysis, when a reader comes across an unknown multisyllabic word, he/she locates the smaller meaning units within the word. Morphemic analysis includes knowledge of the following:

Root words

Prefixes (re, un)

Compound words (outdoors, peppermint)

Syllabication rules (sub-ma-rine, de-pend-a-ble)

Affixes (s, ing, ed)

Suffixes (-able, -ology)

Contractions (can't, isn't)

A child's skill in structural analysis can be assessed with teacher-made inventories administered to an individual or a group. For a thorough presentation of structural analysis, see Shanker, J. L., and Cockrum, W. A. (2009). *Locating and correcting reading difficulties* (9th ed.). Upper Saddle River, NJ: Merrill/ Prentice Hall.

The following is an informal assessment designed to examine a child's ability to identify and apply structural analysis.

Questions 1–3 ask whether the child can identify root words, prefixes, and suffixes.

Question 4 presents prefixes, suffixes, and affixes in context.

Question 5 looks at syllabication rules: a-prefixes/suffixes, b-VCCV, c-VC-V, d–le, e-compound words.

Here are five syllabication rules that children should know. As with any word identification rule, there are exceptions.

1. Divide between the root word and the prefix and/or suffix:
   trans-port   jump-er

2. Divide between two consonants (VCCV):
   rab-bit   wis-dom

3. Divide first between the consonant and vowel (VC-V):
   plan-et   mag-ic

4. Divide between compound words:
   bob-cat   dough-nut

5. -cle, -ble and other -le combinations act as a syllable:
   cir-cle   fly-a-ble

Test of Structural Analysis

1. Underline the base or root word:
   shipped   blowing   tallest   animals   flowery   player
2. Circle the prefix:
   reread export triangle   unfair depart preview
3. Circle the suffix:
   sugarless   livable darkness   joyful friendly   championship
4. Circle the correct word at the right that best fits the sentence:
   a. The key would not ___ the door.   (dislock, locking, unlock)
      b. She sent out ___ to her party.   (invitation, invitations, invitating)
      c. I need to ___ my story again.   (writes, written, rewrite)
   d. When I came home from vacation,   (dispacked, packing, unpacked)
      I ___ my suitcase.
      e. I would love to ___ from sight.   (unappear, disappear, appeared)

f. She stacked her books ___ on her desk. (neatly, neatful, unneat)

g. I borrowed money and now I must ___ it. (prepay, mispay, repay)

h. February is the ___ month of the year. (cold, coldest, coldly)

i. I was late to school because I ___. (sleepy, reslept, overslept)

j. She always smiles and is very ___. (unfriendly, friendly, friendable)

5. Draw a line between the syllables for each word below (Ex.: grand/child):

a. careful　friendly　upward　untie　bossy

b. bottle　forget　pencil　pumpkin　cartoon

c. lemon　lady　robot　atom　zero

d. circle　candle　possible　uncle　horrible

e. backfire　outdoors　stopwatch　keyboard　skateboard

ACTIVITY 3.2-3

Administering a Structural Analysis Test

Administer a structural analysis assessment to a child in grades 2–6. Analyze the results and write a summary of the child's strengths and needs in this word-recognition area.

ASSESSING SPELLING STAGES

Examining a child's spelling strategies may provide you with additional information about his/her reading development. Researchers have categorized several stages of spelling development which have been linked to reading and writing ability. Children's spelling gives us evidence of the phonic skills and language features they have acquired.

There are several ways to describe spelling development. Most researchers have described five developmental spelling stages. These stages have characteristics or features that will be easily recognizable after some practice with children's writing. The following stages and their descriptions are based on the work of Bear, Invernizzi, Templeton, and Johnston (2007).

Emergent Stage

The *emergent spelling* stage is typical of 3- to 5-year-olds. Characteristics are as follows:

1. Writing looks like scribbles. The "word" is made up of letters and letterlike forms, such as numerals and incorrectly formed or made-up letters.

2. The word is usually unreadable; letters and forms are used randomly.

3. The word might be arranged in a horizontal line.

4. Writing usually lacks letter-sound correspondence.

5. Child may have made a distinction between writing and drawing.

Letter-Name-Alphabetic Stage

The *letter-name-alphabetic* stage is typical of very beginning readers, some kindergartners, and most first-graders.

1. The word is made up entirely of letters, usually in short strings of one to four letters; single letters are often used to represent whole words.
2. Letters are used to represent some of the sounds in words.
3. Initial consonant sounds are represented; sometimes final sounds and/or other important, clearly discernible sounds are represented too, but the spellings are very incomplete.
4. The child uses the names of letters to represent sounds in words as well as the sounds of letters (bk = book, U = you).
5. The child understands that letters in print represent sounds in spoken words and indicates the beginning of the ability to segment phonemes.

Within Word Pattern Stage

The *within word pattern* stage is typical of beginning readers who can read a little but are not yet fluent. Most 7- to 9-year-olds fall into this group.

1. Spells most single-syllable short-vowel words correctly.
2. Spells most beginning consonant digraphs and two-letter consonant blends.
3. Learns to spell long vowel patterns and other vowel patterns (r-controlled, etc.).
4. Becomes aware of homophones.
5. Words are usually readable by others.
6. Begins to move away from sound-by-sound approach and begins to include spelling patterns (-ell) or chunks of letter sequences (sete = seat, crie = cry, fownd = found).

Syllables and Affixes

The *syllables and affixes* stage is typical of young children beyond the beginning reading stage and older ones who are still not fluent readers (9 to 12 years of age).

1. All phonemes in a word are represented.
2. Long and short vowel sounds are generally spelled correctly or typically: *hed* (head).
3. The child shows an awareness of marking systems, such as silent letters and consonant doubling, but uses markers inappropriately: *runing* (running), *makking* (making), *ducke* (duck).
4. The student focuses on syllables and can apply what is known about one-syllable words to multisyllabic words.
5. The child shows an awareness of inflectional endings, but the words are often spelled phonemically: *pickt* (picked) *wantid* (wanted).
6. The child shows knowledge of prefixes and suffixes, compound words, and hyphenated words.

Derivational Relations

Children in middle school and higher are usually in this stage. Spelling development is one of refinement and exploration. The focus in the derivational stage is on morphemes and students learn the relationship between spelling and meaning. Here are some characteristics:

1. The child explores common Greek and Latin derivations and related roots.
2. The child begins to examine etymologies.
3. Spelling is mostly correct but may show difficulty with some suffixes (apperence = appearance).
4. The child may have difficulty with silent consonants and with some uncommon roots (solem = solemn).

ACTIVITY 3.2-4

Using the Features List Analysis Form

Directions: In this activity, you are given a list of test words with the child's written responses. Classify each response into one of the five spelling stages.

Place the number of responses for each stage in the appropriate line on the Features List Analysis Form. The number of words at each stage helps to determine whether a student is solidly in a stage, just entering a stage, or close to leaving a stage. A large number of words in any one stage indicates that the student is currently performing at that stage of spelling development. For example:

Stage	Number of Responses
Emergent	2
Letter Name	10
Within Word	3
Syllables/Affixes	1
Derivational Relations	0

Stage of Development: This student is at a Letter-name stage of spelling development.

FEATURES LIST ANALYSIS FORM (BEGINNER)

Student *Lauren*_____ Date *9/17*

Test Word	Student's Response	Classification
1. late	lat	
2. wind	wnd	
3. shed	shed	
4. geese	gez	
5. jumped	jumpt	
6. yell	yell	
7. chirped	chipt	
8. once	wons	
9. learned	lerd	
10. shove	sov	
11. trained	chand	
12. year	yer	
13. shock	shock	
14. stained	stand	
15. chick	chick	
16. drive	driv	

Stage	Number of Responses
Emergent	_____
Letter-name	_____
Within-word	_____
Syllables/Affixes	_____
Derivational Relations	_____
Stage of Development	_____

FEATURES LIST ANALYSIS FORM (ADVANCED)

Student *Muhamed* _____ Date *9/30*

Test Word	Student's Response	Classification	Score
1. setter	str		
2. shove	shov		
3. grocery	gosere		
4. button	buton		
5. sailor	sellor		
6. prison	proson		
7. nature	nature		
8. peeked	peekt		
9. special	special		
10. preacher	precher		
11. slowed	slod		
12. sail	sell		
13. feature	fetre		
14. batter	bater		
		Total _____	

Stage	Number of Responses
Prephonemic	_____
Early-Phonemic	_____
Letter-name	_____
Transitional	_____
Correct	_____
Stage of Development	_____

ACTIVITY 3.2-5

Using Children's Writing to Determine Spelling Stage

Directions: The following are examples of two children's writings. For each child, determine the stage of spelling development. Utilize the same technique applied in the features list by comparing the child's written word with the real word and classifying each word into one of the spelling stages or as correctly spelled. Then total the number of words in each spelling stage to determine the child's stage of spelling development. Use the Developmental Spelling Stage Form to assist you in this activity.

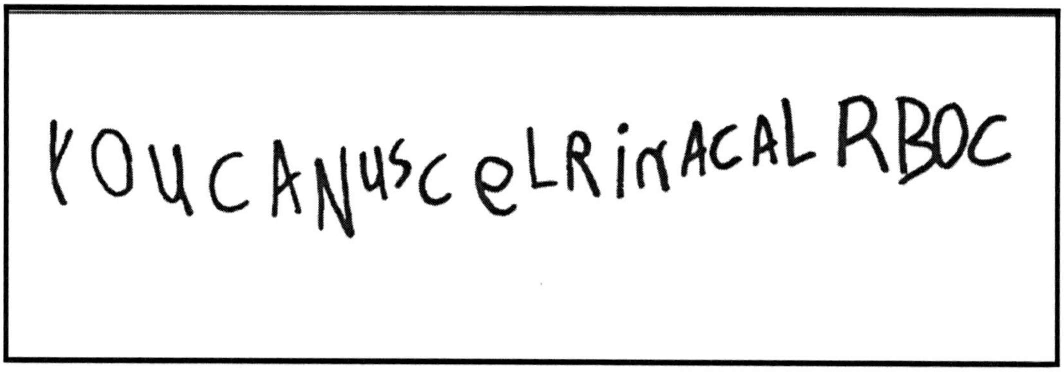

YOUCANusceLRinACALRBOC

FIGURE 3.2-1. "You can use colors in a coloring book."

FIGURE 3.2-6. The White Cat. But I want to keep him, Nick said. But you can't said father. But what if it belongs to his owners? asked Tim.

For additional spelling inventories, you can refer to the work by Bear et al. (2007) *Words their way*. Here you will find inventories at the primary, elementary, and intermediate levels as well as the *McGuffey Spelling Inventory* (Schlagal, 1992) and the *Inventario Ortografico en Espanol* (*Spanish Spelling Inventory*) developed by Lori Helman.

READING FLUENCY

Good readers are fluent. Struggling readers tend to read in a labored fashion, focusing their efforts on decoding words. Fluency is defined as the ability to read efficiently and accurately while maintaining comprehension.

Fluency was the forgotten stepchild of the reading curriculum for many years. However, with the inclusion of fluency as one of five basic components of reading, its importance has been recognized and enhanced. The publication of the Report of the National Reading

Panel (2000) as well as other reviews of research on fluency (Kuhn & Stahl, 2000; Rasinski & Hoffman, 2003) have provided a strong push to include a fluency focus in reading instruction. Moreover, these research reviews noted that reading fluency instruction resulted in improvements not only in students' reading fluency but also, and more importantly, in their overall reading comprehension and achievement. Improved fluency is of value to all students but especially to those who experience difficulty in learning to read and comprehend what they read (Rasinski, Homan, & Biggs, 2009).

Fluency provides the bridge between word recognition and comprehension. Fluency connects to accuracy and automaticity in decoding and connects to comprehension through expressive interpretation (Rasinski, 2004).

We can usually identify a non-fluent reader when we hear one. Typically, there are three common signs of fluency problems:

1. *Choppy reading*—the student stumbles over words, repeats words, uses long pauses, and/or reads word-by-word rather than in phrases.
2. *Monotone reading*—the student has very little expression or variation in his/her voice.
3. *Inappropriate fast reading*—the student reads quickly, often ignoring punctuation. Because of the rapid reading, there might be many pronunciation errors.

In the assessment of fluency, we should examine oral reading rate, oral reading accuracy, the quality of oral reading (prosody), and reading comprehension. In addition, we can assess fluency in both oral and silent reading. If you are examining silent reading fluency, you would not be able to assess reading accuracy or prosody.

Reading Rate

We recommend the following two methods to assess reading rate. In the first method you ask a child to read a passage at his/her instructional level either orally or silently. If the child is reading orally, mark any miscues the child makes. Multiply the number of words in the passage by 60 and then divide by the number of seconds it took to read the passage to give you the Words Per Minute (WPM). To determine the Correct Words Per Minute (CWPM), subtract the word miscues from the Words Per Minute (WPM).

CHAPTER REFERENCES

Cunningham, P. M. (2012). *Phonics they use: Words for reading and writing* (6th ed.). New York: Pearson.

Hillocks, G. & Smith, M. (1991). In Weaver, C., Gillmeister-Krause, L. & Vento-Zogby, G. (1996). *Creating support for effective literacy education*. Portsmouth: Heinemann.

Loman, K. L. (2008). *Targeted reading interventions*. Lee's Summit, MO: Indite Publishing Company.

Stahl, S. A., Duffy-Hester, A. M., & Dougherty Stahl, K. A. (1998). Everything you wanted to know about phonics (but were afraid to ask). *Reading Research Quarterly, 33*(3), 338–355.

Chapter 4

Introductions by Karen Loman and Angela Danley

COMPREHENSION

TEACHING STUDENTS WITH SPECIAL NEEDS

ASSESSING COMPREHENSION

Comprehension

INTRODUCTION TO READINGS 4.1-4.2:

Comprehension

Readers who think about what they are reading comprehend or understand the message of the text. Much of what we understand is not explicit. Readers must infer and interpret the author's intended message (Duffy, 2014). Comprehension is generally thought of in terms of strategies, plans, or sets of steps that can be adjusted and changed as we read. Comprehension strategy instruction helps students become good readers. Readers flexibly use various combinations of strategies as they read. Strategic readers monitor comprehension, determine the most important ideas, make connections/activate and connect to background knowledge, predict, and visualize and infer (Duffy, 2014; Harvey & Goudvis, 2007). Teachers must be selective regarding which strategy will benefit students and meet the needs of the learning process. P. David Pearson and his colleagues studied the comprehension processes of proficient readers, and then developed ways to teach comprehension to struggling readers (1992). There are seven strategies (Power, 2015) for reading comprehension that many literacy researchers and practitioners agree upon. Power's summary of each strategy is

1. Activating background knowledge to make connection between new and known information
2. Questioning the Text—proficient readers are always asking questions while they read

3. Drawing Inferences—proficient readers use their prior knowledge about a topic and the information they have gathered from the text to make predictions
4. Determining Importance—proficient readers look for clues that can help them determine what is needed and what is relative
5. Creating Mental Images—proficient readers create images in their heads when reading and visualize the story
6. Repairing Understanding When Meaning Breaks Down—proficient readers stop and reread what is in the text
7. Synthesizing Information—moves the student from making meaning of the text to integrating their new understanding into their lives

Comprehension strategies are vital components of literacy instruction (Moore, n.d.) Embedding these seven comprehension strategies into the reading classroom will ensure students at all levels are increasing their reading skills.

Anchor texts and anchor charts may be used to exemplify when and how comprehension strategies are used. Students familiar with comprehension strategies use them while engaging in close reading. In a close reading, students identify their own purpose for reading, determine the author's purpose, develop schema, and use systems of thought in the represented discipline (Fisher, 2015). Unlike teacher-structured comprehension lesson plans, close reading plans allow students to use strategies independently.

Comprehension lessons are designed to guide students through a text. Lessons have three components: before, during, and after. Before the lesson the teacher sets the purpose for the reading, telling students how to read the text and what to think about. At this point the teacher may choose to model, or think aloud, using the strategy for students to observe. During the reading, students engage in the text individually, in small groups (with the teacher or on their own), or as a whole group (silent, choral, or echo reading). The teacher may support students during the strategy lesson by reading with them or partnering them to read with a capable reader. Students should be engaged in actual text reading for at least half of the time set aside for comprehension strategy lessons (Fielding & Pearson, 1994). After the reading, students share, orally or in writing, what they thought about during the reading, what they currently understand about the text, and what they still don't understand. Conferring with students individually or in small groups allows the teacher to engage students in a literate conversation. Teachers may meet with students reading the same text or with students reading a variety of texts. The conversations center on the strategies used while reading.

Reading materials should be at a reading level that has the right amount of support and challenge. To accelerate student learning, there should be a balance of grade-level materials students can read with 85% to 96% word accuracy (Stahl & Heubach, 2006) and instructional-level materials students can read with 90% to 96% word accuracy. Materials should represent a variety of opportunities for reading—basal readers, magazines, trade books, and science and social studies texts, along with a variety of genres including fiction, nonfiction poetry, and plays. It is important to link some texts to grade-level expectations in social studies and science (Gelzheiser, 2005 in Allington, 2009; Mathson, 2006 in Allington, 2009). Many students are expected to learn content objectives without ever having an opportunity to read and understand the texts that support the expectations. Reading content-based materials with teacher support will increase student reading achievement and student academic achievement.

Gambrell found most primary grade students read connected text, text with a central meaning, for less than nine minutes per day on average. Some struggling readers read as little as one or two minutes per day. Not all texts are connected texts. Word lists, word phrases, high frequency word books, and decodable texts typically do not have a story line or provide the reader with a set of information. Their purpose is to practice high frequency words or a decoding strategy, not to develop reading comprehension. Although decodable text is often presented as research based, in fact the NRP (2000) stated there was little evidence that decodable texts have any influence on children learning to read. Be sure to select texts that students can and will read and comprehend. A meta-analysis of 99 studies found that the volume of reading is correlated to academic achievement, reading comprehension, writing, and spelling (Risko & Walker-Dalhouse, 2012).

BEFORE READING

Do you see students spending lots of time with books? or completing worksheets? When you observe children as they read, what are their behaviors? Are they decoding? Are they fluent? Why or why not?

DURING READING

How do the articles suggest teachers support comprehension? What are the connections to phonics? vocabulary? writing? How are the teacher behaviors, strategies, and activities in the articles similar? different?

AFTER READING

Are you more comfortable with one approach to phonics than another? Why? How will you use the material to stretch yourself as a teacher? your students as readers?

New Angles on Differentiating Reading Instruction

Five Best Practices That Deserve a New Chapter in the Common Core Era

BY LAURA ROBB

One of my favorite New Yorker cartoons, by Robert Mankoff (1987), is of two men, one a writer, talking at a cocktail party. The caption reads, "*We're still pretty far apart. I'm looking for a six-figure advance and they're refusing to read my manuscript.*" It brilliantly captures sky-high expectations that don't match up to reality.

When I think about the expectations of the Common Core State Standards (CCSS) for reading, it seems to me "we're pretty far apart." In saying this, I am not dissenting from the standards' reading and writing goals, but like many educators, I am concerned that the imminence of the CCSS tests puts pressure on schools that may undermine the goals of the CCSS. Teachers need time. They need time to marry their current practices with those of the Common Core, such as close reading and providing text-based responses. They need quality professional development. The space between many teachers' abilities to help readers make sufficient progress and the requirements for reading proficiency expected by the Common Core is still pretty vast. To some extent teachers are innocent victims of the pendulum swings in education. For example, before the CCSS was adopted by New Jersey, students had been required to add a personal connection when writing about reading on the state exam. But with the CCSS, personal connections are out and text-dependent comprehension is in; only effective, ongoing professional development can help teachers and students transition to a new way of thinking. Indeed, the best professional development experiences will empower teachers to examine the "what works" of their own teaching, and realize that readers make personal connections as they read, and they can continue to, *along with* reckoning with the text's meaning.

Students themselves are far apart from the CCSS requirement that all students read complex grade-level texts by the end of the school year. I recently coached a seventh grade teacher in a middle school close to my home. In September, the range of instructional reading levels among the twenty-eight students was from *third to twelfth grade*! Like many teachers, the teacher thought she could not deviate from the district requirement that each and every student *read* the selections in the seventh grade anthology and take the unit tests. To accommodate the sixteen students reading two to four years below grade level, the teacher read aloud the selections to them. Thus, the very students who should be reading *more* every day—more than proficient and advanced readers in order to move forward, aren't reading. Compelling all students to read the same text frustrates these struggling students and lowers their self-confidence and self-efficacy (Guthrie, Wigfield, Metsala, & Cox, 1999; Guthrie, Wigfield, &. Klauda, 2012). This teacher is a committed, capable teacher—but she needs training and coaching to deepen her expertise in meeting the needs of a vast range of readers.

So our challenge is this: If we are ever to close the achievement gap, either via the CCSS or whatever is next generating change in education, we have to help classroom teachers at all grade levels embrace and "own" their professional development, and allow them to shake off the notion many across the nation express: that with the Common Core in town, everything they've been doing is wrong. Teachers need to know of, lean on, and cite the strong research base of instructional and independent reading practices that have worked for their students. However, they need to look at their current practices and be open to improvements that the CCSS has brought to the professional discussion. Students ultimately suffer when educators go along with "out with the old, in with the new" swings in pedagogy; so what I advocate here is to marry the old with the new.

In this article, I want to focus on differentiation in reading, and use it as an example of how to stay true to best practices that have a strong research base, and yet bring fresh methods to them in light of the Common Core. As you read about how I change up differentiation for today's standards, I want you to see the professional development power of an article, and to see that effective professional development can be—and maybe should be—small, measurable forays, such as trying the ideas you come across in professional books and articles and discussing them with colleagues. How do we meet the CCSS? *Bird by bird*, as writer Ann Lamott's father advised (1994).

So with that in mind, let's focus on differentiation, and how we can use it to meet Common Core State Standards for Reading by staying true to five best practices that need to play a bigger role

1. **Use anchor texts to teach reading.** An anchor text provides a common read aloud text for instruction, and this enables students to have choices with instructional reading. Later in this article I provide sample anchor text lessons you can use to model making logical inferences, discovering the author's purpose and tone, and what it means to read a text closely. The lessons illustrate that teaching with an anchor text offers the freedom to meet students where they are and have them read and learn at their instructional levels so they can improve their reading skills (Allison, 2009; Robb, 2008, 2013).

2. **Use formative assessments to inform teaching decisions.** Formative assessments place differentiated reading instruction on a rock-solid foundation because they consider the child's work, behaviors, and attitudes on a daily basis, and thus decisions about learning, placement, and support emerge from performance-based data, and needn't wait for late- in-the-year standardized tests, when it's too late for the current teacher to act on the data. If schools revalue formative assessment, they stand a far better chance of meeting end-of-year CCSS benchmarks; formative assessments help teachers become more diagnostic in their teaching day to day, and in turn assure students are making sufficient progress week to week, month to month. When students receive frequent, qualitative feedback through formative assessments (conferences, written conversations in reading notebooks, peer feedback, quizzes, and so on) the benefits to the learner accrue quickly (Ser-ravallo, 2010, 2012).

3. **Amplify writing about reading.** English novelist E.M. Forster wrote: "How do I know what I think until I see what I say?" Forster's question captures the point that we can write what we know and understand. Now with the Common Core, there is urgency around students' writing about reading and I think this is a good thing. I encourage you to read the research of Steve Graham and Michael Hebert (2010) in *Write to Read,* which demonstrates that writing that unveils students understandings of a text, his/her thinking with the ideas of the text, improves comprehension. How do we bring writing about reading out of the shadows in order to deepen students' reading experience? I recommend students write something daily—even if it's just a few sentences. In addition, especially beginning in grade three, we can help students to write analytical paragraphs and move to essays in grade five and up.

4. **Recognize that independent reading is the big accelerator.** Students who read voluminously become avid, lifelong readers (Allison, 2009; Allington, 2002 , 2011; Krashen, 1993; Miller, 2009; Robb, 2010, 2013). Students want choice in what they read. The more teachers know about fiction and nonfiction books the quicker they can make great text to student suggestions. We need to help teachers rally around independent reading and toward showing students how to choose texts that they *can* read. We can do that by enhancing teachers' abilities to: (1) understand text complexity; (2) assess students'

interests, (3) extend discussion of texts, beginning with the routine of book talks, and (4) guide eBook reading at home and at school.

5. **Acquire and select books for instructional reading.** Teachers perceive finding books that meet each student's instructional needs a challenge because school funding is limited or there are no funds available. Here are suggestions that work! Raid your school's book room and your class library. Ask your school and local public librarians to select books that link to your unit's genre or theme and organize them by instructional reading level. Gather enough books to give students choices, and keep the books in your classroom to prevent loss. Offering students choice with instructional books is crucial because if a book doesn't motivate a student or if the student finds it too difficult, having other books at students' instructional levels readily available makes changing books easy.

Before delving into best practices in more detail and how they can work in concert, let's review some basic elements of differentiated instruction.

What is Differentiated Instruction?

Differentiation is a method of teaching that asks teachers to know their students so well that they can respond to individual needs and provide tasks and learning experiences that move each student forward. By using formative assessment to observe and understand the differences and similarities among students, teachers can use this information to plan instruction. Here are three key principles that form the foundation of differentiating reading instruction.

Learners reading levels are diverse. The students in our classes have a wide range of expertise with reading, writing, problem solving, and speaking and require differentiated instruction that takes them where they are and moves them forward (Snow & Biancarosa, 2004). Organizing reading around one textbook or one novel is what Carol Ann Tomlinson calls teaching to the middle (1999). This means that only the group reading at grade level has opportunities to improve their reading skill.

Formative assessment. Teachers study and monitor all of students' work and behaviors to determine what students do and don't grasp in order to design scaffolds, reteach, and adjust curriculum.

Tiered instruction helps students' progress. This means that the books students read and the assignments they complete match their learning needs and levels of expertise. The learning experience is the same but the level of complexity differs (Tomlinson, 1999; Sousa, 2001). For example, the class will study historical fiction. Instead of one book for all, the teacher has each student read historical fiction at his or her instructional level.

If the task is to plan and write an analytical essay that cites text evidence to argue for or against a claim or position, tiering means all students will work on analytical writing. However, the teacher adjusts the level of complexity of the writing task by considering students' writing skill. ELL students and those who struggle with writing might plan and write an analytical paragraph and confer often with the teacher who scaffolds the task. Proficient and advanced writers might complete a fully developed essay. Tiering allows teachers to adjust the amount of structure and support they offer students through teacher led conferences as well as the time students require to complete the writing (Dodge, 2005; Tomlinson, 1995, 1999; Sousa, 2001; Robb, 2008).

How the Five Practices Provide New Angles on Differentiating

Historically, teachers applauded the whole class book and/or grade level anthology because it provided them with a common text for modeling how to infer, pinpoint themes and central ideas, complete journal entries, and study literary elements or nonfiction text structures. One-book-for-all can decelerate the achievement of students who can't read and learn in English language arts and content classes. Instead of progressing, they slowly and steadily slide backwards (Allington, 2002; Robb, 2008; Tomlinson, 1999). Does this mean never-ever read anthology selections together, or a whole class novel or work of nonfiction? Not necessarily, but in the course of the year, it cannot be the sole way teachers address literature and reading.

The five angles of differentiation are the antidote to the same-text-for-all: anchor text, formative assessment, writing about reading, independent reading, and acquiring and selecting books at diverse instructional levels.

THE ANCHOR TEXT: TEACHING THE HOW-TO OF READING

The anchor text is a common text that the teacher reads aloud modeling how to apply the CCSS. Lessons are brief—three to five minutes. An eighth grade social studies teacher told me: "I use my textbook and newspaper and magazine articles as anchor texts to introduce vocabulary and show students how to identify big ideas and themes."

A picture book, an excerpt from a novel, informational text, or content textbook, a short story, myth, or legend, or an article from a magazine or newspaper make ideal anchor texts. Match the genre and theme of the anchor text to your reading unit and read aloud one to two paragraphs a day. With this versatile teaching tool, you can make visible how you analyze texts or organize thinking into a journal entry. And because the texts are short and the lessons brief, it's easy to review an anchor text and the lesson in other instructional moments, either while conferring with a student or in another small-group setting.

The series of anchor text lessons that follow apply key Common Core standards to reading an excerpt from a memoir by Frederick Douglass, published in 1845: *Memoir, Narrative of the Life of Frederick Douglass.*

TEACHING THE ANCHOR TEXT LESSON

Anchor text lessons open the door to analytical reading for students who see snapshots of your thinking and writing about reading. Flash the anchor text onto a whiteboard or use a document camera to display it. To heighten students' listening abilities, you might have to read a selection twice or even recap key details for English language learners and developing readers. Bring students into the lessons once you've modeled a process.

First day. This lesson shows students how to use specific text details to make logical inferences.

1. I say something like this: Today I will read aloud two paragraphs from Frederick Douglass's Memoir, *Narrative of 'the Life of Frederick Douglass, an American Slave.* This excerpt discusses Douglass's experiences working as a slave for Mr. Covey. While enslaved, Douglass secretly taught himself to read and write believing that knowledge was the path from slavery to freedom. In 1838, Douglass successfully escaped slavery and worked to abolish it; he also supported woman's suffrage. Listen carefully to the selection, and how I use text details to make logical inferences, find unstated text meanings.

2. Read the selection out loud, then present your think aloud. Here's what I say: Details about how Mr. Covey worked his slaves—in all weathers and long, long days—lets me infer that Covey viewed slaves as his property and cared only for producing crops, for making money. I can infer that Covey's slaves had no human rights because Douglass says that he was whipped every week, his spirit broken, his work hours extremely long with only five minutes to eat and gain renewed energy. Notice what I did: I used details from the text to find unstated meanings called inferences.

3. Invite students to turn to a partner to make [find] another inference, telling them to cite text evidence to support their thinking. Two seventh graders explained that they inferred that Covey's treatment of Douglass violated basic human rights and transformed Douglass from cheerful to angry and that Douglass no longer felt human.

Next, show students how to organize their inferences into a double entry journal response. This type of journal is an easy to implement writing about reading device that greatly improves comprehension. Here's the example that I write on chart paper:

Second day. This lesson shows how to discover the author's tone and purpose by selecting ten to fifteen key words and/or phrases from both paragraphs and then linking the words to tone and author's purpose.

1. Here are the words I write on chart paper (or project onto a whiteboard): *sore back, eat—five minutes, whipping, bitterest dregs of slavery, broken in body, soul, spirit, dark night of slavery, brute.*

2. Read the words and phrases out loud, and then tell students the tone I feel they convey, pointing out that it's the author's choice of words that creates tone. Here's what I say: The tone is anger, anguish, and pain from long, unreasonable work hours, lack of food, and weekly whippings. The frustrating tone comes from Douglass's inability to control his life and decisions. There is also a sad tone with Douglass losing his humanity and feeling brutish. Knowing the tone helps me figure out the author's purpose because the tone contains ideas that signal the meaning of both paragraphs. Douglass's purpose is to show the evils of slavery and what happens when slaves are victims of inhumane masters like Mr. Covey.

3. Invite students to pair-share and use tone to figure out another author's purpose: A pair of seventh graders explained that a second purpose is to show that when a human being is treated worse than an animal, such treatment can turn a person into a brute who loses his humanity.

Third day. This lesson will help students observe how a close reading can enable them to figure out the meaning of a confusing word or phrase. Here's what I

I lived with Mr. Covey one year. During the first six months, of that year, scarce a week passed without his whipping me. I was seldom free from a sore back. My awkwardness was almost always his excuse for whipping me. We were worked fully up to the point of endurance. Long before day we were up, our horses fed, and by the first approach of day we were off to the field with our hoes and ploughing teams. Mr. Covey gave us enough to eat, but scarce time to eat it. We were often less than five minutes taking our meals. We were often in the field from the first approach of day till its last lingering ray had left us; and at saving-fodder time, midnight often caught us in the field binding blades.

If at any one time of my life more than another, I was made to drink the bitterest dregs of slavery, that time was during the first six months of my stay with Mr. Covey. We were worked in all weathers. It was never too hot or too cold; it could never rain, blow, hail, or snow, too hard for us to work in the field. Work, work, work, was scarcely more the order of the day than of the night. The longest days were too short for him, and the shortest nights too long for him. I was somewhat unmanageable when I first went there, but a few months of this discipline tamed me.

Mr. Covey succeeded in breaking me. I was broken in body, soul, and spirit. My natural elasticity was crushed, my intellect languished, the disposition to read departed, the cheerful spark that lingered about my eye died; the dark night of slavery closed in upon me; and behold a man transformed into a brute!

say: In the phrase "My natural elasticity was crushed, my intellect languished, the disposition to read departed, the cheerful spark that lingered about my eye died; the dark night of slavery closed in upon me; and behold a man transformed into a brute!" the words "languished" and "disposition" are unfamiliar. Douglass was transformed into a brute, and he writes that the "dark night of slavery" closed in on him. If reading brings light then disposition could mean desire to read and the word "departed" confirms this hunch. "Languished" refers to intellect or mind. If the desire to read departed, then languished could mean that Douglass didn't use his intellect or mind. He placed his energy on dealing with "the dark night of slavery."

For students who don't experience visualizing, thinking, and feeling about a text, anchor text lessons show them what expert readers do. And these lessons can develop students' in-the-head thinking voices and in-the-heart feelings, bonding them to texts.

ANCHOR TEXT LESSON FRAMEWORK

I've listed the structure of the anchor text lesson so you can plan your own:

- provide background knowledge if necessary;
- tell students what you will model;
- read the passage aloud;
- think aloud, citing details and inferences from the text;
- recap what you did and show students how you used text evidence to support thinking; and
- engage students in the thinking part of the lesson by asking them to infer, determine the author's purpose, etc., with a partner.

When partners discuss ideas and share them with classmates, students can learn from one another and observe the critical thinking process. After you present anchor text lessons, students read their instructional books at school where you are available for scaffolding that can improve comprehension.

Narrative of the Life of Frederick Douglass, An American Slave	
Inference	Evidence from Douglass's Memoir
Covey is a brutal slaver	Covey whips Douglass; gave slaves less than 5 minutes to eat; broke Douglass's body, soul, & spirit; slaves worked late in all kinds of weather

Formative Assessments: The Data for Targeted Teaching

Assessment informs instruction (Afflerbach, 2011; Tomlinson, 1999). I'd say the most effective teachers go to class wondering, what am I going to learn from students as much as thinking about what they need to cover. And they understand students' needs by evaluating observational notes, conducting conferences, reading students' written work, and listening during discussions. But the formative assessment that I think is most valuable to students and teachers is the brief conference. You can achieve it every day as you make the rounds and continually circulate among students, responding to questions, helping them solve problems, offering suggestions, and helping them set goals for next steps (Allison, 2009; Serravallo, 2012; Robb, 2008). By making the rounds I feel the pulse of every student's needs, and it's this continual observation that points to topics for five-to-six-minute scheduled conferences for individuals, pairs, and small groups.

Short conferences while making the rounds form the foundation of differentiated reading instruction. I carry a clipboard with dated sticky notes as I circulate to observe students and listen to their conversations. During this time I am providing immediate scaffolding. Often, I jot the main points of our brief conversation on a sticky note and give it to the student for a reminder so they can revise or complete a task with confidence. After helping Tony, a seventh grader, make logical inferences from several pages of *The Great Fire* by Jim Murphy, I jot suggestions onto a sticky note; *inference is an unstated meaning; reread a paragraph or passage to find details; to infer; think about what you can conclude using details; ask what do these details mean ? What do they tell you?*

Other times, while making the rounds, I notice that a student requires a longer conference, and I jot on a sticky note the student's name and the topic for our meeting. If there's time, I will confer with the student during class that day; otherwise I schedule the conference for the next time class meets.

SOME POSSIBLE READING CONFERENCE TOPICS

Instead of a prepared list of topics, it's best to use your observations of how students apply anchor text lessons to their instructional text as topics. Below are five reading and five writing topics that align with the CCSS and best practices; use these as a starting point until you collect enough data to tap into students' needs.

Five Writing Conference Topics

1. Literary elements: showing understanding by connecting these to a specific text
2. How and why a person or character changes
3. Summarizing
4. Writing about reading (I cut the word "informal" because it's out of favor)
5. Analytical essays

Five Reading Conference Topics

1. Informational text structures: analyzing the organization of nonfiction using these
2. Logical inferences, themes, central ideas
3. Comparing two or more texts to analyze themes, characters, settings, etc.
4. Tone or mood; author's purposes
5. Close reading confusing passages

Recently, I coached a sixth grade teacher who taught four sections of English. She assessed where her students were using completed essays about reading. While it's better than the once-a-year test results, it's not good enough because several weeks passed between each essay—weeks when students received little help.

Clipboard in hand, the teacher made the rounds for a week in each section, and then we met to debrief. "I observed needs every day," she said, "even from my better readers. I polled my students, and they wanted me to continue supporting them every day. The sticky- note reminders got high ratings because on the next day, they had suggestions for inferring or using context clues to figure out the meanings of unfamiliar words." What this teacher experienced is that by making the rounds throughout a class, students had opportunities to learn and to revise their work, avoiding frustrating feelings that the task was an obstacle to learning.

Writing About Reading: Thinking on Paper

Evaluating what student readers put on the page about texts is the most personal, powerful window on a student's life as a reader. We don't want to overdo it by compelling students to write about every book they read—far from it—but as a profession we require it too little. Graham and Hebert (2010) in their landmark report, *Writing to Read* call for extra writing time in all subjects. Yet, a study completed by Arthur N. Applebee and Judith A. Langer in 2006 points to the fact that students in middle and high school ELA classes don't spend enough time writing. Applebee and Langer state: "Overall, this study leaves us with some disturbing findings about how little time many students are spending on writing ... ." (p. ii).

Applebee and Langer call for extended writing across the curriculum, especially in English class. The Common Core also calls for extended writing in English and in content subjects. However, middle and high school teachers with 100 to 150 students avoid extended writing tasks due to the grading demands. Again, ongoing professional development can ease the grading problems as teachers come to see the benefits of forming writing partnerships among students and teaching students how to self and peer evaluate their work using a rubric. Teachers provide support while students plan and draft essays and narratives by conferring but ask the students to revise and edit those messy first drafts. And as I point out in *Smart Writing,* teachers who read and grade much improved second drafts do little red marking and rewriting because the students are doing the work of revision and editing and moving toward independence with these tasks (Robb, 2012).

Extended writing tasks are not enough. Graham and Hebert (2010) state: "Writing about a text proved to be better than just reading it, reading and rereading it, reading and studying it, reading and discussing it, and receiving reading instruction" (p. 12). Why? Back to E.M. Forster's statement: "How do I know what I think until I see what I say?" I'm suggesting that in addition to extended writing, students complete brief responses to teachers read alouds and to their instructional and independent reading.

However, the Common Core suggests that students reread a text they don't understand several times to get the text's meaning. One point I've learned from teaching is that if a student can't read and comprehend a text, he or she can't learn from it. Offer students complex texts via your read alouds because students' listening capacity is greater than their instructional reading level (Woods 8c Moe, 1998). But for instructional reading, offer students materials they can read and learn from.

Clearly, writing about texts is essential if we want our students to improve comprehension. Writing includes drawing and writing about the illustration as well as jotting notes, making lists of ideas, and writing short paragraphs. Informal responses to reading occur every day, and students record their responses in readers notebooks. All learners, including ELL, learning disabled and special education students can complete responses that are short and where the focus is on ideas. As students enter class, have four to five distribute readers notebooks; students immediately head a page with their name and date. Now the notebook is poised and ready to receive hunches, emotional reactions, inferences, drawing, etc. based on the teacher's read aloud.

Short responses are also part of instructional and independent reading. Notebooks are with students while they read at school so they can close write, that is zoom in on applying a skill or strategy to their reading. Even *informal* writing can be differentiated. Some students summarize a paragraph, section, or chapter of a text while others make an inference or pinpoint a theme from a chunk of text, supporting their thoughts with detailed text evidence. I encourage students to talk to a partner before writing because talk clarifies thinking and reclaims ideas. Students use their responses to develop claims or explain a position in an extended essay or a paragraph. Like entries in writers' notebooks, *informal* responses to reading contain idea seeds for more extended writing. And teachers need to differentiate extended writing tasks as this literacy story illustrates.

It was my first day observing in the eighth grade class of a teacher who had invited me in as a coach. While making the rounds, I noticed a girl with her head on her desk. Bending down so I could make eye contact, I gently tapped her shoulder and asked, "Can I help you?" She shrugged her shoulders, and kept her head face down on the desk. Again, I asked, "Can I help you?" No response. After class, I asked the teacher to tell me about her student.

"She's from the Ukraine, been in the U.S. for two years, and she dislikes writing—sometimes, like today, she won't write. She'd rather draw than write, but this is writing class." The teacher and I brainstormed how to differentiate the assignment of writing a narrative. I suggested she let the student draw the events of the story and use her illustrations to write. Asking every student to complete the same writing task, especially when the task is at their frustration level, might satisfy a school's requirements, but it won't result in improving thinking and writing skill.

Independent Reading: The Achievement Accelerator

Read. Four letters. One short word. Powerful skill. Reading is powerful because when students have a rich independent reading life, they can accelerate their reading achievement, enlarge their vocabulary, build prior knowledge, and increase their reading stamina, and ultimately become productive and thoughtful citizens (Allington, 2011; Allison, 2009; Gambrell, Marinak, Brooker, Sc McCrea-Andrews, 2011; Krashen, 1993; Robb 2010). Independent reading should be easy (99–100% accuracy), enjoyable, and on topics and genres that interest learners. So how do teachers motivate students to read thirty to fifty books a year at an appropriate level? Here are four ways:

Understand text complexity. Insights into text complexity can help you guide students to selecting readable books. The Common Core identifies three aspects of text complexity: quantitative, qualitative, and the reader and the task. Here is a summary of each one:

Quantitative measures examine characteristics of a text best analyzed by computer, such as sentence length and word frequency. School districts latch onto Lexiles because it's a number and easy to use. Lexiles provide readability and not grade level. So a seventh grade ELL student might be able to comprehend texts at a Lexile linked to third grade, while an advanced reader in that same class can comprehend texts Lexiled for tenth grade.

Qualitative measures examine a book's content and concepts: knowledge demands (prior knowledge), levels of meaning, text structure, language conventionality, and clarity. This is the area that is the heart and soul of text complexity. Fifth graders can read *The Giver* by Lois Lowry, but should they read it? This dystopian novel deals with complex issues of euthanasia and inhibiting sexual yearnings, concepts appropriate for seventh and eight graders, not fifth graders—concepts that make the book's text complexity more appropriate to middle schoolers and above. So as we rush students toward texts of increasing complexity, continue to ask yourself, "But is this book's content right for this particular child?"

The reader and the task consider students' motivation, knowledge, and experience to determine whether a book is "just right," giving teachers the flexibility to match students to texts so learning can occur. The Common Core asks teachers to make the final decision about what students can read. This is important because you don't have to place students reading three or more years below grade level in texts they can't read. Developing readers will need more than one year to meet the goal of reading complex grade-level texts.

My point is this: we can differentiate instruction and ramp up independent reading if we are aware of what readers can do and keep independent reading a joyful experience (Allington, 2002; Allison,2009; Miller, 2009; Krashen,1993; Snow & Biancarosa, 2004; Robb, 2008). If we "do" Common Core without ever really unpacking its terms, such as text complexity, we probably aren't going to move the needle on achievement very far.

Give an interest inventory and tap into students' interests. When you know students' interests, you can find books that engage them (Allison, 2009; Miller, 2009; Robb, 2010). An eighth grade girl wrote on her interest inventory that she only likes books about vampires. Off I went to the school library, and the public library, and I found ten books about vampires that would be acceptable in an eighth grade classroom. She devoured the books and through book talks inspired classmates to read about vampires. Book talks by her peers and the teacher hooked her onto the Chicken Soup books and then graphic novels. By the end of the year this student had read thirty books! *Read* is a powerful word!

Put book talking on center stage. Book talks introduce students to hundreds of books in the course of a school year. Teachers should book talk all new additions to their class libraries, books by a featured author, and a genre or theme that's spotlighted. Invite students to complete a book talk each month. If a class of twenty- five students presents book talks from September to June, students hear about 250 books. Peer recommendations matter and can transform reluctant readers into book lovers!

Encourage eBook reading at home and at school. The statistics are here: Scholastic's *Kids and Reading Report* (2012). Ten percent more boys read and enjoy eBooks than girls. Half of children age 9–17 say they would read more books for fun if they had greater access to eBooks–a 50% increase since 2010.

Lobby for eBook readers at school, and encourage students to check out eBooks from their public library and read eBooks at home. For today's students, technology can make a huge difference in developing personal reading lives.

Finding Appropriate Texts for Instructional Reading

I organize reading units by genre, a literary category such as historical fiction, biography, or informational texts. This frees me to find books of the same genre that meet students' diverse instructional reading levels. All instructional reading occurs at school so teachers can support students, and meaningful partner and small groups discussions can occur.

Your school and public librarian are the best resources for helping you gather books of the same genre for your students. Use them! About two weeks prior to beginning a unit, ask these librarians to pull books that relate to the genre or theme on the instructional level range in your classes, ask them to identify the readability of each book. If you have a classroom library, mine that for books.

Collect enough books so students at each reading level have choices. Have students put their names on a sticky-note on the cover of the book as students from different sections will choose the same book. You'll find that developing readers select shorter texts than proficient and advanced readers.

Next, give students four to five sticky notes and have them print their name at the top and under that write "Stop to Think;" I call this chunking a book. Divide books into four to five chunks making sure each chunk is at the end of a chapter; this means that skilled readers who select long books will read larger chunks of texts. Place a sticky note at the end of the book, and help students divide their books in chunks of two or more chapters, depending on the book's length.

Since I recommend that instructional reading occur at school, students from different class sections can read the same book. Determine how much class time students need to finish each chunk of text. Those who finish early can complete independent reading. If some students require more time to read a chunk, give it to them. The "stop to think" is students' reminder that they will spend part of two or more classes discussing and writing about a chunk of text before going on to the next chunk. Frequently, I have several students beg: "Can we finish the whole book? Please, please, can we?" Let them; you'll maintain their enthusiasm for reading. I add one caveat: if students finish the book early, they must reread each chunk to refresh their recall of details, but they cannot reveal the book's outcome to peers.

Pair students so partners are no more than one year apart in instructional reading levels and have something to offer each other. Developing readers can pair-up but you need to support them.

DISCUSSING DIVERSE TEXTS WITH SMALL GROUPS OF STUDENTS

Even though students read different books, you can lead small group discussions—just focus them on genre and theme (Serravallo, 2012; Robb, 2008). After students complete their second chunk, schedule two small groups about three times a week to meet for about fifteen minutes during independent work time. Here is a list of topics that students can discuss and compare referring to specific text evidence:

- text structure;
- themes and central ideas;
- author's purposes;
- character's or person's goals, obstacles faced, personality traits;
- significance of information presented; and
- literary elements: setting, plot, conflicts, problems, outcomes, protagonist, antagonistic forces

You can select a focus for the discussion or refer students to the list and ask the group to select a focus. I find that discussions have greater depth if students can prepare for them by jotting notes related to the topic in their readers' notebooks. Students can document their discussions by writing a summary.

Closing Thoughts

A strange disconnect exists in our educational system. We want our students to read, write, think, and speak well; we want them to excel and be the best. We want students to be creative thinkers and problem solvers. To reach this goal, we continually change programs from The Reading First Initiative to No Child Left Behind, to State Standards, and now the Common Core. Programs are not educational solutions; if they were we'd be number one on the PISA (Program for International Student Assessment); but in 2009 we were number 17. In addition, among the 34 nations in the Organization for Economic Cooperation and Development (OECD), the United States ranks 14th in reading (Schleicher, 2011).

The first big takeaway from this article is that it's the teacher who makes the difference in students' progress and learning (Allington & Johnston, 2001), and investing in ongoing professional study is one way to grow great teachers. The second big takeaway is to integrate the five best practices into your curriculum.

Snow and Biancarosa (2004) noted in *Reading Next,* page 8: "A full 70 percent of U.S. middle and high school students require differentiated instruction, which is instruction targeted to their individual strengths and weaknesses." Struggling readers and writers, whether English is their first or second language, deserve opportunities to improve their skills so they can read and comprehend and write and communicate well. Using formative assessments to differentiate reading instruction, to tier writing tasks, and to develop a rich independent reading curriculum provide an efficient pathway to accelerating students' achievement.

Fostering Comprehension

BY TIMOTHY R. BLAIR

What it is and What Research Can Tell Us

Comprehension is the active, internal process of understanding ideas represented in text. Very simply, reading is comprehension. In essence, readers construct meaning from the ideas represented in the text based on their own prior knowledge and experiences. Thus, reading comprehension is the active process of "making sense" of what we read (Pearson, 2009).

The ultimate success of a reading program is the degree to which students can read and understand numerous texts for a variety of purposes. Success in comprehension is achieved through the coming together of a positive attitude, a rich background of knowledge and experiences, the explicit teaching and mastery of reading skills and strategies spanning different cognitive levels in both narrative and expository text, and the ability to monitor and regulate personal reading depending on the situation. Reading comprehension is best viewed as a multifaceted process affected by several thinking and language abilities. The ability to comprehend on different levels exemplifies the types of thinking that can be applied to written and oral language. The three different levels of thinking applied to reading comprehension are defined as follows:

- *Literal comprehension*—Understanding ideas and information explicitly stated in a passage
- *Inferential comprehension*—Understanding ideas and information implied in a passage
- *Critical comprehension*—Analyzing, evaluating, and personally and creatively reacting to information in a passage

To make sense of what they are reading and respond in a critical fashion, students must be shown how to be "strategic" in their reading. "Strategic" readers "think" about their reading before, during, and after reading a selection. They establish purposes for and monitor their reading, recognizing when to slow down, speed up, reread, or pause to understand a point. Knowing how one reads, coupled with the ability to "change gears" while reading, is called *metacognition.*

Central to the development of strategic readers is the important role of you, the classroom teacher. Only through your careful, expert planning, teaching, and guidance will students grow into mature, independent readers. Two major teaching strategies for fostering strategic reading abilities are *informing* and *modeling. Informing* involves explaining the new strategy in small steps, using examples and counterexamples. Informing further means telling students the "what," "when," and "why" of a strategy to help in understanding a generalization. *Modeling* involves demonstrating or showing students how to perform a particular strategy. Helping or assisting students to learn a new strategy is called "scaffolded instruction" (Rosenshine & Meister, 1995). Scaffolds are forms of support given to students in learning something new and the timely withdrawal of those supports as students demonstrate mastery. Examples of scaffolds or forms of support include modeling a strategy, giving students a sheet explaining how to summarize a story, and using a chart of the "reporter questions" *who, what, where, when, why,* and *how* to support the prereading strategy of predicting.

TEACHER BEHAVIORS
- Specify clear instructional goals.
- Explain, model, and scaffold reading comprehension skills and strategies.
- Design collaborative activities with students to discuss and analyze stories.
- Monitor student progress.
- Provide immediate feedback to students.
- Discuss application of skill or strategy in real reading situations.

TEACHING STRATEGIES
1. *Always establish purposes* for students before reading, and train students to set their own purposes.
2. *Use prereading strategies* (e.g., mental imagery, semantic maps, story maps, and other graphic organizers) to activate students' background knowledge, provide information for making predictions, show key relationships, and teach new vocabulary.
3. *Relate the text to be read to your students' background of experiences,* and show your students how to do this themselves, by asking appropriate questions using information from the text and visual aids.
4. *Explicitly explain the various types of text structures* (narrative and expository), and show students how to determine a text structure while they are reading.
5. *Teach students to use the reciprocal teaching approach* of Palinscar and Brown (1984), utilizing the four strategies of predicting, question asking, summarizing, and clarifying.

6. *On a regular basis, ask your students a variety of questions* requiring different levels of thinking. It is imperative to encourage them to think at various cognitive levels. Your art of questioning directly affects students' attitudes toward understanding text and, ultimately, how much they learn. In conjunction with asking a balanced set of questions that require different levels of thinking, practice the proven techniques of wait-time (also called think-time). This term denotes the period of silence after you ask questions but before students respond. Research has shown that if teachers wait three to five seconds before eliciting a response, students are better able to digest the question, and positive results occur (Rowe, 1974). More student participation, linger responses, and more high-level thinking are among the positive effects of this technique. In addition to wait-time, you need to be equipped with "probing questions" to help redirect or expand students' responses to a question. To keep discussions lively and extend students' thinking, ask thought-provoking questions, such as "Can you tell me more?" What are some other ideas?" and "Do you agree or disagree with the author?"

7. *Teach students the Question-Answer Relationships (QAR) strategy* (Raphael, 1982). In this strategy, students learn to identify the source of information required in answering comprehension questions. The four sources of information or relationships between a question, the text, and the reader's own background knowledge are:
    a. *Right there*—The answer to a question can be found right there in the text.
    b. *Think and search*—The answer requires the student to search the text for information and to think about various pieces of information to arrive at the answer.
    c. *Author and you*—The answer requires both information from the text and the reader's background of experiences.
    d. *On my own*—The answer to a question is not in the text but lies within the reader's background.

8. *Directly explain, model, or demonstrate specific comprehension skills and abilities* to students, and practice an abundance of interesting and varied drills for the skill or ability to become automatic. The direct or explicit instruction method—a universal teaching strategy that has been used for years—has as the heart of the lesson the systematic explanation, demonstration, or modeling of the new skill or ability. The basic steps in this approach are readiness, step-by-step explanation of the lesson objective, guided practice, and independent practice.

9. *Using an actual student text, model for students exactly how and why* they should slow down, speed up, stop, use a visual aid (to better understand the ideas expressed in the text), pause to make note of an important point, reread a section (to understand an ideas), and answer end-of-chapter questions.

10. *Teach students the meanings of the "reporter questions"—who, what, where, when, why, and how.* Practice finding the answers to various "reporter questions" in a story or chapter. Model for students how you would ask yourself "reporter questions" while reading and how you would quiz yourself after reading using the same questions.

ACTIVITIES

- *Picture details.* Provide students with a short story or passage appropriate to their abilities and experiential backgrounds. Represent the major story details with pictures placed on separate cards. The pictures can represent major events, characters, settings, and so forth. For example, if in the story the main characters went to a lake to go fishing, set up a tent, wore warm clothing, and cooked their food over a campfire, then each detail can be represented on separate picture cards. Provide students with the cards appropriate to their story. Instruct them to select cards representing the details of the story they read, which are turned over to you after they complete the activity. A variation is to either record stories on audiotape or use read-along stories. Have students listen to the story and then select story details from picture cards.

- *Finish the story.* Provide students with a short story or several connected paragraphs to read. On a separate sheet of paper, provide incomplete information about the story's content. For example: "This story is about Joe, who wanted to _____. Joe's mother did not agree with Joe's choice because _____." Direct students to read the incomplete sentences first and then to read the story to fill in the missing information. Make sure students understand that more than one word is required to fill in the information that is missing.

- *You decide.* Give students two short stories or connected paragraphs. Tell them to read the text and then to decide if information listed on separate story cards belongs to either reading selection, and if so, which one. Students can read an event card aloud, and other students can respond about which story contained the event, character, setting, etc. Students who respond correctly get to keep the story card.

- *A thousand words.* Provide students with a short story or several related sentences to read. Direct them to draw a picture that best represents the main idea of the story. A variation is to have them draw a series of pictures in cartoon fashion that represents literal information found in their reading.

- *Character.* Prepare several short descriptions of different characters. Have students read the descriptions and categorize the characters in terms of their descriptions. A variation would be to give students a visual format, such as a flowchart or wheel and spokes, and have them fill in each part with the descriptive words.

- *Does it make sense?* Cut apart stories and paste the pieces on separate pieces of cardboard. Have students arrange the stories in a manner that makes sense. A variation of this is to have students arrange all but a part of the story in a manner that makes sense. Have students read each other's stories to see if they can find the part that does not make sense. A variation is to have students experiment with the stories to see if they can be combined or organized in several ways and still make sense.

- *Headlines.* Prepare newspaper headlines appropriate to students' reading abilities and experiential backgrounds. Provide students with a headline, and direct them to compose a story appropriate to it. Before writing their stories, students should write out what would be necessary to help them in composing their stories. Use "reporter questions" to assist students in planning their stories. For example, with a headline such as "12-YEAR-OLD BOY CATCHES RECORD-SIZED FISH," students could possibly list information for "who" (name of the boy), "where" he lives, "why" he likes to fish, "where" he caught the fish, "when" he caught the fish, and how he felt when he caught it. Once students have listed the information related to the "reporter questions," have them write their stories. This activity helps students use their experiential background to construct meaning as they read and write stories.

- **Continuations.** Prepare a series of sentences such as, "Joe earned four dollars raking leaves for his mother." Prepare an equal number of sentences that are logical continuations for each of the other sentences. For example, a logical continuation for the previous sentence could be: "He spent three dollars to go to the afternoon movie." Have students read each sentence and then select a sentence that would be a logical continuation. A variation is to have students write their own sentences that would be logical continuations of the given sentences.

- **Finish the story.** Select a connected story, and delete every other sentence from it. Students can either write their own sentences that make sense for the ones that were deleted, or they can select from those that you provide. **EXAMPLE:** "Mary was looking forward to going to the lake with her parents." "Mary spent two weeks at the same lake last summer and made several new friends."

- **Who buys it.** Provide students with a department store catalog and list of items found in the catalog. Direct students to read the description of each item and to infer the type of person or character traits of a person who might purchase such items. A variation of this activity involves using pictures of items in the catalog.

- **What I know.** Provide students with a brief overview of a story and pictures appropriate to the story. Before reading the story, have students list what they know about it. Direct students to read the story to confirm or reject the information they listed.

- **Questions to answer.** Provide students with brief information about a story before they are to read it. Such information could focus on the plot, characters, setting, etc. Then ask students to write a list of questions they would like to have answered as a result of reading the story. Students can write their answers to their own questions after they read the story.

- **Road map.** Give students a written map of a story they are to read (the map would highlight major story information). As students read, they are to predict what comes next in terms of alternate routes on the road map. Students test their predictions as they read the story and complete their map.

- **Who comes to the party.** Give students short descriptions about different characters, and then tell them that one of the characters is having a party and needs help making a guest list. Direct students to help complete a guest list by selecting people to come to the party. Students should write a brief paragraph or two about why they chose the particular characters they did.

Teaching Students with Special Needs

Teachers begin each year with a new group of students. With a new group of students comes a variety of learning needs. Each student learns differently and each student is at a different level of reading. Some students struggle to learn to decode and comprehend. Instructional strategies are techniques teachers use to help students become independent learners and successful readers. Research shows that explicit teaching techniques are particularly effective for comprehension strategy instruction (Adler, 2001). In explicit instruction, teachers inform readers why and when they should use strategies, what strategies to use, and how to apply them (Alder, 2001). The steps of explicit instruction typically include:

1. Direct explanation—The teacher explains to the students why the strategy helps with comprehension and when to apply it.
2. Teacher modeling—The teacher models or demonstrates the strategy by thinking aloud while reading the text the students are using.
3. Guided practice—The teacher guides and assists students as they learn how and when to apply the strategy.
4. Application—The teacher helps students practice the strategy until they can apply it independently.

With explicit instruction in the application of specific strategies and graphic organizers, struggling readers may improve their comprehension.

BEFORE READING
Before reading the following articles, take a piece of paper and fold it into fourths to make a four square graphic organizer. In the top left square, write why special needs students should use graphic organizers in reading or across the content areas.

DURING READING
As you read the articles, which strategies do you find beneficial to teaching reading? Jot notes down as you are reading and add these notes to the top right corner of your four square chart.

AFTER READING
What are two strategies you took away from the reading? What are you willing to try? How will these strategies benefit the students in reading comprehension? Write the responses in the bottom squares of the chart.

Graphic Organizers and Other Visual Strategies to Improve Young ELLs' Reading Comprehension

BY YANHUI PANG

t is well observed that in recent years an increased number of students from culturally, linguistically diverse backgrounds are enrolled in U.S. preK-12 schools. Many English language learners (ELLs) don't get a chance to learn English due to lack of English speaking home environment. In many cases their parents are unable to speak English or their family members prefer to use their native language at home for they want their children to be able to master the native language and retain their cultural heritage. Regardless, it is possible for young ELLs to master both English and their native language from a young age. It might seem that the earlier young ELL children start studying another language like English other than their native language, the easier it is for them to reach a native speaker's level in the second language acquisition. Bilingual learning improves ELLs' cognitive development as well as their self-esteem. Very often young ELLs are very proud of themselves being able to speak two languages and more knowledgeable than- their peers.

However, studying two languages from a young age can put young ELLs at risk of struggling in both languages especially at the initial stage ofbilingual study and when the native language has different phonological system from English. A very common phenomenon known about ELLs is that they switch codes between the two languages and they use their native language to interpret English reading. Language delay is very often observed among young ELLs and many times ELLs have poor reading comprehension abilities. Many young ELLs struggle in English phonics, vocabulary, English grammar, story retelling, or reading

Yanhui Pang, "Graphic Organizers and Other Visual Strategies to Improve Young ELLs' Reading Comprehension," *New England Reading Association Journal*, vol. 48, no. 2, pp. 52-58. Copyright © 2013 by New England Reading Association. Reprinted with permission. Provided by ProQuest LLC. All rights reserved.

comprehension questions. Since phonological knowledge has a direct impact on reading comprehension (Sparks, Patton, Ganschow, & Humbach, 2012), when ELLs don't have adequate phonic knowledge in English, they have a hard time pronouncing some vocabularies, which in turn affects their reading speed. More than phonics, semantics is another key in reading comprehension. Many times vocabulary plays a key role in an entire sentence. If ELLs are unable to understand the key vocabulary, they may not be able to understand the entire sentence or even the whole paragraph. However, understanding only the meaning of vocabulary is far from sufficient. Rather, ELLs also need to know American culture in order to fully understand the meaning of the word within the context of the story they read. For example, when a text reflects traditional American festivals, sports, or American history, young ELLs usually experience difficulty in understanding the context in the story and in retaining what they have just read because of inadequate background knowledge.

Other factors contribute to this issue such as lack of stable home environment, limited literacy materials at home, and children's lack of confidence in mastering and using English since young ELLs are not raised in an English speaking environment. At the same time, some ELLs who are raised in a literacy rich environment might still struggle in English speaking, reading, and writing at a young age. Bilingual education at a young age challenges children especially when the two languages adopt different phonological system and written system such as Chinese and English, Japanese and English, and others. In addition, mastering two languages at a young age requires children to decode two different types of information and switch freely between two different codes. Thus it takes time to process the phonological information and semantic information in the two languages, resulting in a delay in reading, writing, and speaking in both languages.

Reading is Key

In order to improve ELLs' English language proficiency, teachers should adjust their teaching strategies to practice basic phonics and master the meaning of vocabulary and oral proficiency first. These basic skills help with reading fluency, which is believed to impact reading comprehension (Quirk & Beem, 2012). However, mastery of vocabulary alone doesn't guarantee good reading comprehension. Quirk and Beem's (2012) study suggests that although ELL students may be able to pronounce words correctly, they lack full understanding of their meaning. ELLs are not usually familiar with the context wherein the vocabularies are used and the cultural facts related to these vocabularies. As a result, they have difficulty understanding the paragraph or the entire given text.

In order to improve reading comprehension, ELLs should acquire rich cultural heritage. At the same time, teachers should obtain information regarding areas related to language and content that ELLs struggle with, and design instructional plans, or adopt supplemental instruction to increase vocabulary, improve reading fluency, and reading comprehension. One important ways to improve the language skills of ELLs in both the native language and English is through reading. Reading allows ELLs to learn vocabulary, sentence structure, syntax, capitalization and punctuation, function words; they acquire an understanding of American culture, which can lead to an increase in their overall English language proficiency. Mastering good reading habits to improve reading comprehension is beneficial to young language learners and will benefit them in their future academic endeavors.

But how can young ELLs improve their reading comprehension? There are many types of visual strategies that support ELLs' reading abilities such as bilingual picture books, books with visual cues (e.g., add a picture to words that possibly pose a challenge for ELLs to understand), real objects, or drama. In this paper different visual strategies are explained in details with a purpose to improve young ELLs' reading comprehension level and increase their language abilities in English.

Visual Strategies Improve ELLs' Reading Comprehension

HOMEMADE BILINGUAL PICTURE BOOKS

Not all books have a bilingual version. If you cannot find a bilingual version of a book, teachers and parents can work together to make bilingual picture books. There are several ways to make bilingual books. One easy way to do this is by adding a note card with either English translation/native language translation to each page of the book. Ask parents or someone who knows the child's native language to help with the translation. The note card with translation can be glued or taped to each page. When the homemade bilingual book is ready, let ELLs read in their native language first, then in English, and provide assistance when necessary. ELLs can try to read in English only and refer to their native language version when needed. After reading, ask them to retell and write what they have learned from the book, or draw a picture of their favorite book characters. Always remember to ask questions that relate to ELLs' personal experiences. These activities help the ELLs deepen their understanding of the book contents as well as practice their memory and summary skills. If the books are not picture books, teachers and caregivers can ask ELLs to draw a picture for each page they just read. Through visual representation of the page contents they just read, young ELLs learn to recall what they have just read, through which young ELLs practice memory and comprehension skills. This can also help them practice eye hand coordination, fine motor skills and logic thinking. In the process of drawing, teachers can ask children "wh" questions such as "Why did you draw the picture in this way?" or "What do you predict is going to happen in the next page?" These questions can trigger critical thinking for ELLs. ELLs can benefit from the "text-based questioning not only because of the cognitive and language processes it supports but also the interest and motivation it awakes in students" (Taboada, 2012, p.87). ELLs are encouraged to form the questions and bring the questions for discussion with peers after reading. Book club is a good way for students to discuss book characters and therefore practice critical thinking (Park, 2012).

Once the ELLs reach a certain reading level, they will move on to chapter books. However, they might still come across words that they will have difficulty to understand. This will impact their reading rate, fluency, and comprehension of the book contents. If that is the case, use picture word combinations within the text to improve reading comprehension. First of all, picture flash cards of difficult words are appropriate for beginning readers because at this stage they rely more on "word semantic cues to comprehend the meaning of given texts" (Chik, et al., 2010, p.14) than older children and those who read at the intermediate or advanced level. Other researchers (i.e., Quirk 8c Beem, 2012; Stygles,2012;Taboada, 2012) also emphasize the importance of vocabulary in impacting ELLs' reading comprehension. Introducing new vocabulary to ELLs as a pre-reading activity can help speed up their reading and improve comprehension of the given text. Pictures to be used for introducing vocabulary could be hand drawn or printed off the computer. Teachers, parents, or peers can work with the ELLs to practice these words by quizzing them their meaning, their synonyms and antonyms, or composing several sentences using the vocabulary words. During the before reading activity, both word and picture combinations can be applied to introduce a book.

For example, before ELLs read a book about St. Patrick's Day, teachers can show a picture beside the word *leprechaun,* or help ELLs to make an artwork of a shamrock, in case ELLs have a hard time understanding what the words *leprechaun* and *shamrocks* mean. Teachers can also use pictures to describe how St. Patrick's Day is celebrated, and the origin of this festival to assist ELLs' understanding of the story and the festival, which will also help them understand books and stories related to this festival in the future. Related discussions also can be held to expand ELLs' knowledge of the books such as why the U.S. celebrates festivals that European countries celebrate, and why people immigrated to the U.S. in the past. Other topics such as the festivals that people in other cultures celebrate can also be shared in class discussions. ELLs are especially encouraged to share their experiences of celebrating their own traditional festivals. They can bring pictures of foods, clothes, and/or decorations used at celebrating their traditional festivals to class. Throughout, the teachers can create opportunities for ELLs to practice narration, develop writing abilities, and increase social interaction with peers. After obtaining adequate number of vocabulary words and information about American culture and history, ELLs should practice how to summarize, sequence facts or plots contained in stories, analyze the cause and effect, and evaluate what they have just read to develop logical and critical thinking skills. Graphic organizers are excellent tools to help young ELLs reach such a goal.

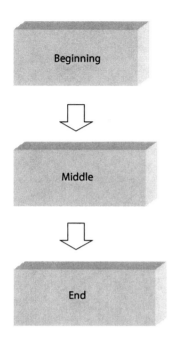

FIGURE 4.3-1. Graphic Organizer: Summarizing a Story.

GRAPHIC ORGANIZERS

Graphic organizers have been widely used by teachers to help students organize and summarize content, classify facts, and analyze and compare contents they read. There are different types of graphic organizers for different reading materials. In this article, real examples are described to explain how to use graphic organizers to help ELLs comprehend book content by classifying facts, analyzing problems, summarizing main points, and criticizing or evaluating the decisions made by authors. When reading narrative stories, it is recommended to use a graphic organizer to help ELLs predict what they expect in the story before reading, check whether they understand what's going on during reading, and retell and summarize what they can remember after reading. For example, Figure 4.3-1 illustrates a graphic organizer that emphasizes the beginning, middle and end of the story, which is a perfect match to summarizing a story. ELLs also can be guided to analyze the problems posed in the story and the solution to that problem by using graphic organizer in Figure 4.3-2. For stories that explain cause and effect, graphic organizer described in Figure 4.3-3 can help comprehension. Graphic organizer introduced in Figure 4.3-4 can be used to analyze stories such as Eve Bunting's (1997) *A Day's Work*, or Jacqueline Woodson's (2001) *The Other Side*, which explains immigrant family, ethnic differences, and the communication among children between different racial backgrounds. ELLs are also encouraged to share their parents' professions and the communities they live in.

When reading books centered on science facts like how trees grow, how to plant a pumpkin seed, or how to take care of beehives, graphic organizers that ask for steps or process can be used to help young ELLs understand sequence and ordering (see Figure 4.3-5, for example). For children's books like Ellen Jackson's (2003) *Turn of the Century: Eleven Centuries of Children and Change* that introduces history from children's perspectives, teachers can use the timeline graphic organizer in Figure 4.3-6 to have ELLs organize the facts mentioned in the book in a sequential order. The timeline graphic organizer provides ELLs a visual way to understand time concept.

After using graphic organizers to analyze the main concepts or plots in the story, young ELLs will be guided to use a graphic organizer to retell the story either through rewriting the story or telling the story to a peer. Teachers can pair ELLs with peers at a higher reading level. After the book reading, the two students are required to relate the book to their own experiences, through which their discourse skills are practiced. Chik et al. (2010) suggest

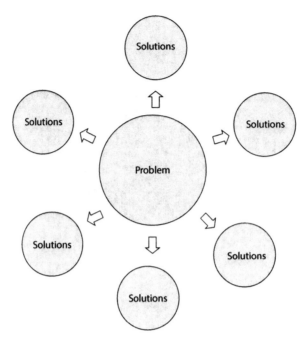

FIGURE 4.3-2. Graphic Organizer: Problem-Solution.

that narrating what happened in their daily life is a very critical factor in improving reading comprehension skills; discourse skills predict comprehension abilities. For example, after reading a book about Christmas, a pair of students is required to compose a book themselves to describe how their own families celebrate this festival. Through this kind of writing activities ELLs practice description skills and skills to examine the connections and sequence between and among events, which also improve reading comprehension skills.

OTHER VISUAL TOOLS

Other visual tools that enhance ELLs' understanding of book contents include maps or globes to improve understanding of books about travel, world, or habitats. For example, teachers, peers, older siblings, or parents can refer to a map or globe while reading a book about travel to help ELLs improve reading comprehension. Even map puzzles and puzzles relevant to the book topics can be used to help ELLs visually understand what is going on in the book. Teachers can develop a toy tote bag to hold all the relevant materials including the book so that an ELL or anyone who struggles with reading can use these materials to improve reading comprehension and cultivate their interest in book reading.

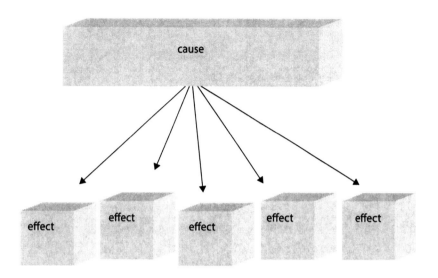

FIGURE 4.3-3. Graphic Organizer: Cause and Effect.

Additionally, use the Internet to search relevant information to expand ELLs' understanding of book content. There are many websites that children can benefit from to improve their reading comprehension and bring words to sounds. For example, when reading books about *Cat in the Hat* series, ELLs can be guided to check the PBS Kids "Cat in the Hat" link to play some relevant games on computer. So are the times when children read books about Caillou, Kai-lan, and Curious George. Another good way to involve young ELLs in reading is to show them relevant movies after the book reading or design a puppet show. For example, after reading books about Cinderella, show ELLs the Cinderella movie. Then ask them to tell what they recall from watching the movie. Teachers can lead a discussion focusing on the differences ELLs can identify from reading the Cinderella book and watching the movie. A puppet show is also a good way to connect the book as well as arouse ELLs' interest in book content. Teachers should also check with their local children's museum for puppet shows. If neither puppet shows nor movies related to books are available, teachers can involve ELLs and their peers in making puppet shows themselves. Puppets also can be homemade. Simply draw or print the book characters, cut out, glue them to popsicle sticks, and then make a stage for the puppet show. ELLs are encouraged to play together with their peers.

Besides movies, games, or puppet shows, ELLs can be encouraged to act out the book contents with their peers. Teachers can help them figure out the appropriate costumes and make up for the characters. This is a good way to visualize book characters. Park (2012) also recommends visualization as an important tool to deepen students' understanding of book characters and contents. If ELLs have a hard time figuring out how to act out certain

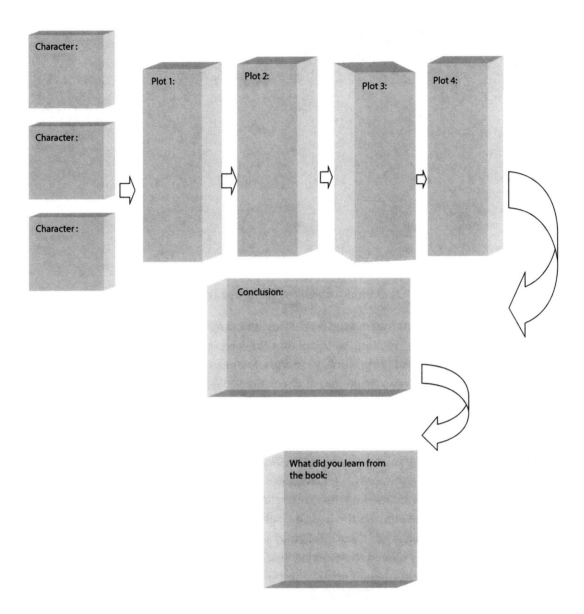

FIGURE 4.3-4. Use Graphic Organizer to Understand "A Day's Work."

characters, teachers can assign other peers who know how to act to demonstrate first. If the books have been converted to film, teachers can show ELLs the movie, and then invite them to pattern their acting out of the character from the movie. Through video modeling, ELLs can visually see how the characters act and how they interpret book contents. ELLs can usually act out the characters independently without adult assistance after watching the video.

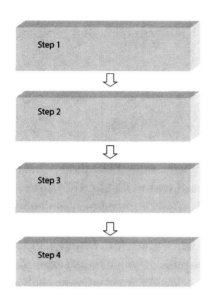

FIGURE 4.3-5. Title of the Book: How to Plant Pumpkin Seeds.

Another visual way to improve ELLs' reading comprehension is by collecting relevant materials to represent the book contents. For example, when reading books about ocean life, teachers can guide ELLs to collect sea shells to expand the knowledge they learned in the book. Also teachers can bring ELLs to a field trip to an aquarium to learn more of the ocean life. When reading books about dinosaurs or other natural science books, children can be brought to visit a natural science museum to explore more of the topics.

Memory, especially short-term memory, also plays an important role in reading comprehension. During breaks or free play time young ELLs can play memory games to relax and practice memory skills at the same time. Playing memory game creates opportunities for ELLs to socially interact with English speaking peers and improve English listening and speaking proficiency. Compared to memory games that are purchased, the homemade memory games can be adapted to focus on ELLs' favorite topics such as beach, ocean animals, dinosaurs, cars, trains, etc. The rules of memory games can be modified to increase ELLs' vocabulary. For example, add words to pictures on memory games. At play whoever matches two same cards is required to sound out the word and make a sentence using this word.

Using picture cards to memorize and analyze the main plots from stories is another visual strategy to improve reading comprehension. Teachers and parents can put the main plots from a story on picture cards; they shuffle the cards, and then ask ELLs to put the cards in a correct order. When readers can identify and understand "causal connectives, some particular features such as time and sequence markers" (Chik et al., 2010, p.13), they gain a faster understanding of the sequence of the events, and the cause and effect, leading to independent reading. One main goal of improving reading comprehension is for students to obtain

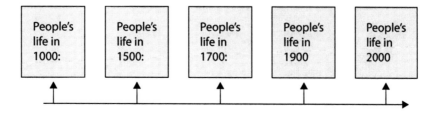

FIGURE 4.3-6. Graphic Organizer: Timeline.

knowledge independently and develop a logical and critical thinking ability, and eventually become lifelong learners.

Conclusion

Reading comprehension is a way for ELLs to obtain knowledge and to become independent lifelong learners. In order to improve their reading comprehension skills, ELLs should first be able to understand vocabulary, its meaning, the context it is used, its function, and how to use it to compose sentences. For example, when ELLs understand causal connectives in sentences, and the time and sequence factors, they are able to predict the events in the story, and analyze the cause and effect that can lead to a better understanding of the given text. Different visual tools that can help ELLs reach this goal are introduced and explained with detailed examples such as using homemade picture books, graphic organizers, and other visual tools such as drama, shuffled flashcard, and memory games. School teachers, parents and/or peers can work with ELLs in using these visual tools to improve their English proficiency; hence also improving their reading comprehension. Teachers should consider modifying their instruction method to accommodate ELLs' specific learning needs, maximize their interaction with peers, and capitalize on their learning potential. Improving reading comprehension is not the end. Rather the ultimate goal should be that ELLs obtain new knowledge through reading to become critical, logical thinkers, and independent lifelong learners.

The Rap on Reading Comprehension

BY JESSICA L. HAGAMAN, KATI LUSCHEN, AND ROBERT REID

Mrs. Brown is the special education teacher for the third-grade team at Casey Elementary School. Recently, the team realized that some of their students had problems with reading comprehension. As a part of their response to intervention (RTI) program, the team assesses students reading fluency every 2 months using Dynamic Indicators of Baste Early Literacy Skills (DIBELS; Good & Kaminski, 2002) to ensure students are improving and meeting district benchmarks. The team noticed that the majority of the third graders were meeting their fluency benchmarks and could decode at grade level thus meeting their instructional goals. However, they also noticed that a few students were well behind their peers in reading comprehension skills despite the fact that their fluency was at or above district benchmarks. This came as a surprise to the team because they had always thought comprehension of text automatically followed fluent reading. They knew they had to address this issue immediately so these students wouldn't fall behind their peers; how-ever, they weren't sure how to improve the comprehension skills of these students. Mrs. Brown suggested teaching the students a reading comprehension strategy. She suggested that they look for a simple and flexible comprehension strategy. They needed a strategy that could be taught individually or in small groups in the general education classroom or resource room. The strategy should also be one that students can master quickly. In addition, Mrs. Brown suggested teaching the strategy using the self-regulated strategy development (SRSD; Harris & Graham, 1996) model because she knew that how a strategy is taught is a critical factor in its success or failure (Reid & Lienemann, 2006).

Many teachers have encountered similar issues with reading comprehension in their classrooms. In fact, reading problems are one of the most frequent reasons students are referred

Jessica L Hagaman, Kati Luschen, and Robert Reid, "The "RAP" on Reading Comprehension," *Teaching Exceptional Children*, vol. 43, no. 1, pp. 22-29. Copyright © 2010 by Council for Exceptional Children. Reprinted with permission. Provided by ProQuest LLC. All rights reserved.

for special education services (Miller, 1993) and the disparity between students with reading difficulties and those who read successfully appears to be increasing (U.S. Department of Education, 2003). As a result, there is now an emphasis on early intervention programs such as RTI. In many cases, early intervention in reading instruction focuses primarily on foundational reading skills, such as decoding. These foundational skills allow the reader to read fluently (i.e., with speed and accuracy; National Reading Panel, 2000). However, with much of the focus on fluency, reading comprehension may be overlooked. It's true that reading fluency is necessary for comprehension. Students who are able to decode and recognize words effortlessly are able to devote more of their cognitive resources to reading comprehension. As a result, readers who are fluent are more likely to have better comprehension skills (Fuchs, Fuchs, Hosp, & Jenkins, 2001). This link between fluency and comprehension can lead teachers to assume that if students can read fluently they should also be able to comprehend what they read.

For many students, this assumption is correct; however, there are students who are fluent readers who experience difficulties with reading comprehension. Up to 10% of students are fluent readers who struggle to understand what they read (Meisinger, Bradley, Schwanenflugel, Kuhn, & Morris, 2009; Shankweiler. Lundquist, Dreyer. & Dickinson, 1996). These students are able to successfully decode text in specific content areas, such as sciences and social studies, but are unable to process and comprehend what they read (Caccamise & Snyder, 2005) One way to improve these students' comprehension skills is by teaching them effective comprehension strategies. Research shows that explicit instruction of reading comprehension strategies can significantly improve students' comprehension skills (Cajria. Jitendra, Sood. & Sacks, 2007; Pressley, Brown, El-Dinary, & Allferbach, 1995). Unfortunately, research also shows that comprehension instruction is often rudimentary and instruction in actual comprehension strategies (i.e., specific procedures students can use to increase their comprehension) is rare (Vaughn, Levy, Coleman, & Bos, 2002) As a result many students do not improve their ability to comprehend text. In addition, few teachers are knowledge able about how to effectively teach a strategy (Reid & Lienemaim, 2006)—and unless all the critical instructional elements are included, students are unlikely to benefit from a strategy.

How can special educators implement an effective reading comprehension strategy with young students who exhibit reading comprehension problems? We taught the RAP strategy (Read Ask-Paraphrase; Schumaker, Denton, & Deshler, 1884) to Cary, Betty, and Jean, third-graders with reading comprehension problems. The results of our Tier II intervention (Hagaman, Casey, & Reid, in press) demonstrate that teaching young students such a strategy can markedly improve their reading comprehension.

The RAP Strategy

RAP (Schumaker et al., 1984) is a simple strategy that is easily incorporated Into existing curriculum without taking time away from critical content instruction. This three-step strategy (see Figure 4.4-1) can improve the reading comprehension of students with and without disabilities and is extremely flexible. It can be used for elementary, middle, and high school students across many different content areas (Hagaman & Reid, 2008).

The strategy requires students to engage in reading materials through questioning and paraphrasing to increase their comprehension of the material. From the questioning and paraphrasing, students process information for better understanding of what they read. Studies using the RAP strategy (Schumaker et al., 1984) have shown it to be effective (e.g., Hagaman, Casey, & Reid, in press; Hagaman & Reid. 2008; Katims & Harris, 1997). Results from these studies showed marked improvement in reading comprehension across multiple age groups (e.g., elementary through high school), and for students with and without disabilities (e.g., learning disabilities). In short, the RAP strategy can easily be incorporated into existing curriculum as a support for a variety of readers who struggle with comprehension.

THE SELF-REGULATED STRATEGY DEVELOPMENT MODEL

Effective strategy instruction requires teachers to explicitly teach students the use of the strategy, model the strategy, cue students to use the strategy, and scaffold instruction to gradually allow the student to become an independent strategy user (Reid & Lienemann, 2006). We used the SRSD model to teach the RAP strategy (Schumaker et al., 1984) because SRSD is a well-validated model with over 20 years of research support that incorporates all the vital components of strategy instruction in the reading process (Harris & Graham, 1996). The SRSD model uses six stages for teaching strategies to ensure student mastery and generalization:

1. Development of background knowledge.
2. Discussion of the strategy steps.
3. Strategy modeling.
4. Memorization.
5. Support of the strategy.
6. Independent performance.

The RAP Strategy

✓ Read a paragraph.

✓ Ask yourself, "What was the main idea and two details?"

✓ Put information into your own words.

FIGURE 4.4-1. RAP Strategy Cue Card.

The stages are flexible and may be combined or reordered. Lessons typically involve activities from multiple stages; for example, memorizing a strategy is incorporated into all the lessons. Table 4.4-1 lists RAP strategy activities for each stage of the SRSD model.

Each of these stages contributes to students' eventual mastery of the strategy. Note that instruction is mastery-based: Students do not move to the final stage until they can use the strategy fluently and without teacher assistance. Fluent use of a strategy is critical because it allows students to use the strategy without taxing their working memory. Struggling students often have difficulty because their working memory is overloaded and information is not processed property (e.g., Gather-cole, Alloway. Willis. & Adams. 2006; Swanson, Howard, & Saez, 2007). This in turn can translate into problems such as difficulty storing and retrieving information. Strategy instruction teaches students how to do each step of the strategy and why each of those steps are important to accomplish their task (e.g., remembering what you read). Strategy instruction also entails teaching students metacognitive information about the strategy (e.g., the "hows" and "whys" of a strategy), because use of a strategy requires much more than rote knowledge of steps. Instruction is *scaffolded* (i.e., responsibility for strategy use is gradually shifted from the teacher to the student) to allow students to become independent strategy users.

TABLE 4.4-1. SRSD Stages in RAP Strategy.

SRSD Stage	RAP Activity
Develop background knowledge	Make sure student knows what main ideas and supporting details are in a paragraph.
Discuss the strategy	Sell the RAP strategy as a "trick" to help with reading comprehension. Discuss current level of performance with the student. Discuss the different steps of the RAP strategy. Obtain a commitment to learn and use the strategy.
Model the strategy	Model the use of the RAP strategy using a think-aload, demonstrating the "hows" and "ways" for each step.
Memorize the strategy	Student memorizes the strategy steps. Automaticity and fluency of strategy steps frees attention for understanding of text.
Support the strategy	Teacher supports the strategy through scaffolding. Responsibility of strategy use is gradually transferred to the student.
Independent performance	Student can use strategy independently. Teacher monitors performance.

Note. SRSD = self-regulated strategy development model (Harris & graham, 1996); RAP = Read-Ask-Paraphrase reading strategy (Schumaker, Denton, & Deshler, 1984).

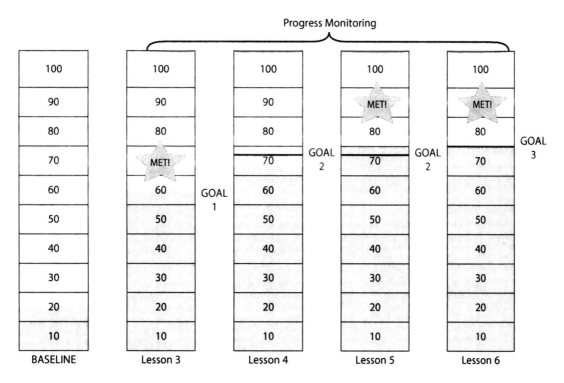

FIGURE 4.4-2. Sample Goal-Setting Chart.

TEACHING THE RAP STRATEGY

Develop and Activate Background Knowledge

In this stage, the instructor identifies if the student has the necessary skills to perform the chosen strategy, in must cases, the instructor will already know this information from working with the student on a regular basis; otherwise a task analysis can be performed. This analysis identifies and defines the skills necessary to use the strategy and then determines whether the student has the necessary skills. Direct observation of the student or curriculum-based measures can work well for this analysis. For the RAP strategy (Schumaker et al. 1984), the instructor might assess whether the student is a fluent reader, as proficient fluency can influence whether students understand what they read (National Reading Panel. 2000). In addition, the instructor will want to ensure that students understand what a paragraph is and what main ideas and details are in a paragraph. After the instructor has determined that students have the necessary prerequisite skills and background knowledge to use the strategy, the students can learn the specific steps of the strategy.

When we taught the RAP strategy (Schumaker et al., 1984) to three third- graders, Cary, Betty, and Jean, we first determined whether the students wore able to read fluently at grade level using DIBELS middle-of-the-year benchmark probes (Good & Kaminski, 2002). We then asked the students to read a short paragraph aloud and identify the main idea and two details. As the students identified each element, we wrote down their responses. This assessment helped us determine whether the students understood the components of a paragraph (i.e., the main idea and details).

DISCUSS THE STRATEGY

In the second stage of the SRSD model (Harris & Graham, 1996), the instructor should help the student continue to understand the uses for the strategy. The instructor should introduce the strategy to the student and activate his/her background knowledge on the topic. For example, the instructor may ask the student to brainstorm what makes a good reader or why reading is important (e.g., good readers understand what they read, enjoy reading). At this time, the mnemonic device "RAP" should be presented to the student and discussed. The instructor should explain each step of the strategy in the reading process (see Figure 4.4-1); the use of a cue card or graphic organizer can help students remember the steps of the strategy. The instructor should present the strategy as a "trick" to help students remember what they read.

An important component of this stage is obtaining student "buy-in." Getting a student to buy in to using the strategy is extremely important. If students are not committed to learning and using a strategy, it is unlikely that they will use the strategy independently, which is one of the goals of SRSD (Harris & Graham, 1996) instruction. For the RAP strategy (Schumaker et al., 1984), student buy-in can be accomplished by reviewing previous measures of reading comprehension (e.g., curriculum-based measures, unit tests). This information should be graphed so students can clearly see a need to improve their reading comprehension (see Figure 4.4-2).

After dismissing with the student how using the RAP strategy (Schumaker et al., 1984) can improve reading comprehension, the instructor should work with the student to set a performance goal (see Table 4.4-2). Graphs are often an effective way to illustrate student progress towards their self-determined goals. For example, the instructor may ask the student to graph current reading performance (e.g., percentage or number correct on a curriculum-based measure) over time to show improvement. Students can compare the current graph with their previous baseline performance. Graphing and goal setting also serve as self-regulation strategies, and feedback serves to reinforce performance. Note that goal setting and graphing also can be highly motivating to students.

For goal selling, we showed Cary, Betty, and Jean a graph of their previous performance gathered during baseline, and discussed how they each might improve their performance by using the RAP strategy (Schumaker el al., 1984). The students then set individual goals related to how much information they could recall from given text. We worked with the students to ensure they set realistic goals directly related to their current performance (e.g., if a student

TABLE 4.4-2. Effective Goal Setting.

Effective goals should be ...	
Specific	Goals must be specific so students know exactly what they hope to accomplish and they will know when they accomplish the goal. For example. "Get 75% on the weekly History quiz" is specific, whereas "Improve my store on the weekly History quiz." is too vague.
Proximal	Goals that can be met in the near future are more effective than those set farther in the future. Students feel a sense of accomplishment when they reach a goal, which motivates them to keep improving their performance. You can set long-term goals by using a series of short-term goals.
Challenging	Goals that are too easy do not enhance student effort; those that are too difficult can be discouraging. Goals that are challenging are those that are attainable, but require effort. Take care when setting goals, because students often will propose goals that are too easy or too difficult.

recalled 17% of text in baseline, an appropriate goal might be 40%). The students would record their future scares on a graph to self-monitor progress toward their self-determined goal. Initial goals for Cary, Betty, and Jean were 35%, 40%, and 50% respectively. When students met a self-determined goal, we worked with them to set a new goal.

We also encouragcd the students to self-monitor their use of the strategy. We taught them to develop a plan to make sure they were following each step of the strategy as they read a passage. Most students monitored their use of the strategy by taking notes or making tally marks while they read a passage to indicate they had completed a step of the strategy. For example, after reading a paragraph, Gary would underline the main idea of a paragraph, circle the details, and briefly orally summarize what was read.

MODEL TILE STRATEGY

For strategy instruction to be effective, students must have a strong understanding of why they use a strategy, how the strategy can help them, and the reasons behind the steps of the strategy. This information is critical if the students are to see the benefit in using the strategy. To provide this information, the instructor should model the use of the strategy. Systematic modeling is a critical component of effective strategy instruction, much more than simply going through the steps of a strategy; good modeling allows the student to see the thought processes of a skilled learner as s/he uses the strategy. This modeling provides critical information on using the RAP strategy (Schumaker et al., 1984), such as why steps are performed and how the steps help them to become a better reader. Modeling helps struggling learners understand that using a strategy is not a passive process, but requires active thought and effort. The procedure used to model a strategy is referred to as a *think-aloud*. In this procedure the instructor demonstrates the use of the strategy while verbalizing his or her thought processes (see box, "Think-Aloud for the RAP Strategy").

When leaching strategies like RAP (Schumaker et al., 1984), it is important to explicitly teach and model both the strategy and the self-regulation components of the strategy. The SRSD model (Harris & Graham, 1996) is designed to include self-regulation strategies such as self-instructions. In our example think-aloud, we have included self-instructions that help students to literally talk themselves through the strategy and reading process. As part of learning the RAP strategy, students should be taught and shown that specific self-statements and self-instruction can help them cope with negative thoughts and get through the strategy. For example, statements such as "If I use my strategy and try hard, I know I can understand what I'm reading" or "I can do this" could be included in the think-aloud.

SUPPORT THE STRATEGY

The support stage of teaching a strategy is a collaboration between the instructor and student. At this stage, students should know the steps of the strategy; however, they will still require practice in using the strategy before mastering it. This stage uses scaffolded instruction to help the student learn to use the strategy independently. During this stage the instructor and student practice using the strategy. At first, the Instructor should support the student through all the steps of the strategy. As the student becomes more comfortable with the strategy, instructor support is systematically reduced. Progress through this stage of the SRSD model (Harris & Graham, 1996) is dependent upon the length of time needed by the individual student. The instructor should decrease support and give students more responsibility for the strategy as they are ready. The end result of this stage should be independent use of the strategy.

Scaffolding can occur at any stage in the SRSD process. For example, in Stage 1, we provided the students with a strategy prompt sheet to help remember the steps of the RAP strategy. Other scaffolding activities occur during instruction and practice activities. For example, scaffolding instruction could begin with reading a story aloud to the student. Students should be allowed and encouraged to perform any steps of the strategy independently; similarly, instructors should support students as needed in any areas of the strategy. At this stage, supports such as graphic organizers can help students remember the steps of the strategy, although both prompts and graphic organizers should be faded as students gain fluency with the strategy. Alter reading the story aloud, ask the student to identify the main idea and details in each paragraph by underlining, highlighting, or saying them aluud. After this step, the instructor should encourage the student to determine whether his or her goal (identified in Stage 2) was met and to graph the results. The instructor should also encourage the student to reflect on how the strategy improved his or her reading comprehension. For further examples of scaffolding, see Table 4.4-3.

INDEPENDENT PERFORMANCE

In this stage, the student should be ready to use the strategy without assistance from the instructor. At this stage, the purpose should be to monitor the student's performance and ensure proper and consistent use of the strategy. Monitoring academic performance is critical: The goal of strategy instruction is increased academic performance. The student's work should show a marked and consistent improvement. There are a number of ways in monitor performance that are simple and effective, such as unit tests or retells. Teachers should also watch to see if students distort the strategy or skip steps when using it independently. If a student modifies a strategy but performance remains high, there is no cause for concern; many students will adapt the strategy to meet their needs. Changes are acceptable as long as the student performance remains high. On the other hand, if a student is performing the strategy correctly and consistently but a high level of performance is not attained (or maintained) then reteaching the strategy or considering a different strategy is probably in order. When using the RAP strategy (Schumaker et al., 1984), the independent performance stage is reached when the student is able to read a multiple-paragraph selection while correctly paraphrasing each paragraph with no assistance from the instructor.

Motivation and emotion are important factors in strategy instruction using SRSD (Harris & Graham, 1996). Changing

Think-Aloud for the RAP Strategy

What am I being asked to do? Mrs. Tuttle said I am going to practice using the RAP strategy to read two paragraphs. I need to understand and remember what I read and Mrs. Tuttle said this strategy is going to help me.

Now, Step 1 of RAP says to *Read a paragraph.* Easy enough—I know how to read and this paragraph only has five sentences! OK I did Step 1. This strategy is easy so far!

Okay, now for Step 2: *Ask myself "what was the main idea and two important details?"* Ub-oh, this step seems kind of difficult. I know that at this step I have to get ready to paraphrase what I just read. If I take my time and look back at the paragraph I just read. I should be able to identify the main idea ... .

Hmmm. I feel like Mrs. Tuttle told me that the main idea is often found in the first sentence of a paragraph. Let me see ... "There are two types of elephants" ... OK! I think this paragraph is definitely about elephants. Now for two important details ... "The two kinds of elephants are Asian and African. African elephants are much larger than Asian elephants." OK, I'm feeling pretty good about this.

Now on to Step 3: *Paraphrase or Put the paragraph into* my *own words.* This is a big step, and very important. This is how I will know if I understood what I read or not. I know that paraphrasing means I have to summarize what I read in my own words. OK, here I go ... .

I'm reading about elephants, and I remember that there are two kinds: Asian and African. Asian elephants are smaller than African elephants. Wow! I can't believe I remembered all that! Mrs. Tuttle was right about this strategy being helpful! But what do I do now?

Hmm. I have one more paragraph to read before I am done reading this story. I guess that means I am going to be doing the RAP strategy again!

All right, here I go again. First, *Read a paragraph* Easy. Here I go, ... Done! Ok, *Ask myself about the main idea and details.* "Elephants can be found in the wild or in zoos" ... OK, so I'm still reading about elephants, but what were the details I read about! "In the wild, elephants live in families called *herds.* A female elephant is usually the leader of a herd and called the *matriarch.*"

OK! I think I'm already read for the third step, paraphrase! Elephants can either live in the wild or in a zoo. Elephants live in herds and a female elephant is in charge of the herd.

Wow! I learned a lot about elephants and it wasn't even that hard! I just used my RAP strategy and I could remember what I read. I bet when I take my test on this reading I'm going to do really well. Mrs. Tuttle said if I used the strategy would get better scores in reading ... . I can't wait to find out if I met my goal!

a student's attitude toward a task and success are important goals of strategy instruction. In our case, we observed whether the students' attitudes toward reading and confidence in their abilities improved. We also checked to see if the students were using the strategy outside the classroom. We observed one student teaching her classmates the RAP strategy. The use of open-ended questions such as "What do good readers do?" or "What do you say to yourself before you read something?" can help teachers determine if a strategy changed students' perception of a task. However, teachers should remember that some changes (such as altitude improvements) take more time than others to obtain.

FINAL THOUGHTS

The RAP strategy (Schumakcr et al., 1984)—when correctly taught using an effective model of strategy instruction such as SRSD (Harris & Graham, 1996)—can be extremely effective for improving reading comprehension. This strategy is extremely flexible and can be used for elementary, middle, and high school students across many different content areas (Hagaman & Reid, 2008). Effective strategy instruction requires using specific techniques (e.g., modeling, scaffolding). Teachers should also remember that strategy instruction should be customized to the student. Instruction should continue until the student has mastered the use of the strategy (i.e., using the strategy correctly and consistently). The number of lessons depends on how quickly the student is able to master the strategy. Luckily, most students can master the RAP strategy quickly, typically in four or five lessons of 20 to 30 minutes. Cary, Betty, and Jean mastered the RAP strategy in

TABLE 4.4-3. Scaffolding Examples.

Type of Scaffolding	Explanation	RAP Example
Content scaffolding	Instructor uses material at an easy reading level (e.g., text below the student's grade level). Instructor uses content of interest to the student to teach the strategy. Instructor teaches the student easier steps of the strategy first, then more difficult steps. In initial practice sessions the student performs the easy steps; the instructor models the more difficult steps.	The student is allowed to read one paragraph, a shorter story, or a story written at a lower grade level. The student reads stories on topic(s) that they know about or that interests them. The instructor leaches the student the R and A in RAP first, then how to paraphrase.
Task scaffolding	Ownership of the strategy is gradually transferred from instructor to student by letting the student perform more and more of the strategy steps.	Phase 1: The instructor asks the student to name the strategy step that should be performed, then the instructor describes the step and performs it. Phase 2: The teacher asks the student to name the step and describe the step; the instructor performs the steps. Phase 3: The student names, describes, and performs the step.
Material scaffolding	Prompts, graphic organizers, and cues are used to help the student use the strategy. Typically, these are faded over time.	The student is given a graphic organizer or cue card. As the student gains mastery of the strategy, the prompts should be faded.

Note. RAP = Read-Ask-Paraphrase reading strategy (Schumaker, Denton, & Deshler. 1984).

four, three, and five lessons, respectively, that were roughly 20 minutes in length (for lesson plans, see University of Nebraska-Lincoln, n.d.). In sum, the RAP strategy, when taught using an effective model for strategy instruction, can be an effective means of improving students' reading comprehension.

Assessing Comprehension

Comprehension may be assessed through oral or written responses. Assessment should include opportunities to express specific knowledge or skills as well as responses to open-ended, higher-level thinking and problem solving, which may have multiple correct responses. Teachers may collect student-created notes, annotations, and graphic organizers, and maintain notes from student conferences and interviews as evidence of learning. The value in authentic documentation is amplified when teachers analyze the documentation and reflect on and infer what students currently understand and what they would benefit from learning next. Group and individual assessments provide further evidence of student comprehension. Formative assessments should occur regularly with the intent to monitor and adjust instruction to meet student needs. Summative assessments occur occasionally as a benchmark of learning.

BEFORE READING
Think about the assessments you have used and/or seen others use. What do they have in common? How were the data used?

DURING READING
How do the assessments in the articles focus on higher-level thinking and problem solving? Do all of the assessments included have value for all students? Why or why not?

AFTER READING
What assessments are you going to use to assess comprehension? How can you use the data to be more reflective of student behaviors? How can you use the data to be more reflective about supporting comprehension?

Assessing the Comprehension of Young Children

BY KATHERINE A. DOUGHERTY STAHL

[...]

Measures Of Decoding, Language Processing, And Domain Knowledge

MISCUE ANALYSIS

Miscue analysis is an evaluation of oral reading errors. A miscue analysis may be conducted independently or as part of an informal reading inventory that includes questioning and retelling. This section of the chapter will focus only on miscue analysis as a lens for assessing comprehension. Some researchers (Clay, 1993a; Goodman, Watson, & Burke, 1987) advocate the use of error analysis as evidence of comprehension processes. According to Goodman et al. (1987), "the ability to produce semantically and syntactically acceptable structures or, if the structures are unacceptable, to correct them, provides evidence of a reader's predicting and confirming strategies."

The examinee is asked to read an unfamiliar passage aloud and the examiner records the examinee's reading of the text using a coding system. After the reading session, the examiner evaluates the reader's errors and self-corrections. Substitutions, omissions and teacher-assists are counted as errors. Typically, repetitions and self-corrections are recorded and evaluated but not counted as errors. Errors are analyzed for their syntactic and semantic acceptability in the sentence and passage, whether they resulted in changes in the meaning of the text, and grapho-phonetic similarity to the text. A coding form is used for the analysis with the consideration of syntactic and semantic acceptability always being given the highest priority. This emphasis on prediction, confirmation, meaning change, syntactic and semantic acceptability may justify the use of miscue analysis as a comprehension measure, especially when used with young children whose reading is often propelled by meaning (Clay, 1991, 1993a; Sulzby, 1985).

Reading Miscue Inventory (Goodman et al., 1987) One distinction of Reading Miscue Inventory is the use of a lengthy piece of text (at least 500 words). For young readers this would involve using multiple books. Teachers and researchers are advised to compile a range of materials suitable for miscue analysis.

Reading Miscue Inventory in its purest form is extensive and time-consuming. A teacher would only be likely to do a Reading Miscue Inventory at the beginning and end of a year or with struggling readers that require specialized instruction. Miscues are analyzed by asking a series of questions about the miscues and self-corrections. The questions may be asked about acceptability at the passage level, sentence level, partial sentence level, and word level.

Running records Running records have the same theoretical base and are very similar to one of the alternative abbreviated Reading Miscue Inventory procedures (Clay, 1993a; Goodman et el., 1987). Although the assessor may ask a few comprehension questions or request a retelling, the error analysis is the primary evaluation of the running record.

Two of the advantages of running records are the ease and flexibilty of administration. The coding format of running records enables them to be used without a typescript, easing the burden of preparation. Text length is not dictated. This enables running records to be conducted with a wide variety of texts. As a result, running records are likely to be administered with greater frequency than the Reading Miscue Inventory or an informal reading inventory. Clay (1993a; 1993b) recommends that running records be administered using any texts that children can read with 90%–95% accuracy. Typically, authentic texts are used. "Little books" that contain complete, cohesive stories or informational text that have been leveled using qualitative criteria (Peterson, 1991; Rhodes, 1981) are often selected as benchmark texts for systematic assessment. For novice readers, the content of these texts is likely to be within the realm of their experience and at or close to their instructional reading level. This increases the likelihood that the novice reader will be able to read the text with fluency, an important factor in the comprehension of novice readers.

Informal reading inventories Informal reading inventories contain a collection of graded reading passages (See Leslie & Caldwell, chapter 19, this volume). The passages typically range from 100 to 300 words for primary level passages (Johns, 1997; Leslie & Caldwell, 2006).

Multiple forms are provided for opportunities to pretest and posttest, determine listening comprehension levels, or to sample comprehension during silent reading with narrative and expository text. The availability of multiple, graded, reading passages with prepared questions and scoring guides with fairly standardized, prescribed procedures are the advantageous features of informal reading inventories. The grade level passages provided are designed to show yearly grade-level growth, but not intermittent progress. As a result, the growth of emergent readers and smaller intervals of growth may not be reflected.

There are several other disadvantages for novice readers. Comprehension and word recognition rates may be negatively affected by passages that are strictly governed by conventional notions of readability. The Dale-Chall readability formula (Chall & Dale, 1995), which has been extended from fourth to first grade, is based on an extrapolation. They caution that lower levels do not have the degree of confidence found in upper levels. This may be true for other readability formulas that are based on word difficulty and sentence length. Chall and Dale list physical features of text, the number of pictures and how they relate to text, language, organization, and cognitive complexity as important variables in the comprehensive nature of readability that have not been included in readability formulas and need to be judged separately. Repetitive pattern, familiar concepts, natural language, good match of illustrations and text, rhyme, rhythm alliteration, cumulative pattern, familiar story, and familiar sequence are features that seem to promote readability for early readers (Gourley, 1984; Peterson, 1991; Rhodes, 1981). Because of the reliance that early readers still have on meaning and language to facilitate decoding, these factors may more significantly impact their performance than the performance of older readers.

Finally, the required speficity of the match between beginning readers' knowledge and the IRI passage can be a limitation of commercial IRI use in the lower grades. Differences in vocabulary learned and tested may impact achievement levels on the IRI (Johns, 1997).

Additional considerations Miscue analysis of oral reading does provide a window for viewing the prediction, confirmation, and meaning-making process during reading. There is substantial evidence that demonstrates that poorer readers, younger readers, and readers with less prior knowledge make errors with less semantic acceptability and more graphic similarity (Chinn, Waggoner, Anderson, Schommer, & Wilkinson, 1993; Schlieper, 1977; Taft & Leslie, 1985; Wixson, 1979). Their errors are also more likely to be nonwords and left uncorrected. However, reading comprehension is dynamic and in many ways situated in the context (Chinn et al., 1993; Taft & Leslie, 1985; Wixson, 1979). Prior knowledge of the topic by the reader, instructional reading program, the type of teacher feedback in response to errors, and the difficulty of the material have all been found to influence student miscues and corrections (Chinn et al., 1993; Taft & Leslie, 1985; Wixson, 1979). These factors influence oral reading miscues and should always be considered in making an evaluation of reading comprehension based on miscue analysis. Additionally, all of these methods are highly reliant on the competence of the teacher in appropriate text selection, recording text reading, error analysis and interpretation. Extensive professional development is essential.

CURRICULUM-BASED MEASUREMENT

Curriculum-based measurement (CBM) refers to a specific subset of curriculum-based assessment (CBA). CBA is typically an informal approach that uses observations and records of student performance on local curriculum as tools for instructional planning (Hasbrouck, Woldbeck, Ihnot, & Parker, 1999; Shinn, 1988). CBA tends to be hierarchical, non-normed, and have questionable validity and reliability. CBM, on the other hand, is a specific standardized set of procedures developed through the Institute for Research on Learning Disabilities as a formative evaluation system to help special educators assess student growth and plan instruction (Hasbrouck et al., 1999). CBM is now widely used by special educators, researchers, and classroom teachers as a valid and reliable measure of student growth.

In the area of reading, CBM usually consists of scoring the number of words correctly read per minute from a passage derived from a basal reader or literature anthology. Although this would seem to be purely a measure of reading fluency, studies have determined that passage reading CBM is highly correlated (.77 to .92) with standardized measures of comprehension (Fuchs & Fuchs, 1992; Kranzler, Miller, & Jordan, 1999; Madelaine & Wheldall, 1999; Shinn, Knutson, Good, Tilly, & Collins, 1992). Kranzler et al. (1999) determined that there was no evidence of gender or racial/ethnic bias of CBM in Grades 2 and 3.

CBM seems to be most sensitive and highly correlated to overall reading competence and reading comprehension before Grade 4 (Kranzler et al., 1999; Shinn, 1988; Shinn et al., 1992). This is consistent with a developmental theory of reading and the recent work by Paris (2005) on constrained and unconstrained abilities. The lack of automaticity of novice readers seems to contribute to difficulties in comprehension (Stanovich, 1980). Recent research indicates that fluency and comprehension may be dependent early in the process of reading acquisition, but they become independent after high levels of reading fluency are achieved (Paris, 2005). Correlations between fluency scores and comprehension scores diminish in the third and fourth grades (Paris et al., 2005). In other words, novice readers who struggle to decode words are less likely to understand the text, whereas an independent relation is evident among older students who read fluently but have poor comprehension. As readers become more automatic in word processing, comprehension difficulties are likely to be the result of unfamiliar content, idea density or some other source.

Teacher training and support are required for reliable application of CBM. As well as taking time away from instruction, the preparation of passages, administration and scoring are time intensive for teachers. Shinn (1988) has given explicit, procedural directions for the selection of reading passages and the development of local norms. Materials are to be randomly selected from the curriculum reading materials, tested for readability consistency and retyped to duplicate the grade-level text for the children and with word counts for the teachers.

The development of passage kits and widespread availability of Dynamic Indicators of Basic Early Literacy Skills has made CBM more accessible to teachers (Madelaine & Wheldall, 1999). Powell-Smith and Bradley-Klug (2001) found that students performed at more proficient levels on generic passages than passages derived from curriculum reading materials. Factors that may contribute to the attractiveness of generic passage kits are control of readability, consistent gradient levels of difficulty, and the inclusion of texts with complete, cohesive structures in their entirety. The compilation and utilization of this commercial packages increases time efficiency, standardization, reliability, and validity of CBM as a measure of student progress.

CLOZE

Cloze was developed by Taylor (1953) as a mechanical approach to test item development and an alternative to the conventional standardized test of comprehension. In its original form, every nth word (usually every 5th word) in a passage is deleted. The examinee fills in each cloze blank. Only a precise replacement is scored as correct and higher scores indicate greater comprehension. One of the most serious criticisms of cloze is the lack of intersentential and intertextual comprehension. Shanahan, Kamil and Tobin (1982) demonstrated that the ability to fill in a cloze blank does not rely upon making sense of the total passage. This is in direct conflict with modern theories of comprehension.

Over the years, researchers have developed a variety of adaptations with modifications to address these criticisms and to moderate the difficulty of writing the precise word in the blank. Pearson and Hamm (2005) list some of the variations in their review of comprehension assessments.

- Allow synonyms to serve as correct answers
- Delete only every 5th content word (leaving function words intact)
- Use an alternative to every 5th word deletion
- Delete words at the end of sentences and provide a set of choices from which examinees are to pick the best answer (this tack is employed in several standardized tests, including the Stanford Diagnostic Reading Test and Degrees of Power).

Cloze and modifications of cloze have been successfully used as a form of ESL and bilingual assessment (Bachman, 1985; Bachman, 2000; Francis, 1999). In an oral reading index, the L2 reader would need to direct attention to the oral production at the expense of comprehension. The cloze method allows the L2 reader to devote processing resources to comprehension (Francis, 1999). Francis (1999) also recommends using cloze passages as instructional tools for L2 learners. Small groups can discuss their response choices for developing language awareness and comprehension monitoring.

MAZE

One of the modifications of cloze that has increased in popularity is the maze task. The maze task is a multiple-choice variation of the cloze task. The maze task is appealing because of its ease of administration and scoring. It can be administered in an individual or group setting, manually or on a computer program. The multiple-choice format makes it easy to score. Teachers value maze as an acceptable indicator of decoding, fluency and comprehension (Fuchs & Fuchs, 1992).

Timed maze tasks have been adopted as another form of CBM. Fuchs and Fuchs (1992) performed a preliminary study of several measures of reading comprehension to determine the potential for a computer-based measure. They evaluated oral and written recalls, oral and written cloze tasks, oral question-answering, and maze. In terms of validity, reliability, correlation with a standard measure, capacity to demonstrate student abilities and progress, and teacher satisfaction, the timed maze task showed the most promise. Since this study, the Fuchs have produced a technology-based CBM maze task series with 30 passages per grade level available commercially.

The preliminary maze work by Fuchs and Fuchs (1992) was conducted with middle school boys with mild to moderate disabilities. The investigation of maze as a valid, reliable, sensitive assessment of younger students was conducted by Shinn, Deno and Espin (2000). Results showed good alternate form reliability (.69–.90 for all monthly passages). Both group improvement and individual gain were reflected. Growth rates were correlated to the children's end-of-year standardized reading tests.

The variations in maze construction may cause variations in sensitivity, reliability, and validity. Care and deliberation in the selection of passages is crucial. The passages should be between 100 and 400 words long to allow for internal coherence (Parker & Hasbrouck, 1992). Passages for younger students would be likely to be at the lower end of this range. Since progress is reflected in gains, passages should have approximately the same readability, although this was not explicitly stated in any of the cited articles. Deletion strategies can also vary in number, ratio deletion, and content. The point at which deletions start in a passage can vary. Typically, they start in the second sentence. However, for younger children a longer lead-in may be desirable.

The greatest source of psychometric concern is the selection of distractors (Parker & Hasbrouck, 1992). The number, quality, and lexical characteristics of distractors can vary greatly. Parker and Hasbrouck (1992) recommend that test designers choose four

... distractors that are (a) the same part of speech as the deleted word, (b) meaningful and plausible within one sentence, (c) related in content to the passage (when possible), (d) as familiar to the reader as the deleted word, and (e) either clearly wrong or less appropriate, given broader passage content. (p. 216)

Evidence indicates that some maze tests are sensitive to the reading comprehension development of novice readers (Francis, 1999; Shinn et al., 1999). The minimal demand placed on working memory is advantageous for younger students. However, the text readability and the characteristics of the distractors would require deliberate consideration and evaluation in the selection or design of maze tasks for young readers.

DEGREES OF READING POWER AND LEXILE MEASURES OF COMPREHENSION

The Degrees of Reading Power (DRP; Touchstone Applied Science Associates, 1995) and Lexile Framework (Stenner, 1996) are two maze modifications that directly relate comprehension scores to readability scales. Student scores are norm-referenced, criterion-referenced, and indicate the level of books that a student ought to be able to read and understand with a predicted 75% comprehension rate. Both tests can be group administered and the multiple-choice format makes them easy to score. DRP passages are all nonfiction and Lexile passages are derived from authentic texts. Both are untimed. Both tests have the advantage of being developed by pschometric experts and have high correlations with standardized tests. The DRP has a deletion ratio of 1/46 to require comprehension of several consecutive sentences on longer passages. Below is one example of a primary DRP passage.

Years ago, there were no electric lamps. People had to _____ their homes differently. One way to do this was with candles.

    (a) paint   (b) shape   (c) light   (d) enter

The extensive sampling, norming, and standardization of these tests helps validate them as comprehension assessments.

[...]

Alternatively, Stahl et al. (2006) describe the utilization of a common instructional passage, assessment of student comprehension of authentic literature specifically designed for use in the classroom instructional setting. The texts were fairly lengthy and complex in content because the teacher provided a scaffolded instructional experience. Instruction made the texts accessible to the students and provided a means of avoiding the decoding obstacles that often hinder the comprehension of novice or struggling readers. The three days of instruction were followed by a curriculum-linked assessment. Students engaged in a retelling and constructed response on Day 4. The common instructional passage assessment can be used to identify the processes that students use to comprehend a common text. Teachers can adapt this assessment format to a wide range of classroom texts. This is another assessment with consequential validity (Taylor, 2006).

The retelling task required the child to orally retell the story in Grade 2 or to provide a written retelling in Grade 4. Additionally, each question that required a constructed response was designed to tap the knowledge and comprehension processes emphasized in a theoretically-based comprehension instructional framework. The instructional framework incorporated vocabulary development, cognitive strategy instruction and responsive engagement (high-level discussion). An example of a question targeting each comprehension aspect and the targeted control for the book *Lazy Lion* is listed below.

Vocabulary/Prior Knowledge: Besides lazy, what other words would you use to describe the lion?
Cognitive strategy: Suppose the lion had asked a hippopotamus to build him a house. What do you predict would happen?
Responsive Engagement: If Lion were a person, is he the kind of person you would like for a friend? Why or why not?

The assessments discussed in this section reflect the social nature of learning and work. However, they raise new questions about issues of validity for individual scores, external accountability, reliability and generalizability (Linn, 1999; Pearson & Hamm, 2000/2005).

CHAPTER REFERENCES

Adler, C. R. (2010). Put reading first: The research building blocks for teaching children to read. National Institute for Literacy.

Duffy, G. G. (2014). *Explaining reading: A resource for teaching concepts, skills, and strategies* (3rd ed.). New York: The Guilford Press.

Fielding, L. G. & Pearson, P. D. (1994). Synthesis of research/reading comprehension: What works. February. *Educational Leadership, 51* (5), 62–68.

Fisher, D. (n.d.). Close reading in elementary classrooms. Retrieved October 5, 2015, from McGraw-Hill site: http://mhreadingwonders.com/wp-content/themes/readingwonders /docs/9430_Fisher_Author_9-4.pdf.

Gelzheiser, L. M. (2005). Maximizing student progress in one-to-one programs: Contributions of texts, volunteer experience, and student characteristics. *Exceptionality, 13 (4),* 229–243. In R. L. Allington. 2009. *What really matters in response to intervention: Research-based designs.* Boston: Allyn and Bacon.

Harvey, S. & Goudvis. A. (2007). *Strategies that work: Teaching comprehension for under-standing and engagement* (2nd ed.). Portland, ME: Stenhouse Publishers.

Moore, D. W. (n.d.). Reading comprehension strategies. Retrieved from http://ngl.cengage. com. Pearson, P. David, L. R. Roehler, J. A. Dole, & G. G. Duffy. (Duffy). Developing exper-tise in reading comprehension. In S. Jay Samuels & Alan Farstrup, eds. *What research has to say about reading instruction* (2nd ed.). Newark, DE: International Reading Association.

National Institute of Student Health and Human Development (NISHHD). (2000). Report of the national reading panel. Teaching children to read: An evidence-based assessment of the scientific research literature on reading and its implications for reading instruc-tion: Reports of the subgroups (NIH Publication No. 00-4754). Washington, DC: U.S. Government Printing Office.

Power, B. (2015). What are the seven comprehension strategies? Retrieved from https://www. choiceliteracy.com. Allington, R. L. & Johnston, P. H. (2000). *What do we know about effective fourth-grade teachers and their classrooms?* Albany, NY: The National Research Center on English Learning and Achievement.

Risko, V. J. & Walker-Dalhouse, D. (2012). *Be that teacher!: Breaking the cycle for struggling readers.* New York: Teachers College Press.

Stahl, S. A. & Heubach, K. (2005). Fluency-oriented reading instruction. *Journal of Literacy Research, 37* (1), 25–60.

Chapter Five

Introduction by Natalie Tye

FLUENCY

Fluency

INTRODUCTION TO READINGS 5.1-5.3

Fluency

Fluency is the process of reading a text as measured by speed and accuracy (Chard, Vaughn, & Tyler, 2002; Kostewicz & Kubina, 2010). Children who struggle to read texts because they read slower than others, or who seem to have difficulty comprehending the text, may be challenged by reading fluency. Teachers often search for strategies to help students develop fluency for later reading success. Unfortunately, without a firm understanding of how to coach for fluency, teachers can sometimes try a myriad of strategies and ideas without having an actual end goal in mind, or even having a plan for improvement.

In order for a child to comprehend the text they are reading, three key concepts must be present: accuracy, automaticity, and prosody (Rasinski, Rikli, & Johnston, 2009). So what are these three words and what do they mean? Accuracy is exactly what it sounds like: the ability to accurately identify words in the text. Automaticity implies that word recognition must be automatic to the reader (Rasinski et al., 2005). Prosody is what brings the text to life through written and verbal expression.

So now that you know reading fluency is an issue for struggling readers, and you are aware of key components to fluency, let's take a look at how to help all readers, developing and struggling, in the classroom. The following three articles will outline how to make a plan to assist readers with fluency. Further, strategies and techniques will be provided to assist with goal accomplishment.

BEFORE READING

Before reading the articles in this chapter, consider how it feels to struggle at something, anything. Take a moment and reflect on that feeling. Write down some words to describe this feeling in your journal.

DURING READING

While reading each of the articles, create a list of the strategies discussed throughout. Each time a new strategy is mentioned, write it down and provide a brief description to go along with it.

AFTER READING

After completing the chapter reading, create a template plan of action to help struggling readers with fluency. Remember that a plan is not just a series of strategies. Before strategies are implemented, the teacher must collect vital information about the child. List the steps required of the teacher before any action can take place.

Implementing Systematic Practice to Build Reading Fluency via Repeated Readings

BY DOUGLAS E. KOSTEWICZ

P eople worldwide appreciate fluent performance. When attending symphonies and plays, we expect performances that move us. When watching professional sporting events, regardless of the sport, we appreciate (and often demand depending on our loyalties) perfect execution. Even during movies and television shows, we can readily notice inaccuracies as we have become accustomed to (lawlessness. How do the performers, actors, and athletes in any of the aforementioned scenarios attain such precise movements? Often the defining feature involves practice (Ericsson, 2006).

Individuals have many ways to engage in practice ranging from simple play (e.g., kicking a soccer ball around or plucking a guitar) to systematic, set practice. Ericsson (2006) suggests that one type (i.e., deliberate practice) differentiates experts from amateurs. For example, master violinists, from the ages of 4 to 20, spend 10,000 hours of cumulative practice (approximately two hours a day for 16 years). Over the same 16 year span, least accomplished experts spend only 3,000 hours practicing with no comparisons made with pure amateurs. While the differences may initially appear staggering, the role of practice has not gone unnoticed by society.

Many parents perhaps not knowing the astonishing numbers of hours necessary fully understand the role of systematic, deliberate practice. Parents involve children in certain activities early and often and support practice in home and abroad. Many industrious individuals hold camps, host tournaments, and run schools dedicated to providing opportunities to practice a given skill. The trend continues for children in schools as professionals and administrators establish the importance of practice on skill areas such as music and sports by dedicating time either during or after school and providing specific practice locales such as music practice rooms and multiple athletic fields.

Oral Reading Fluency and Practice

Given the importance and popular support of practice, one would believe that educators approach academic skills in the same manner. However, oral reading fluency, arguably one of the most important academic skills, has not always received a necessary focus in the classroom (Allington, 1983). Nevertheless, the educational community has placed reading fluency squarely in the spotlight (Allington, 1983; Kubina &. Morrison, 2000; National Reading Panel, 2000; Pikulski & Chard, 2005) and a student's ability to read fluently has become a quality measure of overall reading ability (Fuchs, Fuchs, Hosp, & Jenkins, 2001). As many students both with and without special needs continue to struggle with oral reading fluency (Archer, Gleason, & Vachon, 2003), teachers implementing systematic, deliberate practice with a focus on oral reading fluency can supplement important classroom reading instruction.

Oftentimes teachers employ the silent reading method of practice in the hopes of building reading fluency. Students either receive or choose a book to read and then passively participate in sustained silent reading (SSR). However, student reading fluency outcomes tell a different story. After completing an exhaustive review of reading research, the National Reading Panel (2000) found that students improve oral reading fluency more through systematic, guided (i.e., deliberate) practice, rather than SSR or teachers encouraging students to read more. Fitting with the ties to overall reading ability mentioned earlier (Fuchs et al., 2001), students across grade levels participating in guided fluency practice improved both word recognition and comprehension (National Reading Panel, 2000).

Teachers now find themselves in an exciting position with a formula for student reading success: implement systematic, guided oral reading fluency practice for students. While the charge sounds easy enough, two notable factors for classroom time and teacher attention. First and foremost, classroom instructional time comes at a premium given the high stakes assessments and ramifications of adequate student achievement in education (No Child Left Behind, 2002). Any deliberate oral reading practice would have to, at the same time, include both efficient and effective characteristics. Second, teachers now experience students with a variety of reading levels in the classroom and work with students both with and without special needs (Kavale & Forness, 2000). Teachers must have the ability to quickly individualize reading practice and make use of the sometimes minimal resources available. While provided a seemingly daunting situation, one systematic reading practice has the potential to address both concerns: repeated readings.

REPEATED READINGS

Samuels (1979) and Dahl (1974) initially introduced the method of repeated readings with researchers and practitioners implementing the practice since. The general format for repeated readings has a student reading a grade-level passage multiple times until reaching a goal. Once reached, the student reads a different yet grade-equivalent passage to the same goal (Meyer & Felton, 1999). The process would stop once the student reads new passages fluently or continues with incrementally more difficult text. While, many repeated reading variations and extensions to the original form exist (see Chard, Vaughn, & Tyler, 2002; Kuhn & Stahl, 2003; Meyer & Felton, 1999 for more detailed reviews), teachers must address a series of questions and concerns when building systematic oral reading fluency practice via repeated readings.

DEFINING AND MEASURING ORAL READING FLUENCY

Prior to starting, teachers must determine what student outcome would characterize the effect of reading fluency practice. Ericsson (2006) suggests that those participating in deliberate practice must focus on the most important part of a skill to receive the maximum benefit. For oral reading fluency multiple definitions exist. While some may examine prosody which includes reading with speed, accuracy, and expression (Fountas & Pinnell, 1994; Hook & Jones, 2002; Schreiber, 1980), Archer et al. (2003) provide a clear measurable definition of oral reading fluency for teachers to focus on: reading speed and accuracy. From the concise definition, teachers can quickly determine what to measure by focusing on words read correctly and incorrectly by students in a set amount of time.

PRE-IMPLEMENTATION OF REPEATED READINGS

After determining what to measure, teachers have to examine if individual students will benefit from oral reading fluency practice and what reading level to provide. Reading includes a multitude of behaviors ranging from phonemic awareness to comprehension (Camine, Silbert, Kame'enui, & Tarver, 2010). As reading skills build upon each other (Carnine et al., 2010), all students may not have the prerequisite skills necessary for focused oral reading fluency practice. Students unable to decode text would experience unnecessary failure with repeated readings. Additionally, teachers failing to match appropriate reading text to each student's ability inadvertently cause failure for those reading too far above their level or waste the time of those reading too far below their level.

One way to determine both appropriateness and establish initial oral reading fluency level involves the use of a series of one minute timings. First, identify a series of 200+ word passages for every grade. Teachers can use Fry (Fry, 1989) or similar readability procedures to determine passage readability. Starting with the passage that represents the student's current grade level, have the student read out loud for one minute. Using established scoring procedures (e.g., Shinn, 1989) determine the correct number of words read per minute (CWPM). One range to compare each student's CWPM score comes from Kubina and Starlin (2003) who differentiate CWPM reading scores into three groups (i.e., frustration, instructional, and fluent) regardless of grade level. Students reading 50–150 CWPM fall into the instructional range. Teachers can start the student's reading fluency practice with passages at this readability. Students reading faster than 150 CWPM (i.e., fluent level) would repeat the one minute timing with a passage one grade level higher. For students, reading less than 50 CWPM (i.e., frustration level), repeat the one minute reading with a passage one grade level lower. The process continues until each individual student scores in the instructional range (50–150 CWPM) or scores in the frustration range for first grade passages. The assessment process allows the teacher to individualize each student's practice level and also identify students who require additional pre-oral reading fluency assistance (i.e., students reading at the frustration level on first grade passages).

REPEATED READING IMPLEMENTATION CONCERNS

A teacher having identified both what to measure (correct and incorrect words per minute) and linked the appropriate reading level passages to each student now has other factors to consider before finally implementing systematic reading fluency practice (i.e., repeated readings). The concerns include the amount of time students read, the actual reading process and error correction, providing performance feedback and progress monitoring and the goal that determines when students progress to the next passage.

Length of time. Time plays a major role in systematic practice. As mentioned earlier, the amount of time individuals spent practicing differentiates skill outcomes (Ericsson, 2006). Drawing a parallel to reading fluency practice, the more frequent students engage in reading fluency practice, the greater the improvement. When implementing repeated reading, teachers can consider the time question from three angles: how often students should engage in practice weekly, how long reading practice should last, and finally, how long students should read during each trial.

Most schools schedule instruction in core academic areas to occur once a day with reading fluency surely able to follow a similar model. While daily reading practice may tap already maximized resources, the actual reading time involved does not have to occur for an extended period of time. Most repeated reading research suggests daily reading practice in actual classroom time lasts approximately 5 (e.g., Kostewicz & Kubina, 2011) to 10 (e.g., Staubitz, Cartledge, Yurick, & Lo, 2005; Yurick, Robinson, Cartledge, Lo, & Evans, 2006) minutes depending on the amount of modifications involved. While variation occurs in research regarding the amount of time dedicated to practice each day, a virtual consensus suggests that test readings occur for one minute, meaning that scores on one-minute readings determine oral reading fluency progress. In summary, teachers should include reading fluency practice as often as possible weekly, preferably daily, for approximately five or more minutes with students reading for a one- minute assessment at least once during the practice.

Reading process. Knowing how long to practice only poses the next concern: how teachers should conduct the actual reading process. How individuals practice skills depends heavily on the skill in question and the individual's current level of performance. Beginners, obviously, require a high level of supervision from more competent instructors. Once mastered, individuals can spend more time practicing alone with less supervision. In daily repeated reading practice, coaching and supervision translates to who listens to the reader daily with teachers having multiple implementation options.

Teachers can have each student read out loud to themselves (e.g., Compan, Iamsupasit, & Samuels, 2001) or listen to error-free recordings of the passage before reading (e.g., McDowell, McIntyre, Owen, & Keenan, 1998). Either method presents benefits for teachers in larger classes as all students can practice regardless of class size. The cons, however, present a quandary given that many students require systematic practice due to skill deficiencies. In addition to the extensive time necessary to make recordings of multiple passages, students may have difficulty determining their own reading errors. Daane, Campbell, Grigg, Goodman, and Oranje (2005) found that increased numbers of errors correlated with lower reading comprehension scores. Additionally, Therrien (2004) noted that error correction within reading fluency interventions played a major role in reading comprehension gains. At minimum, students who make errors without error correction are more likely to continue to practice errors further thus compounding reading fluency difficulties.

To provide a student with proper support during fluency practice, a listener can provide error correction. Teachers wanting to include error correction in the practice have two additional options: student-teacher and student-student dyads. The most common form of repeated readings involves the student reading to a teacher or adult (e.g., Kostewicz & Kubina, 2010). The adult's presence allows for competent error correction on every reading trial. The adult-student dyad, however, may prove impossible in some education settings, especially when a teacher sets aside 5–10 minutes for the entire classroom to practice. Students simply outnumber adults. Teachers can instead turn to student-student or peer mediated repeated readings (e.g., Musti-Rao, Hawkins, & Barkley, 2009; Staubitz et al., 2005; Yurick et al., 2006). The teacher then has an opportunity to circulate around the room providing support to the various dyads, helping with difficult words, and modeling effective error correction. Continued oversight allows teachers to identify students' errors while reading and help them minimize practicing errors.

Error correction. Systematic, purposeful practice should help individuals improve the skill in question. Should the individual not receive correction on errors then the individual learns and practices the incorrect way to perform a behavior. The previous section established the importance of the listener in identifying reading errors. Teachers wishing to include reading practice have a variety of error correction procedures to choose from. Some examples in the repeated reading literature include phase drill (e.g., Martens, Eckert, Begeny, Lewandowski, DiGennaro, Montarello et al., 2007), a review of errors on flash cards (e.g., Polk & Miller, 1994), or pre-correction (e.g., Sweeney, Ring, Malanga, & Lambert, 2001). At minimum, teachers can promote and use a model-lead-test error correction procedure (Carnine et al., 2010). After each reading trial, a teacher or peer would identify the mispronounced word for the reader, pronounce the word correctly, and end each error correction with the reader pronouncing the word correctly. Error correction would occur after each reading trial for every reading error.

Performance feedback and progress monitoring. When practicing, individuals need to know how they currently performed and how that performance relates both to past performances and some future goal. In education, research suggests that students can succeed when provided with progress monitoring and performance feedback (i.e., Fuchs, Butterworth, & Fuchs, 1989). While not used in early repeated reading studies (Dahl, 1974; Samuels, 1979), repeated readings researchers (e.g., Kostewicz & Kubina, 2010, 2011; Martens et al., 2007; Staubitz et al., 200S; Yurick et al., 2006) have since incorporated immediate performance feedback for students. When implementing repeated readings, teachers or peers can simply provide a count of correct and incorrect words read per minute to the reader while also maintaining a graphic display of performance, preferably by the reader. As most teachers cannot work with every student, an examination of all student graphs allows the teacher to quickly determine students benefiting from and those requiring adjustments to the practice procedures.

Reading goals. Goalless practice borders on simple play differentiating itself from deliberate practice. Individuals engaged in purposeful practice often move toward results. For example, musicians ready themselves for a concert performance and athletes look toward game execution. Individuals can also use practice to build core skills to fluent levels (Binder, 1996). Fluent displays of scales allow the musician to incorporate new music with less effort. The ability to read fluently has similar ties to reading silently and reading comprehension (Pikulski & Chard, 2005) necessitating similar practice goals. The varied repeated reading goals (i.e., when to move onto another passage or when the student can move onto other reading practice) can involve the student simply reading a passage a set number of times (e.g., Begeny, Daly, &. Valleley, 2006), reading a set number of times within a set amount of times (e.g., Homan, Klesius, & Hite, 1993; O'Connor, White, & Swanson, 2007), or reading until reaching a fixed fluency criterion (e.g., Dahl, 1974; Samuels, 1979). Therrien (2004) found that reading to a set criterion contributes more to reading comprehension than other repeated reading components suggesting teachers include fixed critcrions in oral reading fluency practice.

While multiple fluency criteria exist in the literature ranging from 30 to 180 correct words per minute (Hasbrouck & Tindal, 1992; Koorland, Keel, & Ueberhorst, 1990; Shapiro, 1996), Kubina and Starlin (2003) provide an ambitious practice reading criterion of 200 correct words per minute with 2 or fewer errors. However, teachers should use the Kubina and Starlin (2003) goal for reading fluency practice and not for assessment. Teachers assessing students on oral reading fluency, usually on an untrained passage, can compare reading scores to published rates (i.e., Hasbrouck & Tindal, 1992) to determine students' oral reading fluency progress. Students practicing to such championship rates (Lindsley 1996) not only build confidence, but also experience other successful effects. Kubina, Amato, Schwilk, and Therrien (2008) showed that future readings of a passage decreased similarly when read to two different goals (200 CWPM and 123 CWPM). About four months later, however, students read the 200 CWPM passage faster than passages read to 123 CWPM. Additionally, Kostewicz and Kubina (2011) showed a stronger relationship between one-minute reading scores and oral retells (Good & Kaminski, 2007) than number of times reading a passage and retell scores. Finally considering the average high school student reading at 200 words per minute silently (Meyer & Felton, 1999), students practicing to higher criteria would appear to have a better chance to move seamlessly from oral to silent reading.

Interval Sprinting: One Modification to the Repeated Reading Method

Containing all of the aspects of systematic practice for building reading fluency, interval sprinting (Kostewicz & Kubina, 2010) provides one modified example of the traditional repeated reading method. Addressing all of the included concerns and recommendations, interval sprinting suggests students read instructional range reading passages for approximately three to five minutes daily to an adept listener/scorer who provides error correction, performance feedback, and progress monitoring (Kostewicz & Kubina, 2010). The slight variation occurs during a practice within the practice. Rather than students reading for one-minute multiple times, students read for short times (10–15 seconds) from various predetermined points within a passage.

For example, a teacher wishing to focus on 15 second sprints would divide the first 200 words of a passage into 50 or more word blocks, or sprint passages, making sure each interior passage started at the beginning of a sentence and remained in context with the rest of the passage. Readers would then sprint for 15 seconds from the start of the first sprint passage. After receiving error correction, the reader reads the same passage for 15 seconds again. After two sprints and subsequent error correction, the teacher would direct the reader to start the next sprint from the beginning of the second sprint passage. After two 15-second sprint, the reader moves to the third and then fourth sprint passage. Total reading time equals two minutes and the teacher or peer delivered six instances of error correction. After all sprints, the reader would then read the passage for one minute starting from the first word of the passage striving for the set criterion of 200 CWPM with 2 or fewer errors. Teachers could then provide performance feedback to the reader and graph reading scores.

Conclusion

Practice plays an important role in all aspects of our society. Consistent deliberate practice results in measureable benefits to individual skill performance. In education, teachers have the responsibility to impart knowledge and skills to students. Incorporating deliberate practice in the classroom assists students' academic performance. Teachers, targeting student oral reading fluency, can employ repeated readings, which is one form of deliberate practice. With the many options available, teachers can individualize repeated reading practice across multiple dimensions including reading time, error correction, progress monitoring, and performance feedback. As only one example, interval sprinting demonstrates some potential modifications teachers can employ. The core repeated readings method and associated modifications provide teachers a malleable, effective, and efficient technique for including deliberate oral reading fluency practice in the classroom.

Synergistic Phonics and Fluency Instruction

The Magic of Rhyming Poetry!

BY TIMOTHY RASINSKI, WILLIAM RUPLEY, AND WILLIAM NICHOLS

Phonics (accuracy in word decoding) and reading fluency (automaticity in word recognition and expressive or prosodic oral reading) have been identified as two critical components in early elementary reading instruction (National Reading Panel, 2000). Indeed a long line of research and theory has noted the importance of being able to negotiate print accurately, effortlessly, and with meaningful expression and phrasing. Jeanne Chall's (1996) model of reading development incorporates both word decoding and fluency as key milestones on the road to proficient reading.

According to Chall (1996), once students have established accuracy with print identification they must then become automatic with word recognition. While accuracy is important in identifying words, it is also important to further develop word recognition fluency or the ability to decode a word with relative ease and little hesitation. In addition, as the student's reading becomes increasing more automatic, he or she develops the ability to read with expression (e.g., volume, pitch, phrasing, stress, pace) that reflects meaningful interpretation of the passage. The fluent reader sounds good, is easy to listen to, and reads with feeling that helps those who listen understand and enjoy what is being read. Once children develop this comfort with reading, it becomes easier for them to read for meaning rather than attending to pronouncing all of the words correctly.

The importance of both phonics and fluency in reading development is well established (Allington, 1983; Chall, 1996; Kuhn, 2005; National Reading Panel, 2000; Rasinski & Hoffman,

2003). Literacy scholars ardently make the point that difficulties in word decoding and flu-ency are significant contributors to problems in reading comprehension and overall reading achievement (Duke, Pressley, & Hilden, 2004). Both phonics and fluency need to be taught, practiced, and nurtured in the earliest stages of reading instruction and provided to students at any age who do not acquire proficiency in these aspects of reading. The essential question is not that phonics and fluency are important in learning to read; but how should they be taught?

In most reading curricula phonics and fluency are thought of as distinct instructional elements—that they should be taught separately. Indeed, Chall's own model of reading development proposes that they be developed sequentially, first mastery in decoding then fluency. Although this may seem logical, we are always searching for ways to create synergy in instruction—instructional methodologies in which the whole of the method provides a greater impact than the sum of its parts.

At the same time we recognize that reading instruction should be as engaging and authentic as possible. Traditional phonics and word recognition instruction has had a less than a stellar reputation as students are often asked to complete seeming endless sets of worksheets and engage in monotonous reading and chanting of sounds and words in isola-tion on flashcards, word banks, word walls and the like. Similarly, we see fluency instruction also devolving into rote oral repetitive reading of texts rarely meant to be read aloud (infor-mational texts) and tor the primary purpose of achieving a targeted rate of 80 to 100 words per minute (Rasinski, 2006, in press). Not only docs such instruction run the risk of having students develop the notion that reading fluency and fast reading are one and the same, it also provides students with an instructional routine that is less than engaging and not self-sustaining. This sort of instruction makes students often perceive that reading is boring and uninteresting—something to be avoided.

Beyond the initial reaching of decoding ability, interesting and varied practice is neces-sary to achieve accuracy in decoding and fluency. While it could be inferred that in order to develop fluency, students should be provided with an abundance of opportunities to practice reading, we feel that in order tor this practice to be successful it must come under the direct guidance and scaffolding of the teacher. The bulk of the research on fluency uses analogies that compare fluency development to learning in sports or music where repeated practice leads to fluent reading, in much the same manner as repeated practice of a piece of music leads to mastery of the piece practiced as well as other pieces not previously played.

For many beginning teachers this transfers into just providing time for students to read (Sustained Silent Reading {SSR}, Drop Everything and Read {DEAR} & Accelerated Reader {AR}). While unassisted wide reading for pleasure and practice is clearly important, informed coaches know that it is not practice that makes perfect, it is perfect practice that makes per-fect. In other words having a coach directly working with the student, modeling the desired outcome and providing scaffolded and monitored repeated practice is better than merely practicing on your own, especially when at the initial stages of learning. A music student, for example, will practice a piece under the guidance of teacher who models and provides feedback to the student. The student will practice the selection repeatedly until he can hit all the notes so automatically that he can begin to attend to phrasing, emphasis, and other interpretive features of performing and making meaning from a musical composition. The improvement from practicing the one piece will also carry over to improved playing of subsequent pieces never played previously by the student.

While unassisted wide reading for pleasure and practice is clearly important, informed coaches know that it is not practice that makes perfect, it is perfect practice that makes perfect. In other words having a coach directly working with the student, modeling the desired outcome and providing scaffolded and monitored repeated practice is better than merely practicing on your own, especially when at the initial stages of learning.

We believe that in order for students to develop fluency, they need to be provided with varied opportunities to read text at their independent/instructional level, both recreationally and under the direct guidance of a teacher. Moreover phonics and fluency can be taught in ways that are synergistic, authentic, and engaging. We believe that a secret ingredient to promote such a synergistic relationship and develops word recognition accuracy, automaticity, expressiveness, and uses texts that are meant to be read aloud is rhyming poetry.

Why Rhyming Poetry for Phonics?

Quite simply, the reason we advocate rhyming poetry for teaching phonics is that such poetry contains rhyming words. Ccrtain and relatively common spelling patterns have consistent pronunciations. Perhaps the most useful spelling patterns for beginning readers are rimes (more commonly known by teachers as word families or phonograms). A rime is simply the part of a syllable that begins with the sounded vowel and contains any consonants that follow the vowel. For example, the—*at* in *hat and cat* is a rime or word family as is the—*ight* in *light or sight.* Readers who can perceive a rime in one word they decode can then apply that knowledge to analogous words—other words that contain the same last sound often have the same spelling patterns and that represent the same sounds. Word recognition is made more efficient as readers' process rimes that appear in many words and not as individual letters but as one unit.

The idea, then, is to teach young readers these rimes so that they can use their own knowledge of these spelling patterns in words they encounter in their own reading. This approach to phonics instruction has been recognized and endorsed by leading scholars in reading (Adams. 1990; Cunningham, 2004; Ehri, 2005; Gaskins, Ehri, Cress, O'Hara, & Donnelly, 1996–1997; Gunning, 1995; Snow, Burns, & Griffin, 1998).

There are several hundred word families worth teaching and students who can recognize these word families in one and multisyllabic words have the ability to process such words accurately and efficiently. Edward Fry (1998) demonstrated the utility of word families in his "most common phonograms."

-ab	-at	-ink	-ore	-unk
-ack	-ay	-ip	-ot	-y
-ag	-ell	-ight	-out	
-ail	-est	-ill	-ow (how, chow)	
-ain	-ew	-im	-ow (bow, throw)	
-am	-ed	-in	-op	
-an	-eed	-inc	-uck	
-ank	-ick	-ob	-ug	
-ap	-ing	-ock	-um	

According to Fry. knowledge of the word families listed above gives a reader the ability to decode and spell 654 one-syllable words simply by adding a consonant, consonant blend, or consonant digraph to the beginning of the word family. Beyond one-syllable words, knowledge of these word families can help readers at least partially decode thousands of words in which these word families regularly appear. For example, the rime—am can help a reader with words like *ham, Sam, slam,* and *jam.* The same word family can also help a reader with more challenging words such as *Abraham, Amsterdam, bedlam, camera, hamster, grammar, telegram,* and many more. The value of rimes in helping students decode words is enormous.

Word families are commonly taught by teachers around the country. The typical approach is to teach a word family, list one-syllable words that contain the word family, and practice the words over the course of several days. Teachers may also use the words for spelling instruction and call attention to the words in student' reading.

For some students, simply seeing and practicing the words on a word wall for example may be enough. For others, however, more guided and direct practice may be needed. Indeed, we often see students who can read the words on a word wall or flashcards without any difficulty, but become stumped when seeing the same words in connected reading material. These students especially need the opportunity to read these in authentic texts. What kinds of texts feature such words with sufficient frequency to draw attention to the targeted word family? Rhyming poetry is one text type that fills that bill.

The following rhymes, for example, would be ideal for teaching, practicing, and enjoying the *–at*, and *–old* word families.

> Peas porridge hot
> Peas porridge cold
> Peas porridge in the pot
> Five days old.

According to Ediger (1998) "phonics instruction could become an inherent part of the reading of poems. Sharing poetry in the classroom should become a fun, relaxed opportunity for students to expressively explore language and at the same time develop phonics knowledge (Ediger, 1998). Repeated shared readings of selected poems guided by the teacher, read independently or shared with peers facilitates the learning of words and letter/sound patterns and provides students with a richer understanding of print (Carbo, 1989; Holdaway, 1979). Ediger (1998) argues that providing opportunities for students to explore language through expressive oral reading and creative writing of poetry assists learners in becoming proficient in phonics.

Why Rhyming Poetry for Fluency?

Repeated oral reading of texts (rehearsal), along with modeling fluent reading and supporting students while reading orally by reading with them, have been identified as key methods for teaching reading fluency (Kuhn & Stahl, 2000; National Reading Panel, 2000; Rasinski, 2003; Rasinski & Hoffman, 2003). In repeated oral readings, students read text several times until they can read with a degree of automaticity and expression. Studies have shown that students engaged in repeated readings leads to improved word recognition accuracy, reading rate (a measure of automaticity), expressive and meaningful reading, reading comprehension, and confidence in reading, not only on the passages they have practiced but also on new, nevcr-bctore-seen texts (Dowhower, 1987, 1994; Rasinski & Hoffman, 2003; Samuels, 1979).

Although the value of repcated readings has been well established, the mode of implementing repeated readings remains an issue. In many fluency programs, students engage in rote and somewhat mindless oral repetitions of texts for the primary purpose of increasing reading speed. As a result students may gain a perception of reading as being something that is done fast and is void of enjoyment and interest.

What is needed are authentic reasons to engage in repeated readings or rehearsal—one answer is to perform for an audience. If oral performance is a natural outcome or goal of repeated reading, then what sorts of texts or genre are meant to be performed for an audience?

Certain texts do exist for performance (and by extension, rehearsal)—these include speeches, songs, scripts, and especially poetry. Poetry is meant to be performed. Most poets write their poems to be performed orally for an audience. That is why we have poetry slams, poetry cafes, poetry readings, poetry parties, and requests by parents tor their children to "read your poem to me". Poetry is a natural text choice for performance and practice. Most poems for young children are relatively short, making them easy to read more than once and helping students gain a sense of accomplishment by reading the poems fluently.

Unfortunately, poetry is a genre that has to some extent found its way out of the reading curriculum. Most reading curricula are dominated by informational and narrative texts—poetry has been given a secondary or, in some cases even a tertiary position in most reading curriculum. We feel that with the lack of poetry, students are missing out on a genre that allows them to appreciate the beauty of the language from a number of vantage points—meaning, sound, rhythm, expression. Rhyming poetry is a natural genre for promoting children's phonic knowledge and reading fluency.

Using Rhyming Poetry to Teach Phonics, Fluency, and a Love of Language

So how might a teacher use rhyming poetry to teach both phonics and reading fluency? We'd like to suggest a simple tour step sequence of instruction.

STEP 1

The initial step begins in much the same way that teachers have been teaching rimes or word families for years. A teacher identities a target word family—demonstrates it's spelling and sound, and then brainstorms with students words that belong to that word family. So for, example, if the word family being taught was ay, the teacher and students would brainstorm words such as *day. say, may, jay. pay, play, stay, pray*, as well as some multisyllabic words such as *daylight* and *playmate*. Then, over the course of the next few days the teacher has the students read the list of words that contain that word family, talk about the words, and add other words that belong to that family.

STEP 2

Step 2 moves word family instruction from words in isolation to words in authentic texts—rhyming poetry. In this next step the teacher brings in one or more poems that feature the word family under study. For example, after reading the ay word list, the teacher will put the following rhyme on chart paper and read it with students several times throughout the day and encourage students to read it on their own as well.

> Rain rain go *away*
> Come again another *day*
> Little Johnny wants to *play*.

The teacher or a student points to the words as they are read, drawing the children's visual attention to the words themselves. Once the rhyme is essentially memorized, the teacher will have students read individual words removed from the poem (this includes ay words as well as other interesting words such as *little* and *again)*.

Teachers can work together to collect a community set of rhyming poems and organize them around the word families that will be taught in the primary grades. The poems can be kept in a tile drawer, organized by word families. Manila folders are labeled by word families and as teachers (and students) find appropriate poems, they can be tiled in the appropriate folder. Of course, a similar tile system can be set up electronically as well.

Then, when it is time to teach a particular word family, a teacher simply has to pull the appropriate folder and select the poem or poems she wishes to use with her students. Collecting poems in this way is a project that the entire faculty can participate in.

If the teacher cannot find an appropriate poem to share with students for a particular rhyme, she can easily writer her own. Perhaps the easiest way to do this is to create a parody of an already existing rhyme. For example, when working on the ay word family a few months ago with students in our reading clinic, I (Tim) wrote my own version of *Diddle Diddle Dumpling My Son John:*

> Diddle diddle dumpling *Raymond* and *Jay*
> Love to *play* in the house all *day*.
> From the *crayons* and markers they did not *stray*
> Diddle diddle dumpling *Raymond* and *Jay*.

That very brief text contains eight instances of the—*ay* word family—three in multisyllabic words. The students loved to read that rhyme throughout the day. They were even more delighted to find out that the poem was written by a teacher. We even typed a smaller sized copy tor them to take home to read to their parents. We asked the parents to make a list of ay words with their child and practice the words several rimes through.

STEP 3

After having read and reread the poem in a variety of ways (e.g. whole group choral, anriph-onal choral, echo reading, with a partner together, with a partner alternating lines, reading into a recorder, solo oral reading, solo silent reading, etc.) the teacher guides students in selecting interesting words from the poem. This of course includes many of the word family words, but also words such as *diddle, dumpling, house,* and *love.* The words are written on a sheet of chart paper, put on display in the classroom and read and reread.

Then various follow-up activities such as word sorting (Bear, Invernizzi, Templeton, & johnston, 2007) can draw students' attention to the words and features within the words. For example, students can sort the words by the presence or absence of a rime, by words that do and do not rhyme, words that have one or more than one syllable, words that contain the d sound and words that don't, words that represent things and words that do not, words that contain a word within them and words that do not, and so on. Each time students sort the words they are practicing the words again, but with cach sort, they are examining the words from a different perspective that requires a deep analysis of the words and leads to develop-ing mastery over the words.

Other activities such as close sentences and games such as word bingo (WORDO) can make the study of words taken from a natural text enjoyable, engaging, and worthwhile (Cunningham, 2005). In WORDO, students write the words chosen from the poem for the word wall on index cards or the like, one word per card. Then students select nine words from their index pile and arrange them in a three by three matrix on their desk. The matrix becomes each student's unique bingo card. Then the teacher calls out a word, a definition, or a set of clues tor a particular word (e.g. "a two syllabic word that contains the—ay word family and is a person's name). Students turn over their cards that are indicated by the teacher and the first student to get three in a row, column, or diagonal and calls WORDO is the winner. The game can be repeated as many times as the teacher and students like; the students simply turn their cards back to facing up and rearranging their matrix to make a new card.

Going Beyond Found Poetry—Students can Write their Own Poetry

STEP 4

Step 4 is a natural outgrowth of Step 2. If students see that their teacher can write a poem, they can be encouraged to write their own rhyme that features the targeted word family. They already have a list of rhyming words as well as an example or two of a poem that has been written. We often ask students to work with a classmate, an older partner, or a parent to write their rhyme. Then, for the next class meeting students put their rhymes on chart paper and phonics instruction for that day becomes a poetry festival. We may have four or five poems hanging from chart paper in the classroom. Then teacher and students go from one poem to the next. The student who wrote the poem reads it first, then it is read several times through by the group, and finally individuals and groups of children volunteer to read the rhyme. After several readings, words from the poems are taken out of context and read in isolation and put on a word wall. Then it is off to the next poem, and then the next one.

Last year, we wrote this version of Diddle Diddle Dumpling when studying the -ed word family.

> Diddle diddle dumpling my son *Fred*
> Slept all day on his *bed.*
> Woke up at midnight and said there's a monster under my *bed.*
> Diddle diddle dumpling my son *Fred.*

We find that this four step sequence serves multiple purposes. It allows students to develop mastery of the word families in and out of context, it promotes fluency through repeated and assisted readings, it allows children to take delight in the rhythmical nature of words found in short poems, and it nurtures beginning writing skills as students write (and publish) their own word family rhymes.

Does a Rhyming Poetry Approach to Phonics and Fluency Actually Work?

The answer to the question posed in the heading is "Yes, it does work! Incredibly well/We have observational and anecdotal reports from teachers who use an approach similar to this with extremely positive results. Empirical research is also beginning to weigh in on this approach. One study of a word family/fluency approach called Fast Start (Padak & Rasinski, 2004) involved parents of first grade children reading and rereading short rhymes with their children and then using the rhyming and other words as a vehicle for word study (Rasinski & Stevenson, 2005). At-risk beginning first graders engaged in poetry reading and words study with their parents over the course of twelve weeks, ten to fifteen minutes per day. Parents were given a brief training in the process of rereading the daily poem with their children and engaging in a few minutes of word study. A second control group of at-risk first graders, did not receive specific activities to do with their parents with the poetry, though they did take the same poem home every evening. Both groups of children had the same reading instruction at school. Over the course of the study, the children doing the rhyming poetry instruction at home gained 54 points on a test of word recognition while the control group gained 32 points. On a test of word recognition automaticity, the students using the rhyming poetry with their parents made an average gain of nearly 26 words correct per minute on a grade level passage; the students in the control group experienced a gain of 12 words correct per minute. The at-risk first graders working 10–15 minutes per day at home with rhyming poetry made approximately 50% more progress than the at-risk first graders in the control group and nearly doubled the gain in reading fluency over control group. If these activities were done in the classroom we would expect similar student gains.

Primary grade teachers have long used choral reading of rhymes and poetry to develop a sense of camaraderie and to have some fun in the classroom. More recent thinking on the use of rhyming poetry suggests that the use of rhyming poetry, whether at home or in school, can become an enormously powerful tool to help students develop mastery over phonics and reading fluency, two key goals of the elementary reading program.

Interventions to Enhance Fluency and Rate of Reading

BY MELANIE R. KUHN

n recent years, fluency instruction has come to be seen as a central component in the primary and elementary literacy curriculum (e.g., National Reading Panel, 2000), one that assists students as they make the shift from stilted and uneven oral reading to oral reading that is smooth and expressive and one that contributes to skilled silent reading as well (e.g., Samuels, 2006). And, while fluency instruction has an important place in the general literacy curriculum, such instruction is especially important for students with reading disabilities since these learners are far more likely to experience difficulty making this transition than are their peers (e.g., Kuhn & Stahl, 2003). However, while identifying ways in which we can help struggling readers become fluent is an essential part of this discussion, exploring the ways in which fluency contributes to reading development in general, and comprehension in particular, is also critical if we are to avoid creating fluency instruction—and assessment—that emphasizes reading rate at the expense of understanding. Such instruction not only limits our students' understanding of fluency and its role in the reading process, it leads to a devaluation of instructional approaches that, when implemented properly, can make a significant contribution to the reading development of students experiencing reading difficulties.

The goals of this chapter, therefore, are to discuss several aspects of fluency and fluency instruction in relation to the reading development of students with reading disabilities. First, I explore the role that accuracy, automaticity and prosody play in reading fluency (e.g., Rasinski & Hoffman, 2003). Next, I consider the ways in which overemphasizing certain aspects of the construct, through either instruction or assessment, can negatively influence students' understanding of what constitutes fluent reading—as well as the purposes of reading more broadly (e.g., Samuels, 2007; Walker, Mokhtari, & Sargent, 2006). Finally, I address fluency instruction in order to identify commonalities across effective approaches (e.g., Kuhn, 2009). Hopefully, this chapter will assist you in either rethinking fluency instruction and its role in the literacy curriculum or it will confirm your understanding of the construct and how best to assist students in their efforts to become fluent readers.

Reading Fluency and Its Components

One characteristic that differentiates many reading disabled students from their more skilled peers is their inability to read fluently. By this, I mean they are unable to read passages smoothly or with appropriate expression. While such difficulties might be a bit troubling if they primarily affected the way learners sound when they are reading aloud, these difficulties are worthy of more serious concern when you consider that most disfluent readers also experience difficulties with their comprehension of texts (National Reading Panel, 2000). In fact, according to most researchers, the two facets of skilled reading are linked, with reading fluency seen either as a critical link between decoding ability and comprehension (e.g., Chard, Pikulski, & McDonagh, 2006) or with comprehension seen as an integral component of fluent reading itself (Samuels, 2006). These understandings develop from the role that fluency's component parts—accuracy, automaticity, and prosody—play in skilled reading.

Accuracy and Automaticity. At the level of word identification, skilled readers must accomplish two things in order to comprehend a text.[1] First, they must be able to accurately identify the vast majority of words they encounter in a text (e.g., Adams, 1990; Chall, 1996). This involves developing familiarity with the sound-symbol correspondences that occur regularly in written English as well as with those high frequency words that should be recognized as a unit (e.g., *the, and, it*). Second, their word recognition must be automatic (LaBerge & Samuels, 1974; Logan, 1997). In other words, readers should not have to expend a significant amount of effort on word identification; rather, they should be able to recognize words immediately upon encountering them.

Such instantaneous word recognition is important because individuals have a limited ability to process information (e.g., LaBerge & Samuels, 1974). In the case of reading, this means that attention expended on word identification is attention that is unavailable

---

1 While comprehension of text clearly involves far more than accurate and automatic word recognition, I am only focusing on these aspects of reading at this point in the discussion.

for comprehension. If it is the case that the reader has to spend significant amounts of attention in order to identify most of the words they encounter, he will have difficulty constructing meaning from the texts they are reading. If, on the other hand, a reader has established automatic word recognition, the amount of attention she needs to expend on word identification is minimal, and, as a result, she will retain most of their attention for comprehension.

Prosody. The third component of fluent reading is prosody (Erekson, 2003; Kuhn & Stahl, 2003). Prosody consists of those elements of reading that, when taken together, comprise expressive reading (e.g., pitch, stress, and parsing). It is the case that the accurate use of these elements allows readers to determine shades of meaning that might not immediately be apparent in written text. However, while some aspects of oral expression are represented in text by punctuation (e.g., Truss, 2003), this is not always the case (Miller & Schwanenflugel, 2006). For example, when a person ends a heated discussion with the words "fine," the person they were engaged with usually realizes that the speaker does *not* mean that the two have come to an amicable agreement. However, there is nothing available in a written version of such a conversation to convey this understanding. Instead, the reader has to apply their knowledge of oral exchanges to develop the correct sense of the interaction.

While it is the case that the appropriate application of expressive features can affect the meaning constructed from a given text, it is unclear exactly how this process occurs. There are three distinct possibilities as regards the relationship between prosody and comprehension. In the first scenario, the application of prosodic elements to a text allow for comprehension to occur. In the second case, comprehension of written material needs to take place before prosodic elements can be applied. And in the third and final scenario (and the one that represents my own point of view), an interactive relationship exists in which prosody both contributes to and is reflective of a reader's comprehension. Given the importance of automaticity (which assumes a high level of accuracy) *and* prosody in constructing meaning from text, the value of utilizing instructional approaches that integrate both elements into fluency instruction begins to become apparent.

Automaticity and Prosody in Practice

In addition to thinking about automaticity and prosody in terms of their role in fluent reading, it is also useful to consider how each of these elements can be integrated into classroom practice. When reflecting upon automaticity in reading, Jay Samuels (1979, 2006) argues that it is important to consider the ways in which this construct is developed in other areas (Samuels, 1979); for example, when individuals are learning to play tennis, it is necessary that they practice individual aspects of the game, say their backhand and their serve, to become adept at those moves. However, it is also essential that they learn how to combine various components into a unified action if they are ever to shift from simply practicing to actually playing. Applying this understanding to reading, it is important that students learn how to recognize words quickly and accurately, and, in order to achieve this, they need significant amounts of practice.

As with tennis, some of this practice should take place in isolation, through decoding instruction and word work that allows learners to establish familiarity with English orthography, but, if learners are to develop automatic word recognition when reading connected text, much of this practice needs to take place in context using both supported oral, as well as silent, reading. Without the later type of practice, students may become quite capable of quickly identifying words in isolation, but may not necessarily transfer that ability to their actual reading. In fact, it is often the case that students experiencing difficulties applying their word recognition knowledge to connected text find themselves faced with increasing amounts of decoding instruction in isolation, rather than increased opportunities for guided practice in context (e.g., Allington, 1977, 1983). Unfortunately, by limiting struggling readers to this as their primary form of practice, we are actually minimizing, rather than increasing, the likelihood that they will become skilled readers.

Next, as was mentioned in the previous section, the integration of prosody into students' reading can also lead to a more nuanced understanding of the text (e.g., Erekson, 2003). Further, by developing an awareness of the importance of appropriate expression and phrasing in students, it is possible to prevent them from developing the belief that fluent reading is simply fast reading and the faster the better (e.g., Walker et al., 2006). In fact, by emphasizing the importance of prosodic elements in text, learners are prevented from viewing reading as a race and their comprehension is improved (Dowhower, 1991; Schreiber, 1991). Unfortunately, the overemphasis on oral reading rate may be an unintended consequence of certain assessment tools that emphasize correct word per minute rates without reference to expression or the need to vary reading rate according to the complexity of the text (e.g., Samuels, 2007; Walker et al., 2006). Perhaps even more regrettably, this overemphasis can also lead to a misuse of fluency-oriented instructional approaches such as repeated readings. While it is critical that learners develop automatic word recognition (see Table 5.3-1 for a guide to correct words per minute rates), it is equally important that this not be the only goal. Instead, students should develop the understanding that fluency consists of smooth, accurate, and expressive reading at a rate that replicates that of oral language (see Table 5.3-2 for a guide to prosodic text features).

TABLE 5.3-1. Correct Words per Minute by Grade Level.

Grade	Fall	Winter	Spring
1	—	10-30	30-60 cwpm
2	30-60	50-80	70-100
3	50-90	70-100	80-110
4	70-110	80-120	100-140
5	80-120	100-140	110-150
6	100-140	110-150	120-160
7	110-150	120-160	130-170
8	120-160	130-170	140-180

From Rasinski, T. V. (2004). *Assessing Reading Fluency*. Honolulu: Pacific Resources for Education and Learning. Available at http://www.prel.org/products/re_/assessing-fluency.htm

TABLE 5.3-2. National Assessment of Educational Progress's Oral Reading Fluency Scale.

Level 4	Reads primarily in larger, meaningful phrase groups. Although some regressions, repetitions and deviations from text may be present, those do not appear to detract from the overall structure of the story. Preservation of the author's syntax is consistent. Some or most of the story is read with expressive interpretation.
Level 3	Reads primarily in three- or four-word phrase groups. Some smaller groupings may be present. However, the majority of phrasing seems appropriate and preserves the syntax of the author. Little or no expressive interpretation is present.
Level 2	Reads primarily in two-word phrases with some three- or four-word groupings. Some word-by-word reading may be present. Word groupings may seem awkward and unrelated to larger context of sentence or passage.
Level 1	Reads primarily word-by-word. Occasionally two-word or three-word phrases may occur, but these are infrequent and/or they do not preserve meaningful syntax.

Fluency Instruction

While many readers become fluent as the result of the literacy instruction provided in a typical elementary classroom, this is rarely the case for students with reading disabilities (e.g., Kuhn & Schwanenflugel, 2006). Instead, such students require even greater opportunities to practice their reading in a supported environment than do their peers who are able to develop their reading ability without noticeable difficulty. One way to provide reading disabled students with the instruction they need is by integrating four fluency-oriented principles into oral reading instruction (Rasinski, 2003); these principles are modeling, opportunities for practice, the provision of support and assistance, and the demonstration of appropriate phrasing. While these elements are the basis of a range of fluency strategies that are effective for all learners, the integration of these principles into instruction for students with reading disabilities is critical to their development as skilled readers (McKenna & Stahl, 2003). As such, I will discuss the role each plays in fluency instruction and its particular usefulness for students with reading disabilities. A second way to provide learners with appropriate instruction is to integrate specific fluency-oriented reading approaches into the curriculum. There are many instructional strategies that have proven to be effective over the past three decades (e.g., Kuhn, 2009; Rasinski, 2003), and I highlight three instructional strands (unassisted repeated readings, assisted readings, and classroom approaches), along with ways that recent research may serve to change some of our underlying assumptions regarding effective fluency practices, as part of a broader discussion of trends in this area.

Principles of Fluency Instruction   The first of Rasinski's (2003) principles involves the modeling of expressive reading. Not only is such modeling likely to instill a love of reading in students, it simultaneously provides them with a sense of what good oral reading should sound like. While reading to students is a common practice in the primary grades, it tends to be a fairly rare occurrence in later grades. However, there are many texts, from poems to highly descriptive expository selections, such as speeches, that are ideal for older students and lend themselves to being read aloud. Spending approximately 5 minutes a day reading such a text aloud accomplishes several things. First, it creates a shared experience amongst the learners. Next, and especially critical for struggling readers, it provides students with the opportunity to hear what smooth, expressive reading sounds like. Finally, by making selections from a range of genres, it increases the likelihood that students will find a text that is engaging.

The second principle, that students should have extensive opportunities to practice reading connected texts, provides a caveat for the first principle. That is, as positive as modeling is for students, it is important not to overuse it—a tendency that is especially prevalent when working with reading disabled students. It is often the case that teachers revert to reading aloud as a means of compensating for a text that is beyond their students' instructional level (there is a parallel tendency for teachers to present the information from a difficult text in a lecture format for the same reason; Shanahan, 2007). While this approach is problematic for any student (it is essential that all students have multiple opportunities to read challenging texts in a supportive environment), it is the case that struggling readers need even greater opportunities to read a range of texts (including texts that are challenging for them) in such an environment if they are to become independent readers. By reverting exclusively, or even primarily, to lectures and read-alouds, students are denied the very opportunities they need to develop their own reading ability. However, while the provision of such opportunities make sense in theory, it often seems difficult to accomplish in practice. Luckily, the approaches discussed later in the chapter should provide several options for creating just such expanded opportunities for scaffolded oral reading and, whenever appropriate, for silent reading as well.

The third principle, that of providing students with support or assistance for their reading, is especially critical for reading disabled students. While all students benefit from reading in a supportive environment, students who are experiencing difficulty consolidating what they know about word recognition into their reading of connected texts require additional assistance from a skilled reader. As such, it is essential that they regularly read in situations where some form of support is available. This support can involve the repeated reading of a single text, silently or aloud, until the students have reached a predetermined level of mastery, or it can incorporate the single reading of a range of challenging or instructional level texts through the use of echo, choral, or partner reading. Whichever approach is chosen, the scaffolding that these methods afford students will allow them to develop as skilled readers.

The final principle involves an emphasis on appropriate phrasing. According to several qualitative scales (e.g., Allington & Brown cited in Allington 1983; NAEP, 1995; Zutell & Rasinski, 1991), disfluent readers parse text in ways that do not replicate oral language (e.g., word-by-word reading or inappropriate phrasing). As was mentioned earlier in this chapter, this is at least partially the result of the limitations of punctuation to indicate phrasal boundaries (e.g., Miller & Schwanenflugel, 2006). Unfortunately, this tendency on the part of a disfluent reader has a negative impact on comprehension. One way to help students compensate for this inability is to model appropriate phrasing; this can be especially helpful when leading an echo or choral reading of a text. A second approach is to help students determine where the phrasal boundaries should occur in texts that they are reading by having them identify which breaks sound like language and which ones don't; so, for example, in this excerpt from Tom Sawyer (Twain, 1986, p. 7), students should discuss which sounds better: "The old/lady pulled/her spectacles/down and/looked over/ them about/the room" or "The old lady/pulled her spectacles down/and looked over them/about the room." By holding discussions around appropriate phrasing, it becomes possible to develop students' awareness of these elements and their importance in written text (Dowhower, 1991).

Instructional Strategies

While the above principles can be integrated into virtually any literacy curriculum, there are several strategies that have been designed specifically to increase students' reading fluency. By discussing three strands of instruction that have proven to be effective in developing learners' reading fluency, as well as by looking at new understandings regarding effective approaches that are starting to emerge from classroom-based research, it becomes possible to identify certain trends in classroom-based practice.

Unassisted Repeated Readings. In terms of fluency instruction, the repeated readings approach is probably the most frequently used strategy and is also likely to be the most widely researched fluency-oriented instructional method (e.g., Samuels, 1979; Dowhower, 1994). It also holds the distinction of being the first approach designed specifically to develop the automaticity of disfluent readers. When developing the approach, Samuels (1979) envisioned it as a means of implementing the type of practice that is commonly seen in the fields of music and athletics. As was mentioned earlier, when athletes, for example, begin to take up their art or sport, they take part in the repeated practice of both isolated components of their craft as well as connected routines. At the time this approach was developed, typical classroom practice for struggling readers tended to over-rely on decoding practice in isolation (Allington, 1977) and to underemphasize the scaffolded practice of connected text. When learners did have the opportunity to read connected text, it was often the case that they only took part in a single oral reading of the material and that this reading was broken up into smaller sections as part of a round robin reading of the text. Unfortunately, it remains the case that, far too often, learners face similar types of instruction today, either in a modified form of round robin reading (e.g., popcorn, popsicle, or combat reading; Ash & Kuhn, 2006) or in a lack of opportunities to actually read text (Hiebert, 2004). And while such instruction may be problematic for many readers, it is especially troubling for students identified with reading disabilities (Allington, 1977, 2005).

Thinking about the differences that exist between practice designed to benefit athletes and musicians and that designed to improve reading led Samuels (1979) to consider an approach to reading instruction that paralleled the practice used in other fields and that he felt was likely be more effective than the approaches that were commonly being used. Based on this understanding, he postulated that students might establish automaticity more easily if, instead of reading part of a passage once, they were given the opportunity to practice reading a given selection repeatedly. Samuels not only felt that such repetition should lead to improvements with the practiced material, but that such gains might transfer to the reading of other texts. And, in fact, repeated readings has been shown to be effective for struggling readers not only in terms of rate, accuracy, and where measured, prosody on the targeted text (e.g., Dowhower, 1994; Kuhn & Stahl, 2003), but also on unpracticed material as well.

The procedure itself is a simple one that is easy to use in a one-on-one instructional setting. Since the repetition embedded in the procedure allows learners to increase their automaticity, the approach is ideal for students whose are accurate decoders, but whose reading rate falls below the norms established for their grade. The strategy itself involves the repeated reading of a challenging text (text with an initial accuracy rate of 85% to 90%). As a student completes an initial reading of the text, it is the teacher's role to record the number of words that the learner reads per minute along with the number of miscues she or he makes on the passage. As the student rereads the text, the number of words read per minute should increase while the number of miscues made should decrease. The student should then practice re-reading the passage, either silently or aloud and either for a predetermined number of repetitions, usually between three and five, or until she or he reaches a predetermined target for both reading rate and number of miscues.

While it is important to stress that the repeated readings procedure has been effective at increasing the reading rate of struggling readers (e.g., Dowhower, 1989; Joseph, 2007; Samuels, 1979), some educators have expressed concern that the approach's emphasis on automaticity may, in fact, detract learners from developing the understanding that reading's primary purpose is the construction of meaning. However, a study designed to determine whether learning disabled fifth through eighth graders could increase their comprehension of a passage while simultaneously improving their reading rate through a repeated readings approach had positive results (O'Shea, Sindelar, & O'Shea, 1987). The study's authors found that when students were specifically asked to focus on the passage content, both their comprehension of the passage and their reading rate improved. However, when students were only asked to focus on rate, they only made gains in terms of their automaticity. The implication is that, to ensure learners' focus on both rate and comprehension, they should be encouraged to think about the passage as they are reading it and briefly discuss the selection after the first or second repetition. Similarly, while the primary purpose of the approach is to move students away from word-by-word reading and toward automaticity, this does not mean that students should simply be encouraged to read the passage as fast as possible. Instead, their goal should be to read at a rate that falls within the guidelines established for their grade levels while incorporating the use of appropriate prosodic elements. By having students focus on rate, meaning, and expression (see Tables 5.3-1 & 5.3-2), the likelihood that they will use this approach as a stepping stone to skilled silent reading increases.

Assisted Readings. While repeated readings is a highly successful strategy that is easy to implement in a one-on-one setting, most classroom teachers do not have the opportunity to work with individual students for significant periods of time. As such, several effective alternatives to this procedure have been developed; these include reading-while-listening (Chomsky, 1976, 1978; Pluck, 2006), closed-caption television (Koskinen, Wilson, & Jensema, 1985), computer-assisted technology (e.g., Adams, 2003), and a modified version of the neurological impress method (NIM; Hollingsworth, 1970, 1978). Each of these alternative approaches makes use of a model of fluent reading—be it an audio recording or the use of the text that accompanies a television show—rather than relying solely on repetition to serve as the scaffolding. As such, they may be more readily integrated into a classroom center where a student can work independently.

Rather than explore each version of assisted reading, I will use reading-while-listening (Chomsky, 1976) as an exemplar. In this approach, students are asked to read along with audio recordings of a text, either silently or orally, to increase their fluency. The procedure was developed as a way of assisting several third graders who were reluctant, disfluent readers. Despite taking part in intensive phonics instruction, these students were unable to apply their decoding knowledge to the reading of connected text and were reading well below grade level. Rather than provide these learners with yet more decoding instruction, Chomsky thought the students would benefit from the opportunity to read significant amounts of connected texts. She therefore provided them with recordings of two dozen books ranging in reading level from second to fifth grade. This provided the learners with accessible versions of the material, allowing them to practice their reading independently.

Since these students were struggling readers, the level of the selections were challenging for them, however, the procedure gave them a chance to apply their knowledge of word recognition to connected text—a step that had been missing in their instruction to date. Further, by simultaneously listening to and *reading along with* the tape, the students were able to establish the connection between written text and oral language. They did this by rereading a particular text until they were able to render the material fluently for the teacher. And, because it holds the students responsible for the material, the procedure ensures their active participation in the process and provides a level of accountability. Since the students who take part in this procedure are experiencing reading difficulties, it may take them a while before they are able to coordinate their reading with the recording. However, once they become comfortable with the procedure, this should no longer be an issue. And, it is important to note that while some students will develop this comfort by practicing orally (this is often the case with younger students who can be encouraged to use whisper reading or pvc "phones" to minimize the level of noise in the classroom), others will prefer to practice silently (a more likely scenario for older students). Further, research conducted on reading-while-listening procedures (e.g., Rasinski & Hoffman, 2003) indicates that the approach is not only an effective one for struggling readers, it is a motivating and enjoyable one as well.

Classroom Approaches. A third strand of approaches (and the last to be discussed in this chapter) involves incorporating fluency-oriented instruction into the broader literacy curriculum through whole class or flexible grouping. There are several approaches that have been designed for such a purpose. Some of these are supplemental, for example, Reader's Theater, the Fluency Development Lesson, and Paired Repeated Reading (see Kuhn, 2009), while some can be used in conjunction with guided or shared reading instruction, for example, the Oral Recitation Lesson (ORL; Hoffman, 1987), Wide Fluency-Oriented Oral Reading (Wide FOOR; Kuhn, 2005), or Fluency-Oriented Reading Instruction (FORI; Stahl & Heubach, 2005). All of these classroom approaches are effective at improving students' reading fluency, and they appear to be especially beneficial for students who are experiencing difficulty making the transition to fluent reading (see Kuhn, 2009, or Rasinski, 2003, for an in-depth discussion of these and other fluency-oriented reading approaches). Further, these approaches all share a number of characteristics.

To begin with, all of the procedures mentioned in the above paragraph incorporate support in the form of a model, usually the teacher, who provides an expressive rendering of a given text. As with the assisted reading approaches discussed in the previous section, rather than expecting struggling readers to determine each word as they encounter it, the students are provided with scaffolding for their word recognition. This scaffolding takes the form of either an echo or choral reading of a text. Next, although these strategies emphasize appropriate pacing, they do not stress reading rate at the expense of comprehension. Instead, they focus on the construction of meaning both through a discussion of the selection and through the emphasis of appropriate prosodic elements. Third, they ensure that students spend significantly greater amounts of class time engaged in the reading of connected text than is the case with many instructional alternatives. However, while many of these approaches incorporate repeated practice of a given text, there are some that instead rely on the Wide Reading of multiple texts to accomplish this goal (e.g., Wide FOOR; Kuhn, 2005).

Wide Reading, in this context, refers to the scaffolded reading of a large number of challenging texts, as opposed to the independent reading of multiple texts that is usually part and parcel of the reading habits of skilled readers. As has been stressed in the discussion of fluency instruction throughout this chapter, repetition has been viewed as a critical element in helping disfluent readers make the shift to automatic, expressive reading. However, a recent review of the research on fluency interventions (Kuhn & Stahl, 2003) observed that, when comparing students using repetition with students who read equivalent amounts of scaffolded text, both groups made equivalent gains. In this context, scaffolding of Wide Reading consists primarily of echo or choral reading of challenging texts (texts that students generally read with an initial accuracy level of between 85% and 90%), although paired or partner reading can serve the same purpose depending on the length and difficulty of the text (e.g., Kuhn, 2009).

Further, it appears that Wide Reading is designed not only to provide learners with support in the reading of challenging text, it also allows learners to encounter a broad range of words in multiple settings as opposed to the same text multiple times. So, for example, it is likely that students would see high frequency words and common nouns such as *warm* and *dog* in the phrases *the warm day* and *the barking dog* between three and five times as part of a repeated readings exercise. During Wide Reading, on the other hand, students are likely to come across these words in multiple phrases, for example *the warm day, warm mittens,* and *warm toast,* during the same period of reading. And, it seems possible that, by encountering words not only multiple times, but also in multiple settings, students are likely to learn them more easily (e.g., Logan, 1997; Mostow & Beck, 2005).

After considering the above findings, I designed a research study that compared two forms of small group fluency instruction to determine the relative accuracy of the conclusions. The research consisted of two instructional approaches, one based upon repetition and one based upon the wide reading of a larger number of texts for an equivalent amount of time. To control these groups for simple exposure to text, I also included a group that listened to, but did not read, the selections used by the intervention groups along with a traditional control group. The intervention was designed for use with second grade struggling readers who, according to both their teachers and the pre-test assessments, had established basic word recognition abilities, but were experiencing difficulties applying this knowledge to connected text. The intervention consisted of small group instruction (5–6 students per group) for 15- to 20-minute periods three times a week.

The goal of these sessions was to scaffold these struggling second graders as they read a series of challenging texts, or texts that would normally be considered to be beyond their instructional level. Given the students were reading below grade level, the texts I selected ranged between a late first- and an early third-grade reading level (e.g., Fountas & Pinnell, 1999). Since the goal of this evaluation was to explore the effectiveness of a repeated readings procedure and a wide reading approach, the first procedure, Fluency-Oriented Oral Reading (FOOR), incorporated a modified repeated readings approach. This involved the reading of a single trade book over the course of a three sessions. The second condition, Wide Fluency-Oriented Oral Reading (Wide FOOR), on the other hand, consisted of a single echo or choral reading of a different text at each session. As previously mentioned, a third group of students listened to, but did not read, all the stories that were used with the Wide FOOR group. Finally, there were 6 students who did not take part in any literacy activities beyond those that occurred in their classroom.

While the approaches used in this research were similar to many other fluency-oriented classroom approaches insofar as they increased the amount of text that students read aloud with scaffolding, the results were important for confirming the conclusions noted in the earlier review (Kuhn & Stahl, 2003). That is, both the FOOR and the Wide FOOR groups made greater gains than the students in either the listening-only condition or those in the control group in terms of their word recognition in isolation, the number of correct words read per minute in connected text, and their prosody. However, the Wide FOOR group also made greater growth in terms of their comprehension. It certainly seems possible that these differences resulted from the differing nature of the tasks; so, for example, students in the FOOR group might have felt that the implicit purpose of the repetition was to improve their word recognition, reading rate, and prosody, whereas the students in the Wide FOOR group may have considered the implicit purpose for reading multiple texts included not only these three elements, but the construction of meaning as well. If this is the case, it could explain why these differences were seen in the outcome measures.

Following from this, it is useful to note that, although some embedded discussion occurred around both the stories and the vocabulary, the sessions did not incorporate direct instruction in either of these areas. As such, it may be that the inclusion of a comprehension focus as part of the FOOR approach would lead to increases in those students' comprehension scores as well. This could be as simple as embedding a range of questions into the reading of the story (see Kay Stahl's, 2008, use of questioning in the shared reading of *Big Old Bones: A Dinosaur Tale* (Carrick, 1992) for an outstanding example of this process) or it could involve the use of more formalized procedures such as the Directed Reading-Thinking Activitty (DR-TA; Stauffer & Cramer, 1968) or reciprocal teaching (Palinscar & Brown, 1986) that have been developed specifically to increase students engagement with texts. By integrating a comprehension element into fluency-oriented instruction, it becomes less likely that students will develop into word callers who recognize words automatically but who fail to construct meaning as they read (Schwanenflugel & Ruston, 2008)

When discussing the research around Wide Reading, it is worth noting that additional studies based upon the reading of multiple texts have shown similar promise, whether in an approach that replicates and extends the work undertaken in the original FOOR study (Schwebel, 2007) or in different contexts, such as shared reading (Kuhn, Schwanenflugel, Morris, et al., 2006) or computer-aided instruction (Mostow & Beck, 2005). It is also the case that the exposure to multiple texts increases students' access to a greater range of concepts and an expansive vocabulary than is the case with repeated readings (e.g., Kuhn, 2009). Since students experiencing reading difficulties are less likely to read extensively than their more skilled peers, it is important to provide them with additional opportunities to engage with print whenever possible. By assisting students in the reading of multiple selections rather than just one, it becomes possible to provide struggling readers with access to a broad range of ideas while simultaneously aiding their fluency development.

Conclusions

There are several possible reasons why the approaches discussed above are effective in assisting students who are experiencing reading difficulties become more fluent readers. It may be that the improvement results from the sheer amount of reading students are required to complete as part of these fluency-oriented instructional approaches (Kuhn & Stahl, 2003). In other words, the strategies may simply increase the amount of time on task for students when compared to a traditional reading curriculum. Alternatively, the improvement may be due to specific effects that result from the scaffolding that occurs either as part of the repetition of texts (Laberge & Samuels, 1974) or from the supported reading of a wide range of materials (Kuhn, 2005) or to the prosodic components that result from the students exposure to modeling (Dowhower, 1991; Schreiber, 1991) or to a combination of these factors. Further, certain elements appear to be consistently important in the creation of effective fluency instruction, including the use of challenging, connected texts and the need to develop students' reading rate in conjunction with their prosody and comprehension.

Although the fluency development of reading disabled learners is certainly deserving of further investigation, I would consider any of the above approaches, along with the principles that underlie them, to be an effective means for helping these students make the transition to fluent reading. As such, they should be thought of as a tool for incorporating oral reading instruction that will actually support learners in becoming skilled readers.

Notes

1. While comprehension of text clearly involves far more than accurate and automatic word recognition, I am only focusing on these aspects of reading at this point in the discussion.

References

Adams, M. J. (1990). *Beginning to read: Thinking and learning about print.* Cambridge, MA: M.I.T. Press.

Adams, M. J. (2003). The pedagogical goals of soliloquy learning. Developing research-based resources for the balanced reading teacher. Retrieved from http://www.balancedreading.com/soliloquy.html

Allington, R. L. (1977). If they don't read much, how they ever gonna get good? *Journal of Reading,* 21, 57–61.

Allington, R. L. (1983). Fluency: The neglected reading goal. *The Reading Teacher,* 36, 556–561.

Allington, R.L. (2005). What really matters for struggling readers: Designing research-based programs, (2nd ed.). New York: Allyn & Bacon.

Ash, G. E., & Kuhn, M. R. (2006). Meaningful oral and silent reading in the elementary and middle school classroom: Breaking the Round Robin Reading addiction. In T. Rasinski, C. Blachowicz, & K. Lems (Eds.), *Fluency instruction: Research-based best practices* (pp. 155–172). New York: Guilford.

Carrick, C. (1992). *Big old bones: A dinosaur tale.* Boston, MA: Clarion Books.

Chall, J. S. (1996). *Stages of reading development* (2nd ed.). Fort Worth, TX: Harcourt-Brace.

Chard, D. J., Pikulski, J. J., & McDonagh, S. H. (2006). Fluency: The link between decoding and comprehension for struggling readers. In T. Rasinski, C. Blachowicz, & K. Lems (Eds.), *Fluency instruction: Research-based best practices* (pp. 39–61). New York: Guilford.

Chomsky, C. (1976). After decoding: What? *Language Arts,* 53, 288–296.

Chomsky, C. (1978). When you still can't read in third grade? After decoding, what? In S. J. Samuels (Ed.), *What research has to say about reading instruction*, (pp. 13-30). Newark, DE: International Reading Association.

Dowhower, S. L. (1989). Repeated reading: Theory into practice. *The Reading Teacher*, 42, 502-507.

Dowhower, S. L. (1991). Speaking of prosody: Fluency's unattendedbedfellow. *Theory into Practice*, 30(3), 158-164.

Dowhower, S. L. (1994). Repeated reading revisited: Research into practice. *Reading and Writing Quarterly: Overcoming Learning Difficulties*, 10(4), 343-358.

Erekson, J. (2003, May). Prosody: The problem of expression in fluency. Paper presented at the annual meeting of the International Reading Association, Orlando, FL.

Fountas, I. C., & Pinnell, G. S. (1999). Matching books to readers: Using leveled books in guided reading, K-3. Portsmouth, NH: Heinemann. Hiebert, E. H. (2004, April). *Teaching children to become fluent readers - year 2*. Discussant at the American Educational Research Association, San Diego, CA.

Hoffman, J. (1987). Rethinking the role of oral reading in basal instruction. *The Elementary School Journal*, 87, 367-373.

Hollingsworth, P. M. (1970). An experiment with the impress method of teaching reading. *The Reading Teacher*, 24(2), 112-114.

Hollingsworth, P. M. (1978). An experimental approach to the impress method of teaching reading. *The Reading Teacher*, 31, 624-626.

Joseph, L. M. (2007). Getting the "most bang for your buck": Comparison of the effectiveness and efficiency of phonic and whole word reading techniques during repeated reading lessons. *Journal of Applied School Psychology*, 24, 69-90.

Koskinen, P. S., Wilson, R. M., & Jensema, C. J. (1985). Closed-Captioned Television: A new tool for reading instruction. *Reading World*, 24(4), 1-7.

Kuhn, M. R. (2005). A comparative study of small group fluency instruction. *Reading Psychology*, 26, 127-146.

Kuhn, M. R. (2009). *The hows and whys of reading fluency*. Boston: Allyn & Bacon.

Kuhn, M. R., & Schwanenflugel, P. J. (2006). All oral reading practice is not equal (or how can I integrate fluency instruction into my classroom?). *Literacy Teaching and Learning*, 11, 1-20.

Kuhn, M. R., Schwanenflugel, P. J., Morris, R. D., Morrow, L. M., Woo, D., Meisinger, et al. (2006). Teaching children to become fluent and automatic readers. *Journal of Literacy Research*, 38, 357-387.

Kuhn, M. R., & Stahl, S. (2003). Fluency: A review of developmental and remedial strategies. *The Journal of Educational Psychology*,95, 3-21.

LaBerge, D., & Samuels, S. J. (1974). Toward a theory of automatic information processing in reading. *Cognitive Psychology*, 6, 293-323.

Logan, G. D. (1997). Automaticity and reading: Perspectives from the instance theory of automaticity. *Reading & Writing Quarterly: Overcoming Learning Difficulties*, 13, 123-146.

McKenna, M. C., & Stahl, S. A. (2003). *Assessment for reading instruction*. New York: Guilford.

Miller, J., & Schwanenflugel, P. J. (2006). Prosody of syntactically complex sentences in the oral reading of young children. *Journal of Educational Psychology, 98*, 839–853.

Mostow, J., & Beck, J. (2005, June). Micro-analysis of fluency gains in a reading tutor that listens. Paper presented at the Society for the Scientific Study of Reading, Toronto, Canada.

NAEP. (1995). *Listening to Children Read Aloud, 15* [oral reading fluency scale]. Washington, DC: U.S. Department of Education, National Center for Education Statistics.

National Reading Panel. (2000). Teaching children to read: An evidence- based assessment of the scientific research literature on reading and its implications for reading instruction. Reports of the subgroups. Bethesda, MD: National Institutes of Health. Retrieved from http:// www.nichd.nih.gov/publications/ nrp/

O'Shea, L. J., Sindelar, P. T., & O'Shea, D. (1987). The effects of repeated readings and attentional cues on the reading fluency and comprehension of learning disabled readers. *Learning Disabilities Research, 2*, 103–109.

Palinscar, A. S., & Brown, A. L. (1986). Interactive teaching to promote independent learning from text. *Reading Teacher, 39*, 771–777.

Pluck, M. L. (2006). "Jonathon is 11 but reads like a struggling 7-year- old": Providing assistance for struggling readers with a tape-assisted reading program. In T. Rasinski, C. Blachowicz, & K. Lems (Eds.), *Fluency instruction: Research-based best practices* (pp. 192–208). New York: Guilford.

Rasinski, T. V. (2003). *The fluent reader: Oral reading strategies for building word recognition, fluency, and comprehension.* New York: Scholastic.

Rasinski, T. V. (2004). *Assessing Reading Fluency.* Honolulu: Pacific Resources for Education and Learning. Retrieved from http://www. prel.org/products/re_/assessing-fluency.htm

Rasinski, T. V., & Hoffman, J. V (2003). Oral reading in the school curriculum. *Reading Research Quarterly, 38*, 510–522.

Samuels, J. (2006). Reading fluency: Its past, present, and future. In T. Rasinski, C. Balachowicz, & K. Lems (Eds.), *Fluency instruction: research-based best practices* (pp. 7–20). New York: Guilford. Samuels, S. J. (1979). The method of repeated readings. *The Reading Teacher, 32*, 403–408.

Samuels, S. J. (2007). The DIBELS Tests: Is speed of barking at print what we mean by reading fluency? *Reading Research Quarterly, 42*, 563–566.

Schreiber, P. A. (1991). Understanding prosody's role in reading acquisition. *Theory into Practice, 30*(3), 158–164.

Schwanenflugel, P. J., & Ruston, H. P. (2008). Becoming a fluent reader: From theory to practice. In M. R. Kuhn & P. J. Schwanenflugel (Eds.), *Fluency in the classroom* (pp. 1–16). New York: Guildford.

Schwebel, E. A. (2007). A comparative study of small group fluency instruction — a replication and extension of Kuhn's (2005) study (Unpublished master's thesis). Kean University, Union, NJ.

Shanahan, T. (2007). Differentiating instruction when embedding literacy. Invited speaker at the 39th Annual Conference on Reading and Writing. Rutgers Centre for Effective School Practices. April 20. Somerset, New Jersey.

Stahl, K. A. D. (2008). Creating opportunities for comprehension within fluency-oriented reading. In M. R. Kuhn & P. J. Schwanenflugel (Eds.), *Fluency in the classroom* (pp. 55–74). New York: Guildford.

Stahl, S. A., & Heubach, K. (2005). Fluency-oriented reading instruction. *Journal of Literacy Research*, 37, 25–60.

Stanovich, K. E. (1986). Matthew effects in reading: Some consequences of individual differences in the acquisition of literacy. *Reading Research Quarterly*, 21, 360–407.

Stauffer, R. G., & Cramer, R. (1968). *Teaching critical reading at the primary level. Reading Aids series.* Newark, DE: International Read- ing Association.

Truss, L. (2003). *Eats, shoots, and leaves: The zero tolerance approach to punctuation.* New York: Gotham Books.

Twain, M. (1986). *The adventures of Tom Sawyer.* New York: Penguin Classics.

Walker, B. J., Mokhtari, K., & Sargent, S. (2006). Reading fluency: More than fast and accurate reading. In T. Rasinski, C. Blachowicz, & K. Lems (Eds.), *Fluency instruction: Research-based best practices* (pp. 86–105). New York: Guilford.

Zutell, J., & Rasinski, T. V. (1991). Training teachers to attend to their students' oral reading fluency. *Theory into Practice*, 30, 211–217.

CHAPTER REFERENCES

Chard, D. J., Vaughn, S., & Tyler, B. J. (2002). A synthesis of research on effective interventions for building reading fluency with elementary students with learning disabilities. *Journal of Learning Disabilities*, 35(5), 386–406.

Kostewicz, D. E. & Kubina, R. M. (2010). A comparison of two reading fluency methods: Repeated readings to a fluency criterion and interval sprinting. *Reading Improvement*, 47(1), 43–63.

Rasinski, T., Padak, N. D., McKeon, C. A., & Wilfong, L. G. (2005). Is reading fluency a key for successful high school reading? *Adolescent and Adult Literacy*, 49(1), 22–27.

Rasinski, T., Rikli, A., & Johnston, S. (2009). Reading fluency: More than automaticity? More than a concern for the primary grades? *Literacy Research and Instruction*, 48(4), 350–361.

Chapter Six

Introduction by Angela Danley

VOCABULARY

Vocabulary

INTRODUCTION TO READINGS 6.1-6.3

Vocabulary

When do students learn vocabulary? Why is teaching vocabulary important? What strategies are used to teach vocabulary? Vocabulary is just one component of reading, but one of the most critical components in reading comprehension. Children who hear more words spoken at home learn more words before entering school. Children who learn words at home while being exposed to reading at home have the advantage of beginning school with larger vocabularies. Larger vocabularies benefit children as they progress through their school years.

Which words are important for children to know, and in what context? Choosing words to teach can be complicated. One way teachers can choose words is to consider that words have different levels of value. One way of looking at the levels is to think of tiers. Tier 1 words are the basic words like *book, bed, baby, clock,* which do not require a lot of instruction in school. Tier 2 words are the high-frequency/multiple-meaning words—*required, merchant, reinforce*—which are the most important words for direct instruction in school. Tier 3 words are low-frequency/content-specific words—*produce, landforms, motion*—which are taught when students are exposed to them in the subject areas, such as social studies, mathematics, and science. When teachers make a decision about which words to teach, they need to take into consideration how many words to teach. Teachers want to provide opportunities for students to successfully learn the words.

Perhaps one of the important ways to help students gain a stronger vocabulary is to link the language (Ebbers, 2008). Rather than teaching words in isolation, teachers should look for opportunities to teach words with the same root. This approach will be beneficial for English Language Learners and students who need help making the connections to the words. Students need to build their background knowledge by gaining an understanding of morphemes, such as prefixes and suffixes. To offer this process, teachers should expose the root in clusters of related words. For example, *bio* means "life"; some words containing *bio* are *biology, autobiography, biography, biologist.* This set of words is called a morphological family of words; the relationships of words such as these help foster the reading process.

Regardless of which strategies and activities are integrated into the classroom when teaching vocabulary, students need exposure to literature. Students need to be in a classroom with rich print and access to reading materials. Students need to be exposed to words multiple times to understand and make meaning of the vocabulary (Alber, 2010). Teachers need to provide opportunities for students to select their own vocabulary words to explore and make meaning of when reading the text (Alber, 2010). This allows the student to make personal connections and build their background knowledge. This also helps the students take ownership of the targeted vocabulary words.

Word knowledge is world knowledge (Stahl, 2005). Knowledge of a word includes the definition and how the word defines our world. Vocabulary knowledge can never be fully mastered; vocabulary is something that expands over the course of a school career and lifetime (Diamond & Gutlohn, 2006). The National Reading Panel (2000) concluded that there is no single research-based method for teaching vocabulary, but the panel does support that vocabulary instruction should include a variety of strategies in both indirect and direct instruction. A classroom teacher needs to be able to find strategies to engage the students in the learning process. No one strategy will work for every child. Teachers need to be willing to try new strategies to move the students forward in vocabulary development.

BEFORE READING

Think about how you learned vocabulary words. Think about your childhood. Did your caregivers read to you? Were you exposed to children's literature? How did your teacher help you learn new vocabulary? Think and write about all the ways a teacher can help students learn vocabulary words. Create K-W-L chart in your journal or notebook. The K: What do you know about teaching vocabulary? The W: What questions do you have about teaching vocabulary? Fill out these two sections before you begin reading.

DURING READING

As you are reading, think about your classroom. As you read the chapter, which strategies do you find beneficial to teaching vocabulary?

AFTER READING

Go back to your K-W-L chart. The L: What did you learn after reading the chapter? Write a vocabulary mini-lesson on the grade level of your choice and use one of the strategies from the chapter to guide your mini-lesson.

Strategies for Effective Vocabulary Instruction

BY DONNA C. KESTER PHILLIPS, CHANDRA J. FOOTE,
AND LAURIE J. HARPER

The following article is born of necessity. After observing student teachers, novice teachers and veterans, we have noticed that many teachers, no matter the content area, fail to stimulate and engage students when they address vocabulary concepts. Unfortunately, too many teachers resort to copying definitions as the strategy of choice in vocabulary instruction. When asked why they use this method, teachers respond that it saves time and enables them to progress to the actual content in a more efficient manner. A student-centered focus on learning would counter this response suggesting that time is actually wasted when students aren't actively and mentally engaged in language study. This article will suggest five vocabulary teaching strategies that stimulate the adolescent or child mind in a time efficient manner.

The American Federation of Teachers notes that research on vocabulary instruction consistently supports practices that include "a variety of complementary methods designed to explore the relationships among words and the relationships among word structure, origin, and meaning. (Moats, 1999, p. 8)." It can be said that *all* teachers are reading teachers and therefore it is necessary that all teachers develop the knowledge and skills in language artsinstruction to promote student learning in the content areas. The National Board Professional Teaching Standards in language arts require accomplished teachers to *strengthen student sensitivity to and proficiency in the appropriate uses of language* (NBPTS, 2006). The majority of teachers, especially at the secondary level, have not taken coursework in their teacher preparation programs that provides the background knowledge to effectively address reading and language arts in their classes (Moats, 1999).

TRIED BUT NOT TRUE

The following strategies are presented in an effort to illustrate to teachers the less effective methods that are often used in hopes that they might recognize themselves and establish an awareness of a need to change. In essence these strategies are "well tried" but least successful or true.

Definition Copying

The strategy of copying definitions takes many forms. Some teachers will list the vocabulary words on the board and have students look up the definitions in the dictionary or textbook glossary. Others will list the vocabulary and definitions on the board arid require students to copy these postings. Hybrid versions of this strategy include definition copying as homework or searching on-line for definitions using a website like dictionary.com or www.m-w.com.

Context Clues

The practice of asking students to use context clues to help them understand word meaning is a step above the definition search strategy in that it requires engagement and questioning on the part of the student. Teachers who use this method identify a reading passage, typically part of the assigned textbook, which includes challenging vocabulary words imbedded within the reading. Students essentially guess at the meaning based on the parts of the text that they do comprehend.

Both of these widely accepted methods for helping students learn new words fail to develop relational knowledge that is necessary for true understanding of the concepts represented by the vocabulary words (Blachowicz & Fisher, 1996). Each version utilizes the lowest levels of cognitive processing from the perspective of Benjamin Bloom's (1956) Taxonomy of Thinking and are therefore, highly unlikely to lead to true understanding, learning, or transfer to new situations.

TRUE BUT LESS TRIED

The following "true but less tried" strategies are evidence of research-based, best practices in vocabulary instruction that go underutilized. Irvin (1990) suggests that vocabulary instruction should involve students in deep processing of words.

The following vocabulary instruction strategies require more active engagement on the part of students and higher level cognitive processing in the sense of Bloom's Taxonomy.

Selecting Words

Deciding which words to include as part of vocabulary instruction does not typically demand a great deal of teacher planning. Some districts identify the vocabulary terms for specific units of study, and textbooks often list vocabulary words for a chapter or passage. More planned and thoughtful study should be taken when selecting the words students will learn (Moates, 1999). This requires that teachers themselves are sensitive to vocabulary. In being so, they can model and promote the sensitivity to words that they expect their students to have. The words must build upon prior knowledge and connect to current student understanding. Words should be selected based on their relationship to other words the students will be learning or already know. This requires the teacher to have a thorough understanding of the students with whom he or she is working. Students also benefit from having a purpose for learning, and selecting words that are central to understanding a text or reading passage helps to highlight this purpose. One strategy to connect students more closely with their vocabulary development is to have *them* identify the words they will study based on the difficulty of words they encounter in their reading.

One way to think about the selected words is to sort them by dividing them into three categories.

Category 1
- words that students have probably heard and probably know the meaning of

Category 2
- words that students have probably heard but may not know the meaning of

Category 3
- words that students have probably not heard and most likely do not know the meaning of

Since many lessons or topics of study contain many vocabulary words, doing this will help teachers prioritize words in terms of importance. This will assist them in selecting the words that may need to be taught explicitly and directly allowing students to explore the remaining words. Providing opportunities for students to explore words engages the 'deep learning' necessary for them to become more word conscious and more likely to retain the words in their working vocabularies (lexicon).

Graphic Organizers

A graphic organizer is a two-dimensional, visual representation that shows relationships among concepts (Rice, 1994). A typical graphic organizer or word map places the vocabulary word at the center and includes additional links or cells connected to the central word or concept. The research on the use of graphic organizers in vocabulary instruction has yielded overwhelmingly strong results. Graphic organizers facilitate higher level thinking (Clarke, 1991), they serve as retrieval cues to promote learning (Dunston, 1992), and they are especially effective in teaching technical vocabulary (Readence, Bean & Baldwin, 1989). Additional research has revealed that they may be more useful in post-reading situations and when the organizers are actually constructed by the students rather than the teacher (Moore and Readence, 1984).

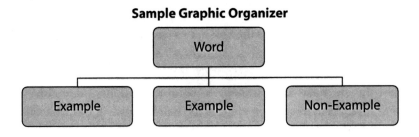

FIGURE 6.1-1. Sample Graphic Organizer.

There are many websites dedicated to graphic organizers for vocabulary study that teachers can access for easy downloading:

www.enchantedlearning.com/graphicorganizers/vocab
www.educationoasis.com/curriculum/GO/vocab_dev. him
teacher.scholastic.com/reading/bestpractices/vocabulary/pdf/sr_allgo.pdf

Some students may benefit by sketching a picture of the word in one of the graphic cells. Another link may ask the student to use the word in a sentence. This encourages ownership of the word based on experiences and deeper understanding. Other cells that may be used are "definition: in your own words", "I can remember this word by". By using "word to self", "word to word" and "word to world", connections students can become more aware, or metacognitive, about language and the importance of vocabulary.

Logic and Prediction

Asking students to predict the meaning of words in isolation and again in context helps them to use their logical, problem solving skills to examine the roots or origins of words and find connotative and denotative meanings (Moats, 1999). Some words sound like they should mean something other than the definition. For example, one student predicted that the word germinate meant to "dip a piece of food in some sauce, take a bite, and then dip it in again. This act was to germinate the sauce." Using a graphic organizer, students can first make their predictions in isolation. Then they can read the word in context, and then revise their predictions in a "before" and "after" structure. Deep learning can be enhanced when students compare their predictions and discuss the results with peers and the teacher. The act of discussing the relational understandings of words is an important component of each of the vocabulary strategies identified (Naughton, 1993–1994). This allows students to ask questions, clarify thoughts and use vocabulary in conversation; important aspects of vocabulary learning.

Synonyms and Antonyms (Weighting Words)

The process of identifying synonyms and/or antonyms also builds a stronger and deeper understanding of the concepts behind vocabulary words (Moats, 1999). Asking students to identify words that have similar or opposite meanings and place all of the words on a continuum from "weakest" to "strongest" helps students understand the subtle nuances in word choice and may even assist them in building their writing skills. How many times has a teacher said "you need a stronger word here" when helping a student edit a writing piece? Word Walls often list words by categories in a vertical format. They can also be horizontal by creating a continuum line from weakest to strongest. Students can discuss where on the line the word should be placed in relation to others. Words can be selected by the teachers or the students from vocabulary lists. They can also be incidental, rising from writing or conversation. For example, a student used the word *prattle* in her writing. While sharing her writing, the teacher took time to ask the class if they knew what it meant or what other words could be used in its place. After the words *ramble* and *babble* were generated, the words were written on post-it-notes and the class decided where each should be placed on the continuum in relation to each other. They were also encouraged to add additional words if they came across them in their reading or in other classes. This activity did a number of things. First it recognized and celebrated a student's use of a unique word. In addition, it exposed other students to the word who may not have heard it before and the discussion and the creation of word awareness that reached outside the context of that classroom helped students develop their own "word awareness".

Classify Words

Asking students to group or sort words according to teacher or student-directed properties builds additional connections for students (Moats, 1999). It is suggested teachers need to create an awareness for their students and provide them with multiple forms of discourse (Payne, 1996) to allow them to function effectively and communicate in different settings. Many students do not know, nor do they have the vocabulary to move from conversing with friends to conversing with those in authority to conversing in professional settings. Sorting words by those they a) know, b) have heard but don't know, or c) have not heard and do not know is one strategy to create word awareness. To create an awareness of application it would be beneficial to have them classify words by those they would use a) in conversation with friends, b) in conversations with adults or important people, or c) in specialized conversations related to a discipline science, social studies, etc. Actually practicing this is also very helpful. "How would you say this to a friend? How could you say the same thing to a teacher, a minister, or a police officer and what words would/should you change? What words could you choose?" Finally, "How might you engage a professional in this conversation and how might you change the words you used?" Any form of classification and discussion will help students build associative linkages.

Blachowicz and Fisher (2003) suggest 5 Evidenced Based Guidelines for the effective teaching of vocabulary.

Guideline 1:

The effective vocabulary teacher builds a word rich environment in which students are immersed in words for both incidental and intentional learning, and the development of "word awareness". In doing so they provide rich oral language, wide reading models, and word play.

Guideline 2:

The effective vocabulary teacher helps students develop as independent word learners. They provide opportunities for students to practice control of learning, use of context, and dictionary skills.

Guideline 3:

The effective vocabulary teacher uses instructional strategies that not only teach vocabulary but also model good word learning behaviors. Stategies such as graphic organizers, clustering, personalizing learning, and mnemonics promote these behaviors.

Guideline 4:

The effective vocabulary teachers provides explicit instruction for important content and concept vocabulary, drawing on multiple sources of meaning. They include content area vocabulary, definitional information, synonyms and antonyms, semantic maps, feature analysis, contextual information, and usage examples.

Guideline 5:

The effective vocabulary teacher uses assessment that matches the goal of instruction. They consider depth (how much is known about the word) and breadth (how words arc connected to other words)

Conclusion

Some final thoughts to keep in mind come from National Center on Education and the Economy (2003). This document provides as list of things to keep in mind while working with vocabulary in the form of a "Decrease" list and an "Increase" list. It is suggested that teachers decrease:

- looking up definitions as a single source of knowledge
- writing sentences for new words before that have studied the word in-depth
- assuming all words need to be defined
- assuming that context clues are a reliable source for increasing comprehension
- assessing on single definitions

It recommends that teachers increase:

- time for reading
- opportunities for students to hear and use words
- use of graphic organizers to illustrate, define, or denote
- opportunities to use words in meaningful ways through listening, speaking, and writing
- opportunities to connect new words to known concepts
- the study of concepts that encompass multiple, related words
- explicit concept construction
- use of strategies that lead to independent word learning
- finding the word or concept that will have the greatest impact on comprehension
- focus upon inference

The strategies listed above are simply a small set of ideas for teachers to improve vocabulary instruction. It is important to keep in mind that using the same strategy repeatedly is not the way to help students develop their word knowledge. The strategy selected depends on the words, the content, and the purpose of knowing, utility and importance of each word. It is important to keep in mind that many students view vocabulary as something done to them, and often it is. They need to develop a sense of "control" and be encouraged to think more broadly and deeply about words. They need to know that these words are not necessarily left in the classroom when they leave. They should begin to see the connections of vocabulary words to themselves and the world around them. They need to see themselves as empowered and as "word collectors".

We hope that the brief articulation of these strategies will make teachers more aware of the importance of vocabulary. We hope they think more deeply about the strategies they use to address vocabulary concepts and we hope that our future observations of pre-service, novice and veteran teachers will reflect these practices.

Dare to Differentiate

Vocabulary Strategies for All Students

BY DANNY BRASSELL

Ilesenia arrives to the classroom nearly an hour before the first bell rings. She has completed all of her homework perfectly, organized her desk in preparation for the day's lessons and helps herself to different learning center activities to occupy herself while she awaits the start of school.

José shows up ten minutes late to class every day. He never has a pencil, and he does not seem to have the ability to sit in his seat for periods beyond eight minutes.

Anthony completes math exercises well ahead of his classmates, but he struggles during reading time and usually acts up.

Welcome to Ms. Kwon's fourth grade classroom. It could be just about any classroom in America. One of the epiphanies teachers reach within their first week of teaching is how, no matter what, every classroom is filled with students of mixed abilities and interests. Every student is different. This is the challenge good teachers face: how to differentiate instruction to meet the needs of every student. Differentiating instruction is especially critical in enhancing students' reading aptitudes and attitudes.

What is Differentiated Instruction?

Teachers need to keep in mind that instruction begins where the students are, not at the front of the curriculum guide (Tomlinson, 1999). Differentiated instruction permits all students to access the same classroom curriculum by providing entry points, learning tasks and outcomes that are tailored to students' needs (Hall, Strangman, Meyer, 2003). Differentiated instruction is an approach, not any single strategy.

In aiding students' progress in reading (particularly in their vocabulary and, ultimately, comprehension development), teachers can create classrooms that meet state and federal standards and maintain high student expectations by supporting all students' learning modalities and differentiating through content, activities (process) and product, based on students' readiness, interests, profiles of learning and environments. Brassell and Rasinski (2008) describe a simple mnemonic trick to help teachers always keep differentiation in mind: each student is RIPE for learning when the teacher uses his/her thinking CAR "RIPE" stands for Readiness, Interests, Profiles of Learning and Environments; "CAP" stands for Content, Activities (process) and Product.

Why is Vocabulary Instruction Important?

Who are the more successful vocabulary teachers: optimists or pessimists? The answer is "optimists," and the reason is that optimists keep in mind that if at first they do not succeed they always try again. Optimistic vocabulary teachers display a passion for teaching that infects their students. We need plenty of optimistic and passionate teachers in our classrooms if we want our students to enhance their vocabulary development.

But that is only half the battle. If teachers want to make their vocabulary lessons "stick," teachers have to create rich and engaging activities that attract the enthusiasm of their students. Good vocabulary teachers need to have "weapons of mass instruction," a variety of research-based strategies for their vocabulary-teaching arsenals.

Before Carol Ann Tomlinson talked about differentiating instruction, Howard Gardner (1983) proposed that teachers recognize students' "multiple intelligences." Essentially, Gardner pointed out what Gary Coleman already preached: it takes different strokes for different folks. Some students learn vocabulary best by playing games, and others prefer drills. Teachers need to realize that they have to create classrooms that provide students with a variety of different vocabulary development activities to accommodate all students' learning interests and needs.

Although research has shown that vocabulary knowledge plays a critical role in students' literacy development, many teachers devote hardly any class time at all to vocabulary instruction (Scott, Jamie son-Noel, & Asselin, 2003). Moreover, teachers that do devote time to vocabulary instruction often use strategies that fail to increase students* vocabulary and comprehension abilities (sec reviews in Blachowicz & Fisher, 2002; Nagy, 1988). Finally, Graves (2000) and his colleagues (Graves & Watts-Taffe, 2002) have advocated broader classroom vocabulary programs for students that: (1) facilitate wide reading, (2) teach individual words, (3) provide word-learning strategies, and (4) foster word consciousness.

What Does Differentiated Vocabulary Instruction Look Like?

A thorough examination of various vocabulary enhancement strategies is detailed in *Dare to Differentiate: Vocabulary Strategies for All Students* (Brassell, 2009). This article is meant to provide teachers with a broad starting point on the road to their students' vocabulary development. Without sacrificing a large part of time reserved for other curriculum, teachers in an urban Southern California elementary school showed how they facilitate vocabulary growth by utilizing a variety of differentiated instructional strategies with their highly culturally and linguistically diverse students.

Word Sorts. (Bear, Invemlzzi, Templeton, & Johnston, 1996; Cunningham, Moore, Cunningham, & Moore, 1995; Gunning, 2003) is an instructional strategy used to help students see the generative nature of words. Students "sort" words written and chosen by the teacher on individual cards into groups based on commonalities, relationships and/or other criteria ("closed sort"), or students select categories for sorting their words ("open sort"). The strategy is used to: (1) assist students in learning the relationships among words and how to categorize words based on those relationships; (2) activate and build on students' prior knowledge of words; and (3) allow students to understand recurring patterns in words (e.g., rhyming words, number of syllables, etc.).

Key Science Vocabulary Words (selected by Mrs. Hiroshi)				
recycle	conservation	reduce	contemplate	disappear
consume	disintegrate	respect	construct	container
disabled	reusable	consider	disaster	resource
discover	responsibility	distance		

TABLE 6.2-1. Word Sorts by Mrs. Hiroshi's Fourth Graders.

Tamiko Hiroshi's fourth graders were studying a science unit on recycling. She had introduced a variety of books to the class, and in the third day of her unit she selected a couple of passages from the book *Fifty Simple Things Kids Can Do to Save the Earth* (Earthworks Group & Montez, 1990). These passages continued to focus on the three R's she had been teaching her class: recycle, reuse and reduce. She selected words from the passages that she believed were unfamiliar to most of her students. As a number of words contained similar prefixes, she asked students to work in pairs to categorize each word based on its prefix (closed sort). Knowing that this would be a fairly simple activity for her fourth graders, Mrs. Hiroshi then asked her students to create their own categories for words (open sort).

After students completed both the closed sort and open sort, Mrs. Hiroshi asked them to share their work with the class. Students explained why they placed words in various categories for the closed sort, and they told the class why they had created the categories they had for the open sort. Mrs. Hiroshi allowed students to make any changes they deemed necessary for their final word sorts. Table 6.2-1 shows the target science vocabulary words that Mrs. Hiroshi selected for the class, as well as examples of two student groups' closed and open word sorts. As the table demonstrates, open word sorts particularly lend themselves to product differentiation, as some of Mrs. Hiroshi's students chose to categorize words by "parts of speech" while others categorized words by their "number of syllables."

Word Sorts allow students to classify groups of words as they see fit. It is one of the favorite vocabulary activities offered by many teachers, especially elementary school teachers. Pat Thompson, a second grade teacher, says that she uses Word Sorts with her students as a way of seeing how their minds operate. "I use it as an assessment, but not in the way some 'test-crazy' folks think," she says. "When my students sort their words, it allows me to ask them about their thought process...(which) helps me determine new ways to present information to certain students in ways that are meaningful to them.* Like Thompson, many teachers use Word Sorts as a way of relating students' prior knowledge to new concepts, making target vocabulary words much more comprehensible to students.

Vocab-O-Grams. (Barr & Johnson, 1997; Blachowicz & Fisher, 2002), also known as "Predict-O-Grams," allow students to make predictions about how authors use particular words to tell a story. Vocab-O-Grams are used with a charting process that asks students to organize vocabulary in relationship to the structure of the selection. This strategy is used to: (1) allow students to go beyond the definition of a word and consider its application in text, and (2) encourage students to form predictions about a selection based on vocabulary words.

Deron McGinnis planned to read the West African folktale *Why Mosquitoes Buzz in People's Ears* (Aardema & Dillon, 1975) to his third graders. He knew that many of the words in the story would be new to his students, so he chose a list of new vocabulary words for the class to review before reading the story. He wrote the list on the overhead projector and

Closed Sort (teacher-created categories)		
Prefixes		
con-	dis-	re-
conservation	disappear	recycle
contemplate	disintegrate	reduce
consume	disabled	respect
construct	disaster	reusable
container	distance	responsibility
consider	discover	resource
Open Sort (2 student-created categories)		
Syllables		
2-syllable words	3-syllable words	4-or-more syllabic words
consume	contemplate	conservation (4)
construct	container	disintegrate (4)
distance	consider	reusable (4)
reduce	disappear	responsibility (6)
respect	disabled	
resource	disaster	
	discover	
	recycle	
PARTS OF SPEECH		
nouns	verbs	adjectives
conservation	contemplate	disabled
construct	consume	reusable
container	construct	
disaster	consider	
distance	disappear	
respect	disintegrate	
responsibility	discover	
resource	discover	
	recycle	
	reduce	
	respect	

TABLE 6.2–2.

asked students to discuss what they knew about the words. Next, he passed out Vocab-O-Gram handouts to the class. Mr. McGinnis organized students into groups of four students and asked each group to predict where each vocabulary word could be found as it related to the story structure.

As an example, he asked students to place the word "village" in the most appropriate category. A group answered "setting," and Mr. McGinnis then asked students to think of a

"Why Mosquitoes Buzz in People's Ears"	
New Vocabulary Words	
alarmed whining iguana plotting burrow feared killed reeds council gathered mosquito sticks farmer	
Setting farmer	Which words tell you about when and where the story took place? On a farm
Characters burrow farmer iguana mosquito	Which words tell you about the characters in the story (their feelings, thoughts, appearance)? There's a donkey and an iguana and a mosquito on a farm.
Problem/ Goal alarmed whining killed	Which words describe the problem or goal? One of the animals pulls a fire alarm because one animal was whining about mosquitoes biting him and he wants to kill it.
Action whining feared killed reeds	Which words tell you what might happen? The animals fear the farmer because they know if they arc loud he will be mad. So when the mosquitoes come and they make noise, the farmer comes and kills the mosquitoes.
Resolution sticks	Which words tell you how the story might end? Maybe the farmer uses sticks to swat the mosquitoes off the animals.
What question (s) do you have?	Why don't the animals kill the mosquitoes? Why do mosquitoes buzz in people's ears?
Mystery words: council, plotting	

TABLE 6.2-3. Vocab-O-Gram by Mr. McGinnis's Third Graders.

prediction they could make about a story with the word "village." A student predicted that such a story would take place in a small town. Mr. McGinnis told students that they would be reading *Why Mosquitoes Buzz in People's Ears*, and they had to guess where their new vocabulary words fit in the story (characters, setting, problem/goal, action or resolution). If a group could not decide what category to place a word under, they could place the word in the mystery word category.

Students worked in groups for about ten minutes, placing words in categories and making predictions about the story. Mr. McGinnis asked groups to share their predictions and to explain how they came up with them, and then he asked each student to write at least one question about the story, based on previous predictions. He read aloud the story and discussed with students whether their predictions were accurate. Students shared their thoughts about the story and about different ways the author used the words. Their feedback is listed in Table 6.2-3.

Students enjoy predicting how they think stories are going to turn out, and Vocab-O-Grams allow students not only to predict what they think is going to happen in a story but which words to focus on, as well. Teachers comment that the strength in Vocab-O-Grams seems to be in allowing students to work in pairs or small groups to test their different predictions with peers before sharing them with the entire class. Sal Parker asks his sixth graders to come up with different ways to present their Vocab-O-Grams to the entire class. For example, Mr. Parkers students have created skits, facilitated talk shows, performed puppet shows, shot short videos and even created their own WebQuests. When using Vocab-O-Grams, Mr. Parker points out, teachers can differentiate content, process, product—or a combination of all three.

Vocabulary Self-Collection Strategy (Haggard, 1986; Readence, Bean, & Baldwin, 2001; Ruddell, 1992), also known as Vocabulary Self-Selection (VSS), is an instructional strategy that places the responsibility for learning words on the students. It is a group activity in which students each bring one or two words to the attention of the group that they believe the group should learn. Students, rather than the teacher, generate the majority of words to be explored and learned. Students use their own interest and prior knowledge to enhance vocabulary growth. The strategy is used to: (1) help students generate vocabulary words to be explored and learned by focusing on words that are important to them, (2) simulate word learning that occurs naturally in students' lives, and (3) guide students in becoming independent word learners by capitalizing on their own experiences.

Joyce Tan had been working with her first graders on a thematic unit emphasizing the importance and responsibility of good citizenship. Her students had been reading a number of stories about how to respect themselves and others, play fairly and behave like model citizens. Today, the class had read the book *Dear Mrs. LaRue: Letters from Obedience School* (Teague, 2002), and afterward Ms. Tan asked her students to arrange themselves in groups of four.

Word	Student Definition*	Rationale **
canine	dog	"The police have K-9 units. Those are the cops with dogs."
prison	jail	"A prison is where you go when you are bad and can't get along with other people so they put you alone by yourself."
discussed	said; talked about	"We're discussing now!"
prevented	stopped	"When you prevent something it means you stop it from happening. That's why they say not to have fires in the forest because they can cause bigger fires... so you can prevent big fires by not making little fires."
refused	say "no" won't do	"It's like when Munro (another story students read) told his parents he wouldn't take a bath or eat his dinner. He refused to."
shocking	surprise	"Something shocks you when you don't know it's going to happen."

* Ms. Tan asks students to double-check their definitions by comparing them with definitions found in their dictionaries.

** Ms. Tan does not write students' rationale for choosing a word on the overhead projector/chalkboard. Rather, she asks students to tell her why they chose a word. It is written here to demonstrate how students feel about certain words.

TABLE 6.2-4. Vocabulary Self-Collection Strategy for Ms. Tan's First Graders.

She told students that she would read the story again more slowly and asked each group to try and find one word from the story that they would like to learn more about. She told her students that the word could be a word that they did not understand very well, a word that they think they needed to know, or a word they were curious to know more about. The most important thing to remember, Ms. Tan emphasized, was for each group to nominate a word, define the word by looking at how the author used it in the story, and tell the class why they thought it was important that the class learned the word.

Some groups came up with a number of words, and Ms. Tan said that was all right because different groups might nominate the same words for the class vocabulary list. After allowing students about five minutes to discuss their nominations, Ms. Tan asked representatives from each group to share with the class the words they chose. She wrote each word on the overhead projector and asked the class to define each word. She also asked students to share whatever they knew about a word.

When she asked students to defend why they chose a word, students discussed why their word was important to know. Once the entire class had shared their words, definitions and rationales, Ms. Tan rewrote the key vocabulary words on the board with the definitions decided by the class. She passed out "Vocabulary Self-Collection Strategy" sheets and asked students to copy the words and definitions from the class list on the overhead (see Table 6.2-4). Ms. Tan informed the class that they could refer to their new words when they wrote stories later in the day. She also told the class that she would use their vocabulary list to include in future word finds and word jumbles.

Freedom of choice among students is the key to the Vocabulary Self-Collection Strategy. By allowing students to select the words that they are interested in learning more about, teachers are empowering and encouraging their students to take active interest in their own learning. Frederica Pimmel cautions that some students may require some extra guidance in terms of what types of words students need to focus on. According to Mrs. Pimmel, "By modeling to students which words in a story play critical importance to comprehending a story, teachers can interest students in discovering 'the important words to know.'" She says that she uses Vocabulary Self-Collection Strategy as a game where she challenges her third graders to act like "word investigators" who have to uncover the most important words in any passage. By calling the activity a game, she has learned, her students take an immediate interest and even practice the activity outside of school.

Final thoughts

Learning vocabulary can be fun with the right attitude. There are all sorts of ways for teachers to engage their students in acquiring more vocabulary. Introducing students to great books is always the best idea. Games are fantastic. It is necessary for more teachers to realize, though, how they can differentiate the content, process and/or product of any given lesson in order to meet the needs and readiness levels for all of their students.

The strategies discussed in this article are all utilized as part of a number of vocabulary development activities offered at one school, in addition to increased access to books. It should be noted that all teachers at this school considered their extensive classroom library reading resources as critical in attracting their students' interests in vocabulary activities. Again, a more comprehensive list of strategies can be found in *Dare to Differentiate: Vocabulary Strategies for All Students* (Brassell, 2009). If teachers want to build students' word knowledge without sacrificing a significant portion of their instructional time, they need to practice more enticing vocabulary-building activities that focus on the specific needs of each individual child. In that way all students may succeed.

Building English Language Learners' Academic Vocabulary

Strategies and Tips

BY CLAIRE SIBOLD

Introduction

According to Beck, McKeown, and Kucan's Three Tier Model (2002), when it comes to language instruction the distinction between academic vocabulary words and content specific words has a significant bearing on the language success of English language learners (ELLs). By using the strategies described in this article teachers and parents will have the means to develop ELLs' vocabulary through reading, direct instruction, and reinforcement activities and games. Teachers and parents can use these strategies before, during, and after reading, and thus provide students with a set of tools they can use independently as they read.

Often vocabulary instruction receives inadequate attention in elementary and secondary classrooms (Biemiller & Boote, 2006). Academic vocabulary, specifically the language that may occur in multiple contexts or the precise words that are presented in a specific context, can help students acquire new learning strategies and skills (Marzano, 2005).

Academic vocabulary, however, is notably more difficult to learn than conversational language because it is more specific and sometimes abstract, making it difficult to grasp. Knowledge of this kind of technical vocabulary in any specific content area—for example, social science, science, mathematics, or language arts—is directly linked to content knowledge. Stahl and Fairbanks (1986) found that such vocabulary instruction directly improves students' reading comprehension of textbook content.

While the majority of teachers develop students' vocabulary across the curriculum, it is essential that English language learners have explicit instruction about the academic vocabulary that is necessary for their success in school.

The Importance to ELLs

When English language learners struggle with reading comprehension, it can often be attributed to their difficulty with understanding the vocabulary. Many studies report that low academic language skills are associated with low academic performance (Baumann, Edwards, Font, Tereshinski, et al, 2002; Biemiller & Boote, 2006; Carlo, August, McLaughlin, Snow, et al, 2004). These studies also report a discrepancy among students of diverse ethnicities related to the amount of vocabulary they know and the depth to which they know and use that vocabulary. According to Beck, McKeown, and Kucan, "there are profound differences in vocabulary knowledge among learners from different ability or socioeconomic (SES) groups" (2002, p. 1).

Thus, students with smaller vocabularies are at a greater disadvantage in learning, and this lack of knowledge too often is the main barrier to their comprehension of texts and lectures (Newton, Padak, & Rasinski, 2008). According to Graves (2006) and Zwiers (2008), ELLs require assistance in developing content-related vocabulary in their second language if they are to experience success in school.

Both native English speakers and ELLs need support in learning the language that is used in the classroom as part of instruction, reading, discussion, and assignments. Interweaving

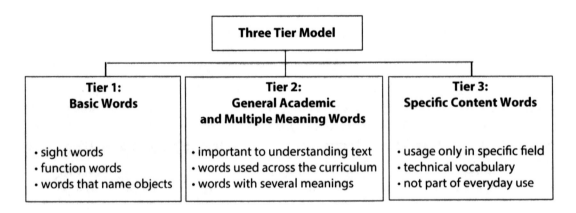

FIGURE 6.3-1. Graphic Organizer of Three Tier Model.

direct instruction in academic language helps students acquire an understanding of abstract concepts, multiple meaning words, and content vocabulary. When students are able to understand the vocabulary for the that content they are reading and hearing, they will have a better understanding of the material. While wide reading promotes vocabulary growth, ELLs who do not read enough cannot acquire the word wealth that would help them with language learning.

Three Tier Model

Beck, McKeown, and Kucan's (2002) Three Tier Model places vocabulary words into three categories: Tier 1 which consists of basic or common words, Tier 2 which involves words that are used across the curriculum and multiple meaning words, and Tier 3 which is content specific vocabulary. In this model (see Figure 6.3-1).

Tier 1 words are the most common words in English and they make up a significant percentage of the words students read. These words generally require little or no instruction, e.g., *table, swim, cars,* and *dog* (Wosley, 2009). Sight words, function words, and words that name objects are included within Tier 1 vocabulary.

Tier 2 words are useful terms found with high frequency. These are words that are important to understanding the text and are used across the curriculum. For example, *analyze, compare,* and *conclusion* are words commonly used in academic settings during instruction, in discussions, on tests, and in assignments. Multiple meaning words such as *set, bat, base,* and *check* have several meanings and must be presented in context in order to be understood. Students who are proficient in English typically have a better grasp of these words and are able to use them to communicate.

Tier 3 vocabulary words are found with less frequency and are typically limited to specific content areas. According to Vacca and Vacca (2008) these words have "usage and application only in a particular subject field," e.g., *centimeter, kilogram,* and *deciliter* in a mathematics or science class, or *abolitionist, emancipation,* and *secession* in a history class (p. 145).

It is relatively easy for teachers to identify these Tier 3 words in their textbooks. Students, on the other hand, struggle to define or explain the meaning of these vocabulary words, words that are not part of the language they use every day. Therefore, this technical vocabulary needs to be taught explicitly and thoroughly (Vacca & Vacca, 2008).

Effective Vocabulary Instruction

Effective vocabulary instruction emphasizes direct instruction. For example, presenting both key words that help ELLs understand difficult text and multiple-meaning words that require students to use context to figure out the meaning will be necessary. By using direct instruction, teachers can incorporate relevant vocabulary into the before, during, and after reading stages of instruction (see Table 6.3-1).

In order to help students remember new words, teachers can ask ELLS to associate the new words with things that are already familiar to them, or the teacher can translate the words into the students' primary language (Colorado, 2007). After students read, teachers can use word play to reinforce the understanding of new words and create enthusiasm for learning those new words. For example, "Find the Antonym" (*divide* → multiply) and "Which One Doesn't Fit" (square, circle, ruler, triangle) are two possibilities.

While students may learn new words by encountering them in their reading, it is critical that teachers give ELLs the tools for acquiring vocabulary through explicit instructions. To create enthusiasm for learning new words, teachers can help students hunt for clues that unlock the meaning of unknown words such as synonyms, descriptions, explanations, and visual aids.

It is important to connect the new words to students' prior knowledge. To do this, teachers can actively involve ELLs in learning new words, create a vocabulary rich environment, and teach through a variety of strategies. For younger children, *realia*, actual objects or items, are useful for making abstract words more concrete. For example, in teaching *shapes*, teachers can bring to the classroom objects of different shapes.

Real objects, pictures, and photographs that clearly match unfamiliar words provide visuals that help ELLs make sense of the new words, e.g., photographs of frogs and salamanders to illustrate "amphibians." Teachers can also use anchor words for new words, e.g., "baseball cards" as the anchor for "collection," "frogs" for "amphibians," and "rice" for "grains."

To create a rich vocabulary environment teachers can use a word wall that contains words from different content areas, word books, and develop a reading room with books that teach and reinforce new concepts. Word walls engage students visually and can be used to display content vocabulary from the curriculum or involve students in activities that will help them learn new words. It is also helpful to integrate the new vocabulary into students' writing assignments.

Strategies for Teaching Academic Vocabulary

It is important to explicitly teach vocabulary using effective strategies that will engage students in learning new words—for example, association strategies, imagery, and graphic organizers. When introducing a new word, it is helpful to avoid a lexical definition as dictionary

TABLE 6.3-1. Three Stages for Incorporating Relevant Vocabulary.

Before Reading:
- Pronounce the word and use the Spanish equivalent; then have students repeat the word in English several times
- Tap students' prior knowledge and identify anchor or familiar words for new vocabulary words, e.g., "walk" as the anchor for "saunter"
- Pre-teach words before students read the material
- Introduce graphic organizers that show relationships among words
- Show realia, actual objects, pictures, picture books, and video clips to introduce vocabulary
- Use the Spanish equivalent
- Teach students how to use the structure of words, e.g., compound words, prefixes, roots, and suffixes, to break down a word into the meaningful units

During Reading:
- Define words in context, using sentences from students' reading material
- Help students find the context clues that will help them determine the meaning of an unknown word as they read
- Use graphic organizers to help students process the content
- Show students how to use the dictionary to confirm their predictions about the meaning of the vocabulary they meet in their reading u Talk-through the words as students hear these during oral reading
- Use a variety of strategies to help students process the meaning of difficult words

After Reading:
- Focus on a limited number of key words, particularly interrelated words, to increase the depth of their understanding and concept development u Give students multiple exposures to words throughout the day in order to cement their understanding of the word meanings
- Reinforce new words through activities, discussions, and assignments following students' reading
- Help make the words meaningful to students by linking the words with familiar things, people, or experiences
- Have students incorporate the new words into students' writing assignments
- Help students integrate new words into their speaking and writing vocabularies
- Display word walls and other graphic organizers with the new vocabulary and definitions

definitions often include other words that are equally difficult and do not make sense to the students. Instead, teachers can provide students with a description or explanation of the word or an example as shown in Figure 6.3-2.

Repetition is one of the keys to learning a new word. First, have the students listen to the pronunciation of the new word and at the same time view a picture or an actual object that goes with the word. Have them repeat the word out loud at least three times. Then have them use the word in a sentence similar to what appears in the material the students are reading. For example, the teacher reads, "There are four geographic *regions* in California." Then the teacher explains that regions are *parts* of the state of California. She shows these regions on a map. Students can work in pairs to come up with a new sentence using the word in question. This procedure can be repeated with each key word as shown in Figure 6.3-3.

When teaching academic vocabulary using this repetition cycle, carefully select a few content-specific words from the textbook that are critical to students' understanding of the main concepts, topics, or sub-topics. After developing activities that provide multiple exposures to the words in context, then present opportunities for the student to practice using these words. Through the use of a variety of strategies, teachers can scaffold students' learning of new vocabulary. Since learning vocabulary through reading may not be sufficient, direct teaching of vocabulary words will ensure learning and greater opportunities for academic success.

Sample Strategies for Elementary Students

SIGNAL WORD OF THE DAY

In an elementary classroom the teacher selects a word for the day from students' reading as the "signal word" of the day. The teacher pronounces the word; then the students echo the word. This word is used as a signal for the children to start or stop an activity.

When the students are seated, the teacher checks their understanding of the word. The teacher asks: "What does this *character* mean?" "Can you use the word in a sentence?" To help the class pay attention to the word the rest of the day, the teacher states the definition of the word and has the students say in unison the word. Through this method the use of repetition and the multiple exposure to the word throughout the day increases the students' retention of new words.

"TALK-THROUGH" STRATEGY WITH READING ALOUD

Both teachers and parents can help students learn new words by "talking-through" the definitions and giving examples during oral reading. This allows students to hear the word in context. For example, in reading a passage from the science textbook on the earth's water, teachers would stop and talk through the meanings of *cover, surface,* and *atmosphere.*

Introduce the new word → Provide synonyms → Describe or explain the word → Use the word in a sentence

FIGURE 6.3-2. Presenting a New Word

Repeated readings of the text are essential for learners with more limited vocabularies and help them link the pronunciation of new words with their meanings. After reading, reinforcement activities can help cement the students' newly obtained knowledge.

ACADEMIC VOCABULARY JOURNALS

In a fifth-grade class, the teacher asks students to guess what a new word means; the teacher then gives the students the formal definition. Next, the students use the word in a sentence and draw a pictorial representation of the word. Students record the new words alphabetically in their journals. These academic journals may also be created in chart form and include ratings, pictures, and ideas that are connected to the new words (see Figure 6.3-4 for a sample Academic Vocabulary Chart).

GRAPHIC ORGANIZERS

Graphic organizers are visual representations that show arrangements of concepts and/ or vocabulary words. Such organizers are effective when coupled with direct instruction. Because graphic organizers use visual images, they are particularly appropriate for English language learners. The use of graphic organizers, such as word trees, concept maps, and

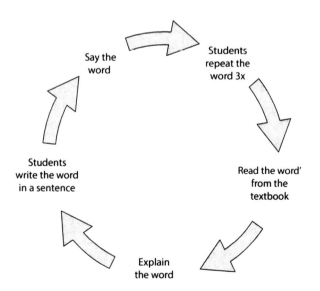

FIGURE 6.3-3. Repetition Cycle.

relational charts, help students understand concepts and the related vocabulary. Graphic organizers also help to link the definitions to examples (Colorado, 2007).

Teachers can also use a flow chart to look at a multiple-meaning word. This graphic organizer helps students break the word down into syllables, note the parts of speech, bring into view different definitions, and provide sample sentences. Both teachers and students can draw pictures to illustrate the words. See an example in Figure 6.3-5 for the word "difference."

THE POWER OF GAMES

Games can also be powerful tools for reinforcing ELLs' vocabulary. Commercially published games such as *Balderdash* and *Scrabble* promote general vocabulary usage, however, other interactive games and teacher-created games are equally useful in reinforcing students' understanding and encouraging enthusiasm for learning new words. Bingo cards are an example of these.

Sample Strategies for Secondary Students

Explicit instruction of technical words is even more critical in content areas at the secondary level "where students need a shared set of vocabulary to progress in their learning" (Biemiller & Boote, 2006, p. 190). ELLs must not only be able to define the words but must also be able to understand these words in context as well as use the words in discussions and integrate the words in their writing. Some of the previously mentioned strategies for elementary students can be appropriate at the secondary level, but three strategies that are particularly effective with secondary students are the PAVE procedure, Student VOC Strategy, and Quick Writes.

PAVE PROCEDURE

Bannon, Fisher, Pozzi, and Weasel (1990) developed the PAVE procedure, a four-step process that encourages students to compare their guess at the meaning of a word with its lexical definition. PAVE stands for **P**rediction, **A**ssociation, **V**erification, and **E**valuation. Students first read the new word as it appears in the textbook and then based upon the context clues they predict the meaning of the word.

Students then try to personalize the word by connecting the word to their own mental images. To verify the meaning of the word, they look up the word in the dictionary, read the definition, and compare this definition to their predicted meaning. Through this process, students learn a strategy that helps them become more independent learners.

STUDENT VOC STRATEGY

The Student VOC Strategy is a Tier 3 strategy that targets content vocabulary. It helps students acquire a deeper meaning of the word. To implement this strategy, teachers provide a list of the key words from the chapter the students will be reading. Before reading, the students meet in small groups and choose one or two words they don't know or which may be unclear (West Virginia Department of Education, 2010).

After reading, students discuss what they think the word means and consult an "expert"—their textbook, a web-site, or a friend for the actual definition. After learning the definition of the word, they use the word in a sentence and draw a picture to remember the word. For example, one group chose the word "proclamation" and came to a consensus that the word meant "an announcement." To verify their guess, one student sent a text message to his father who provided this definition: "Proclamation means 'announcement or declaration. It can also be a document declaring something.'"

This strategy allows teachers to assess their students' prior knowledge, and it helps the students realize the possible sources of information they can tap to verify the meaning of a new word.

QUICK WRITES

Quick writing invites students to write brief responses to questions about a key word, e.g. What do you think *freedom* means? The student writes "to do what you want." Then the teacher asks, what other words do you think of when you hear this word? For example, students write "the Statue of Liberty," "the Bill of Rights," "wearing what you want," and "listening to the music you like." Students' Quick Writes can be used to start a dialogue that taps their prior knowledge and allows the teacher to build upon this knowledge. As

Word	Rating	Description or Example	Picture	Ideas
nutrition	No, never heard it	Foods that make your body work Vegetables are good for you		Not fast food Good for you Makes you healthy
balanced	Yes, have heard it	Eating some of each type of food Eating things that are good for you Not eating too much sugar		Sandwich with tuna, celery, & mayannaise, wheat bread A banana Milk Use the Food Pyramid

FIGURE 6.3–4. Academic Vocabulary Chart.

Images copyright © Depositphotos/ lineartestpilot; copyright © Depositphotos/lenmdp.

an alternative, English language learners can work in pairs to generate an answer to the questions.

Partnering with Parents to Develop ELLs' Vocabulary

Teachers can partner with parents in developing ELLs' academic vocabulary, particularly when it comes to content words that students need to master in each unit. Teachers can provide word lists that include the words in English as well as the home language and the definition of the word. They can supply parents with tips on how to build vocabulary and share examples of strategies they can implement at home. For example:

- Provide synonyms in the students' home language whenever possible.
- Use flash cards with the vocabulary word and definition.
- Create charts with anchor words that link students' knowledge with new words.
- Find simple books that focus on one topic in the content area and related content vocabulary, especially books with illustrations.
- Use a dictionary in the child or teen's home language.
- Keep a vocabulary journal for younger students and review the words periodically to ensure the words have become part of their vocabulary.
- Collect and review words with their children after reading and before tests.
- Play games to teach and reinforce new words with their children.

During parent-teacher conferences, teachers can promote the importance of vocabulary development, review some of the strategies, provide dictionaries, and respond to parents questions. For parents who are not proficient in English, it is important to translate or have someone proficient in the home language translate the tips and participate in the conferences.

Conclusion

English language learners who struggle with academic vocabulary can have difficulty comprehending reading materials and class instruction. By explicitly teaching multiple meaning words and technical words, teachers can assist students in developing word wealth and increase their understanding of content material. It is important for teachers to make connections between the learners' prior knowledge and the new vocabulary.

Direct instruction of academic vocabulary includes the use of a variety of strategies, many of which use visual aids for students and present the words in context. There are many effective strategies such as the use of signal words, talk-through with read-alouds, vocabulary games, the Student VOC Strategy, and Quick Writes that help ELLs learn new words and provide tools for them to use in class and independently. By partnering with parents, teachers increase the opportunities for students to receive the help they need in learning academic vocabulary.

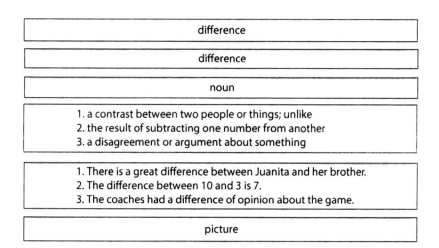

FIGURE 6.3-5. Flow Chart.

CHAPTER REFERENCES

Alber, R. (2010). Doing it differently: Tips for teaching vocabulary. Retrieved from http://www.edutopia.org/.

Diamond, L & Gutlohn, L. (2006). Teaching vocabulary. Retrieved from http://www.readingrockets.org/.

Ebbers, S. (2008). Linking the language: A cross-disciplinary vocabulary approach. Retrieved from http://www.readingrockets.org/.

National Reading Panel (2000). Retrieved from http://www.nichd.nih.gov/.

Stahl, S. (2005). Four problems with teaching word meanings (and what to do to make vocabulary an integral part of instruction). In E. H. Hiebert & M. L. Kamil (Eds.), *Teaching and learning vocabulary: Bringing research to practice* (pp. 95–114). Mahwah, NJ: Lawrence Erlbaum.

Chapter Seven

Introductions by Karen Loman

WRITING PROCESS

WRITING ASSESSMENT

Writing

INTRODUCTION TO READINGS 7.1-7.2
Writing Process

Reading and writing develop simultaneously. The more we read, the better we write; the more we write, the better we read. Writing is supported in a workshop approach much like reading: mini-lessons for modeling writing and engaging in units of study, opportunities for students to write while the teacher confers with individuals and small groups of students, and time for sharing. Writing may be viewed as a process (how students write) *and* a product (what students write). A writer's workshop supports both writing as a way of knowing (process) and writing as a way of telling (product). In the workshop, students compose texts and receive feedback from peers and the teacher. When the focus is on the process, very young writers are free to make books and other authentic texts (products). The writing process includes planning, drafting, revising, editing, and publishing. Responding to teacher-initiated prompts and filling out worksheets do not support the writing process; planning and organizing are predetermined. Revising and editing may be redundant, as it is about completing rather than processing. Teachers support writing by modeling, developing inquiry studies, and engaging students in conversations about what authors do and how writing works.

Teaching students how to write is supported by the Six + 1 Traits proposed in 1983 by the Northwest Regional Educational Laboratory. The Six Traits—ideas, organization, voice, word choice, sentence fluency, and conventions plus presentation—guide students to assess their writing and determine what they do well and what they need to improve. The Traits provide a common language to teachers, regardless of grade, to talk about student writing. Teaching students what to write is supported by inquiry studies or looking at "stacks of books" (Ray, 2004). Studies may include anchor texts that exemplify each trait, various genres, authors, themes, topics ... whatever the teacher determines meets the needs of the students and the grade-level expectations. Studies generally include anchor charts that document key elements of the author's craft in the study.

Unfortunately, writing instruction is often limited to or has as its primary focus on grammar, punctuation, and spelling. In 1986 Hillocks reviewed 20 years of research on the teaching of writing. He found the teaching of grammar did not improve writing quality. If the traits are aligned with grammar, punctuation, and spelling, we see that they comprise only one part of a seven-component curriculum and only one part of the writing process. Grammar and spelling are best taught in the context of student writing during the revision and editing process. Penmanship is best taught as short 5- to 10-minute fine-motor lessons then transferred and reinforced during conventions and presentations.

Students should write daily on topics of choice with many opportunities for peer feedback and revision.

BEFORE READING
Think back to your own writing instruction. Were you taught *how* to write? *what* to write? Or were you given prescriptive activities that didn't allow students to determine how and what to write? What do you see happening in classrooms today?

DURING READING
What practices do both articles recommend? Where do they differ?

AFTER READING
What challenges do you anticipate when implementing a writer's workshop with mentor texts? Do you think your students are capable of writing as well as the student examples provided? Why or why not? What would it take to get students there?

When Kids Make Books

BY KATIE WOOD RAY

When we encourage young children to think of themselves as writers, their achievement soars.

This is Meredith Glover's first literary nonfiction," a kindergartner writes in the author's note for her book, *The Rabbit and the Snake*. So much is captured in this confident statement. At the ripe old age of 6, Meredith has a sense of her own history as a writer. She has a fairly sophisticated understanding of the features of a particular genre, and she knows that incorporating these features into her latest book sets it apart from others she has written. And perhaps most important, Meredith is beginning to understand writing as a way to get things done. "She made this book to teach her friends," she writes.

Writers like Meredith offer an important lesson for us as teachers of young children. When we invite students to *make* something with writing instead of just asking them to write, they go about their work differently. Especially when students have seen examples of the kinds of things they could make, they are more likely to craft a piece of literature—as Meredith has done in her first work of literary nonfiction—than to just string words together.

Joining the Club

We know that young students profit from using approximation to invent spellings for words that they have in their spoken vocabulary but don't yet recognize in print (Wilde, 1992). If we expand this understanding of approximation to include every aspect of writing, young students can do more than we ever thought possible. They can craft such literary nonfiction as *The Rabbit and the Snake* (see p. 17), complete with two levels of running text (facts at the top and narrative at the bottom); illustrations that support and enhance the meaning; "clues" that foreshadow what will happen on coming pages; a "Did You Know?" section with more facts; and an author's note. Meredith may not quite be ready to write feature articles for *National Geographic* or to publish her picture books with HarperCollins, but she certainly has approximated this kind of writing in smart 6-year-old ways.

When young students see themselves as people who make books, they develop beginning understandings about genre, craft, style, voice, organization, audience, process, and purpose. This sense of identity is key to much of their development as writers.

Meredith writes with such intention because she has a strong sense of what she is doing: She is making a book. As adults we may call it *approximating* the making of a book, but Meredith doesn't see it this way. She clearly sees herself as a "member of the club" of people who make books (Smith, 1988). What's more, she is making a particular kind of book: a piece of literary nonfiction, a book like *One Tiny Turtle* by Nicola Davies (Candlewick Press, 2001) or *Gentle Giant Octopus* by Karen Wallace (Candlewick Press, 1998). Meredith cannot yet read these books on her own; supportive adults have done the reading for her. But she can write books like these, if the adults supporting her accept the fact that she will write her books as a 6-year-old does.

Many teachers are discovering the value of inviting young students to join the club of people who make books. These teachers staple paper together so that it looks like a book and ask students to try their hands at it (Ray, 2004). Why make picture books? Developmentally, most children need to draw along with their writing to make meaning. But perhaps even more important, picture books are the mainstay of most young children's reading diet. In creating picture books, they are approximating the kind of writing that they know best.

Meredith's clear vision for her book has come from seeing other writers do these same things in their books. She is *reading like a writer* (Ray, 1999; Smith, 1981), even before she's actually reading for herself. Writers read differently than other people do. Writers notice and think about how texts are written, in addition to what texts are about. They can't help but notice; it's a habit of mind they adopt when they come to think of themselves as writers.

Everything Meredith notices about how books are written becomes an idea she might try when she makes her own books. When adults read more sophisticated books to children than they can read independently, the children's writing development can actually outpace their independent reading development for some time.

Rethinking Challenging but Achievable

The joint position statement of the International Reading Association and the National Association for the Education of Young Children defines developmentally appropriate practice as "challenging but achievable, with sufficient adult support" (1998, p. 8). I'd like to consider the idea of *challenging but achievable*, and then the related matter of *sufficient adult support*.

Adults commonly make judgments about what is challenging but achievable on the basis of our assumptions about typical child development. Often, schools design curriculum, instruction, and assessment with these judgments in mind. But what happens when students show us kinds of achievement that we never imagined they were capable of?

For example, look at what Meredith knows in addition to the genre features I mentioned before. Her level of achievement would not appear on any developmental continuum that I have ever encountered for writers her age. She understands the sequencing of a narrative, the consistency of verb tense, and the interactive nature of narrating a story in present tense. She understands that punctuation is a tool used to communicate in specific ways with a reader, that print can be embedded in illustrations, and that words can be laid out on a page in different configurations. She knows that writers reread and self-correct, as we can see by the words she's marked through and revised. She understands that texts of this kind don't just stop —they end with some sort of closure. She even knows that writers often use third-person pronouns to talk about themselves in author's notes. And besides reflecting all these understandings, *The Rabbit and the Snake* also shows us that Meredith is developing sophisticated spelling insights.

Clearly, Meredith's accomplishment exceeds the achievement that we have typically expected from writers in kindergarten. How can we make sense of it? How can we understand its implications for our practice?

Recently, literacy specialists from the Lakota Early Childhood Center in West Chester, Ohio, met with me to look closely at books written by kindergartners at the Center. As we discussed these books, we realized that students at all levels of development were defining "achievable" on their own terms, not on ours. The more advanced writers often stunned us with the decisive, intentional crafting of their writing, but the beginning writers also demonstrated understandings that neither these reading specialists nor I had thought possible. Their achievement was especially impressive when we listened to them telling us what they were *trying* to do, instead of just looking at the pages of their books. Often, understanding their intentions was the key to understanding their remarkable achievement.

Ryan is a good example. During a guided reading lesson, Ryan and his teacher encountered a book about gorillas. The writer of this text moved back and forth between telling about a gorilla in the wild and a gorilla in a zoo. As Ryan and his teacher talked about the book and its predictable structure, they batted around several ideas about how Ryan might use a similar structure in his writing. Ryan's teacher casually offered, "You could try that sometime if you'd like." It was up to Ryan to decide whether he could rise to that challenge. A few days later he decided to try, and produced the following text:

Title Page:	*Real Baseball/Fake Baseball, by Ryan Middendorf*
Page One:	*I play real baseball, I play fake baseball on PlayStation and both of them are fun, really, really fun.*
Page Two:	*And I throw a baseball and I press X or $\triangle$ or $\square$ or $\bigcirc$.*
Page Three:	*I hit the baseball and I press X or $\square$ to hit on PlayStation.*
Page Four:	*And I press < > to move on PlayStation.*

Ryan set out with the specific intention of writing a classic comparison/contrast text about two kinds of baseball he knows well. Was this an achievable challenge for him? He obviously thought so! As a teacher, I have learned to value the whole breadth of approximations that young students make when they set out to try things with writing, making anything they want to try achievable.

IMPLICATIONS FOR INSTRUCTIONAL TASKS

Operating with the new understanding that young students can decide for themselves what is achievable, many teachers have stopped asking students to perform inherently limiting exercises in the name of writing. Such tasks as drawing a picture and writing a sentence underneath or filling out a predetermined story frame don't help students build identities as writers. And perhaps more significantly, these tasks have a predetermined level of achievement in mind. They force students "to operate within the teacher's assumptive bounds" (Harste, Woodward, & Burke, 1984, p. 14) and may or may not match what the students can actually do.

When we replace these limiting tasks with a more open-ended and ongoing invitation to young students to make books, the students build identities as writers around their daily work of composing texts. The making of books becomes a fundamental part of the students' routine at school, and out of that routine we create a context for their writing in which they can define their own achievement. Because such a context was in place, Ryan's teacher could offer him a writing challenge and then step away and see whether he could achieve that challenge.

As the Lakota teachers and I reflected, we realized that we had likely been shortchanging our young writers in the past by failing to create a context for writing in which students could set their own goals for achievement. This was true for all writers, but perhaps especially true for our more developmentally advanced writers. How much, we wondered, had students been held back by adults who defined what is "challenging but achievable" for students on their own adult terms instead of letting the children define it for themselves?

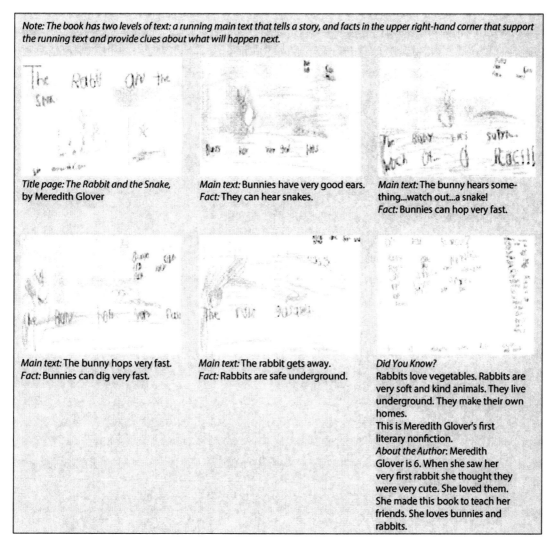

Note: The book has two levels of text: a running main text that tells a story, and facts in the upper right-hand corner that support the running text and provide clues about what will happen next.

Title page: The Rabbit and the Snake, by Meredith Glover

Main text: Bunnies have very good ears.
Fact: They can hear snakes.

Main text: The bunny hears something...watch out...a snake!
Fact: Bunnies can hop very fast.

Main text: The bunny hops very fast.
Fact: Bunnies can dig very fast.

Main text: The rabbit gets away.
Fact: Rabbits are safe underground.

Did You Know?
Rabbits love vegetables. Rabbits are very soft and kind animals. They live underground. They make their own homes.
This is Meredith Glover's first literary nonfiction.
About the Author: Meredith Glover is 6. When she saw her very first rabbit she thought they were very cute. She loved them. She made this book to teach her friends. She loves bunnies and rabbits.

FIGURE 7.1–1. Meredith's Book (Selected Pages).

IMPLICATIONS FOR ASSESSMENT

Understanding that we need to create contexts for writing in which young students can show us what is achievable has also led us to think differently about assessment. So much of the assessment of students' writing has focused on the question, "What does this piece of writing show me that the student needs to know?" Although writing teachers need to ask this question in our assessments, we also need to ask, "What does this piece of writing show me that this student already knows?" and, "What is this writer trying to do here?" To find out the answer to this second question, we often have to ask the student about his or her intentions.

Finally, in our continual process of assessment, we must also ask, "If this writer can do all this, then what else might he or she be capable of achieving?" Our assessment needs to help us not only define deficits but also imagine possibilities. Our assessment should lead us to wonder what would happen if Meredith, who writes literary nonfiction of such high quality, were immersed in poetry. What if we read her books rich with dialogue? What if we showed her series books? As long as teachers let students define what is achievable on the students' own terms, almost anything is possible.

Providing Sufficient Adult Support

How do we teach students like Meredith and Ryan well? How do we help them realize their full potential while honoring them as children? Answering such questions involves a continual process of reflection and action on the part of teachers. Here are several recommendations:

- Create supportive contexts for student writing—environments that value and recognize approximation and that encourage students to define for themselves what their achievement will be.
- Help students develop vision for their writing by inviting them to make things with writing: mostly books, but also poems, letters, and songs—any kind of compositional writing with which they have had experience as readers or listeners (remembering that adults will have to do much of the reading for them until they can read independently).
- Read to students often from richly crafted literature from a wide variety of genres. These readings need to be carefully rendered so that students can tune their ears to what good writing sounds like (Fox, 1993). Repeated readings are also important.
- Talk with students about what they notice writers doing in books (the craft of the writing) and help them imagine how they could write like that in their own books.
- Ask students often about the decisions they made and the thinking they engaged in as they were writing. Often, much more is going on than we realize.
- Be a good audience for students' writing, responding in ways that show them you value their work. In addition, find them other audiences that will appreciate their work.

STILL LEARNING . . .

More than 10 years ago, on the 30th anniversary of the publication of *Research in Written Composition* (Braddock, Lloyd-Jones, & Schoer, 1963), Julie Jensen asked 24 leading scholars to name "the single most important thing we as a profession know now that we didn't know

30 years ago about the teaching and learning of writing in the elementary school." Peter Elbow responded,

> *Writing is the realm where children can attain literacy first and best feel on top of it—feel ownership and control over the written word. (Jensen, 1993, p. 291)*

This statement is as true today as it was then. With each passing year, teachers are learning more about the profound implications of helping young students gain a sense of ownership and control over literacy. When students see themselves as writers, they can achieve more than we have ever imagined.

Making the Most of Mentor Texts

BY KELLY GALLAGHER

We must teach students to imitate model texts before they write, as they write, and as they revise.

When George Lucas was making *Star Wars*, his special effects team was at a loss as to how to film realistic-looking dogfight scenes. They began by storyboarding them, but they found that simply drawing the scenes on paper didn't help them understand the pacing and rhythm of the fights. They solved their dilemma by splicing together footage of real dogfights from World War II documentaries into one film sequence and copying this sequence frame by frame.

This story reminds me of the first time I was asked to write a grant proposal. Never having written one before, I was feeling very unsure of myself. My bosses were counting on me to write something I didn't know how to write. Can you guess what I did next? I found a previously successful grant proposal and studied it, paying close attention to its structure and language. Like the *Star Wars* team, I found a strong model and emulated it.

Isn't this how people learn to do something unfamiliar? We stand next to someone who knows how to do it. We watch him or her carefully, analyzing what the person does and then copying those actions as closely as we can.

There's a lesson for writing teachers here. If we want our students to write persuasive arguments, interesting explanatory pieces, or captivating narratives, we need to have them read, analyze, and emulate persuasive arguments, interesting explanatory pieces, and captivating narratives. Before you can film a dogfight, you have to know what one looks like. Before our students can write well in a given discourse, they need to see good writing in that discourse.

But effective modeling entails much more than handing students a mentor text and asking them to imitate it. It's not that simple. Rather, students benefit from paying close attention to models before they begin drafting a piece of writing, as they compose their first draft, and as they move that draft into revision. Mentor texts are most powerful when students frequently revisit them *throughout* the writing process—and when teachers help them take lessons from writing exemplars.

Prewriting: Discerning What to Imitate

If we want beginning writers to learn lessons from model texts, we need to teach them what to look for. For instance, if students are going to be writing poetry, we should begin by giving them lots of poems to read. But while students are immersed in the poems, we also need to teach them how to read like writers—to notice the techniques, moves, and choices that poets make.

Students are used to being asked *what* is written, but asking them to recognize *how* a text is written is a shift for many of them. This shift is essential in meeting three of the 10 Common Core anchor standards for reading:

- Standard 4: Interpret words and phrases as they are used in a text, including deter-mining technical, connotative, and figurative meanings, and analyze how specific word choices shape meaning or tone.
- Standard 5: Analyze the structure of texts, including how specific sentences, para-graphs, and larger portions of the text ... relate to each other and the whole.
- Standard 6: Assess how point of view or purpose shapes the content and style of a text (National Governors Association Center for Best Practices & Council of Chief State School Officers, 2010).

All these standards ask readers to answer the same basic question: What did the writer do? To help students sharpen their ability to discern the moves writers make, I give them passages like this excerpt from Martin Luther King Jr.'s 1963 "Letter from Birmingham City Jail" and ask them to identify the techniques that elevate this to a great piece of writing:

Perhaps it is easy for those who have never felt the stinging darts of segregation to say, "Wait." But when you have seen vicious mobs lynch your mothers and fathers at will and drown your sisters and brothers at whim; when you have seen hate-filled policemen curse, kick, and even kill your black brothers and sisters; when you

see the vast majority of your 20 million Negro brothers smothering in an airtight
cage of poverty in the midst of an affluent society ... then you will understand why
we find it difficult to wait.

With some prodding, my students notice King's use of complex sentence structures, intentional repetition, semicolons to separate lengthy items in a series, strong diction, and metaphor.

Having students recognize these techniques positions them to infuse them into their own compositions—and I explicitly assign students to do so. For example, as students read *Of Mice and Men*, I highlight Steinbeck's description of the men's living quarters:

The bunk house was a long, rectangular building inside, the walls whitewashed and
the floor unpainted. In three walls there were small, square windows, and in the
fourth, a solid door with a wooden latch. Against the walls were eight bunks, five of
them made up with blankets and the other three showing their burlap ticking. Over
each bunk there was nailed an apple box with the opening forward so that it made
two shelves for the personal belongings of the occupant of the bunk. And these shelves
were loaded with little articles, soap and talcum powder, razors, and those Western
magazines ranch men love to read and scoff at and secretly believe ... . Near one wall
there was a black cast-iron stove, its stovepipe going straight up through the ceiling.
In the middle of the room stood a big square table littered with playing cards, and
around it were grouped boxes for the players to sit on (Steinbeck, 1937/1993, p. 17).

Students then imitate this passage. Here's Eduardo's description of the subway he takes to school each morning:

The #6 trains are rectangular cars linked together, making a silver metal sausage,
with the decal number 6 on the side rectangular windows of the cars. Inside, the
baby-blue seats line both sides of the car, above a black-and-white speckled floor.
People sit opposite each other, sleeping, gazing off into space, or silently wondering
about the lives and problems of their fellow passengers. Metal poles are strategi-
cally placed through the middle of the car, giving standing passengers a place to
grab. Above the seats hang advertisements for sleazy lawyers or television shows,
many of which are inappropriate for the youngsters on the train.

I'm constantly on the lookout for good mentor sentences. Reading Donna Tartt's novel, *The Goldfinch*, I noticed this whopper of a sentence describing the rat race of modern society:

People gambled and golfed and planted gardens and traded stocks and had sex and bought new cars and practiced yoga and worked and prayed and redecorated their homes and got worked up over the news and fussed over their children and gossiped about their neighbors and pored over restaurant reviews and supported political candidates and attended the U.S. Open and dined and traveled and distracted themselves with all kinds of gadgets and devices, flooding themselves incessantly with information and texts and communication and entertainment from every direction to try to make themselves forget it: where we were, what we were.

My students and I examined this sentence, discussing how its intentional excessive length and list of verbs reinforces the pressures of daily living. Students then imitated the sentence, noting the pressures of school. Here is Shaniah's:

Students press their alarm clocks and roll out of bed and get ready for school and wait a long time for the train and arrive to school late and get lectured by the attendance lady for their tardiness and read lots of long novels and study SAT vocabulary and wrestle with chemistry formulas and tackle pre-calculus problems and annotate primary source Civil War documents and work their way through a 6.5 hour day and meet with teachers and have mountains of homework and get report cards and get yelled at by parents and go to study halls and take numerous tests and stress over their grades and sacrifice sleep, just to get to this finish line we call graduation.

Language traditionalists may be shocked that I use such a lengthy sentence for emulation. But I believe it's OK to break the rules if you understand the rules—and if you have a stylistic reason for doing so.

Drafting: Keep Your Eye on the Model

When I sat down to write my first grant proposal, I propped up a previously successful proposal right by my side. As I drafted, I repeatedly returned to this model, taking careful note of its structure, language, syntax, and tone. When my students sit down to write their first drafts, they also benefit from having exemplary models to analyze and imitate as they compose.

These models shouldn't come solely from professional writers. I start students on the process of writing with a model at hand by trying something light. They emulate one of the essays found on the "100 Words" website, which encourages any budding writer to compose and post a piece of writing that's exactly 100 words long. We examine techniques that lead to economical writing. Composing something that's precisely 100 words teaches kids to economize their language, combine and branch sentences, and repeatedly revise until they hit the exact word count.

From there, I move students into deeper waters. Last year, my seniors wrote historical investigations into the events of September 11, 2001. Some of them had never written a three-page paper, but at the end of the unit they'd written papers averaging 25 pages. I used numerous strategies to move my inexperienced writers into writing such in-depth pieces, but perhaps the most effective was allowing them to study exemplary papers from previous years. When students hold models of such research papers in their hands, they pay close attention to structure. They notice tone and voice. They see how research is properly embedded and learn how to write works cited pages. Students need to be allowed to study mentor papers long enough to understand the task at hand (but not long enough for plagiarism to occur).

Students also gain from studying models produced by the adult writer in the classroom—the teacher. I'm not suggesting that we should make students sit still while the teacher drafts an entire essay in front of the class. But teachers should frequently write in 5–7-minute blasts in front of their students, thinking out loud while composing. For those who are reluctant to write in front of students for fear that they may be revealed as mortal, remember that students benefit greatly from seeing their teacher struggle with writing. It reinforces a central notion: that struggle is a central part of the writing process for everyone, even the teacher.

Mentor texts are also effective in improving the writing of highly skilled student writers. Consider, for example, how you might prepare your students to answer this prompt on the 2013 advanced placement exam for the AP English Literature and Composition course:

> *A bildungsroman, or coming-of-age novel, recounts the psychological or moral development of its protagonist from youth to maturity, when this character recognizes his or her place in the world. Select a single pivotal moment in the psychological or moral development of the protagonist of a bildungsroman. Then write a well-organized essay that analyzes how that single moment shapes the meaning of the work as a whole. (College Board, 2013)*

The best advanced placement teachers I know prepare students for rigorous questions like this by having them analyze previously scored essays.[1]

---

1 The College Board posts examples of high-, middle-, and low-quality student essays on its website for teachers and students.

Revision: Modeling Improvement

Comparing model texts with examples of lower-quality writing gives students a lot of insight into how to improve a first draft. Earlier this year, I showed my 8th grade students who were drafting personal narratives two drafts of the beginning of a piece I was working on (see Figure 7.2-1). I wrote Draft A as a typical student would, straightforward in sequence and devoid of the many craft moves we'd want students to make. For Draft B, I wove in craft techniques such as imagery, deliberate repetition, and sentences of varying length. I asked students to pick the draft they thought was best.

Once students recognized that Draft B is better, I had them identify specific elements that made it better. For instance, Grace noted that the first line of Draft B builds suspense; that intentional repetition (of *daring*) is used well; and that dialogue makes this draft livelier. Another craft move Grace highlighted is that this draft first "reveals the moment," then uses

Decide which draft is better and identify elements in the writing that make it better.	
DRAFT A	**DRAFT B**
The day that changed my life was the day my father died.	A tiny blinking red light changed my life.
My father, Big Jim, and his wife, Sylvia, were home that fateful Saturday, preparing to meet some friends for dinner. Before leaving the house, however, my dad decided he needed to water a couple of plants in his greenhouse. He told Sylvia he would be right back. When he did not return, she grew worried and stepped outside to check on him.	It had sat there blinking for a couple of hours before being noticed. Flashing. Daring someone to pay attention to it. Daring someone to push it.
	While it sat there flashing, I went on as if life was normal. I swept the leaves off the back patio. I threw the ball to my dog, Scout. I relaxed, reading my *New Yorker* in the backyard, continuing my "normal" Saturday, oblivious to the little red light flashing a few feet away from me.
She found him slumped over in the greenhouse. She hurriedly ran and called 911. When the paramedics arrived, they told her there was nothing to be done. He had passed away. In a panic, she called my house, but I wasn't home. She got my voicemail and that is where she left the message that my father had died.	As it turns out, I would not be the one to discover the little red flashing light. My daughter, who was home visiting for the day, saw it first. It was my daughter who pushed "play" on the telephone answering machine, and it was she who was the first to hear the fateful words: "Kelly, I have terrible news. We lost your father today ..." It was my daughter's horrific screams that brought me rushing into the house.
I came home shortly after she left the message. Unfortunately, I did not see the red light flashing on the answering machine. A couple of hours went by before my daughter noticed the blinking red light. She was the one who first heard the terrible news.	My father, Big Jim, had died.

FIGURE 7.2-1. Which Draft is Better?

flashback to show what led to that moment. Grace immediately went back to her first draft and started experimenting with sequence.

Yolanda, an inexperienced writer, was drafting a narrative about being stood up by a boy at a dance. She wrote this lead:

> *I was in summer camp and there was a dance that was happening tomorrow night. I decided to ask my first crush, who was Australian. His name was Vincent and we were friends since the second day of camp.*

After examining introductions in other mentor texts, Yolanda changed her lead to this:

> *Where is Vincent? Did he forget? Did he change his mind? Standing alone in a ravishing dress, I am shocked, feeling a heat wave come across my face. Where is that boy?*

If It's Good for Star Wars ...

Before I sat down to write this article, I read through previous issues of *Educational Leadership*, paying close attention to the style and tone of the articles. Once I began drafting, I again revisited these articles, checking to see if what I was writing was aligned with what has traditionally been published in these pages. (For instance, is it OK to use first-person point of view?) Revisiting the articles once more before I actually submitted my article told me my first draft was too long and that I needed to trim a few hundred words.

Having issues of *Educational Leadership* next to me before I wrote, while I wrote, and after I wrote was invaluable. Providing the same level of modeling support to students will prove invaluable to them. If it worked for me—and George Lucas—it will work for your students.

Writing Assessment

Assessing student writing is a challenge. Teachers often focus on what is easy to see: capitalization, punctuation, spelling, and grammar. The message to the writer: "Just make it look good, it doesn't really have to say anything." A scoring guide, or rubric, narrows the focus. If well written a scoring guide clearly describes what the author is expected to do in his or her writing. It guides the writer and it guides the reader.

Scoring guides should be both formative and summative. Students should self-assess as they are composing. Peers should formatively assess one another using the scoring guide. Teachers should use the scoring guide to give feedback for improvement. After many opportunities for success, the same scoring guide is used to provide summative feedback. Not every piece of writing is assessed summatively. There should be many opportunities for students to compose and give feedback without publishing or a formal, final assessment.

Scoring guides may be holistic or analytic. Holistic scoring guides provide a single score on a broad range of skills; they assess the work as a whole. An analytic scoring guide assesses each component of the writing. Both provide helpful feedback to the author. Trait-based scoring guides are most often analytic with established criteria for each trait. Scoring guides should be revised, just like a great piece of writing, to provide clear expectations for the writer and the reader.

BEFORE READING

When have you used scoring guides? Were you the writer or the assessor? What was your experience?

DURING READING

How does the author's experience with scoring guides match yours? differ from yours?

AFTER READING

What challenges do you anticipate when using scoring guides? What will you do that you aren't currently doing? Do you think it is important to focus most of your instruction and student attention on craft (ideas, organization, voice, word choice, sentence fluency, and presentation) with limited focus on conventions? Why or why not?

What Student Writing Can Teach Us

BY MARK OVERMEYER

"If you read carefully, a poem will teach you how to read it."

This comment came from Jake York, a poet and teacher who was facilitating a summer institute workshop offered by the Denver Writing Project. I immediately copied this statement into my writer's notebook. Jake had been helping us unravel the meaning behind a tricky poem. He kept encouraging us to stick with it and assured us we would be rewarded with greater understanding. Because my work as a district literacy coordinator means I lead teachers in carefully examining and assessing student writing, I began to wonder whether it is possible to read student writing in the same way Jake suggested we read poetry.

Can student writing "teach" us how to read it if we look carefully at what the writer has to say, where the writer shines in saying it, and what instruction would increase the writer's polish? And if so, can we use this technique of careful reading as a kind of formative assessment to guide instruction? And can the rubrics now so common in evaluating student writing help teachers read more deeply?

Moving Beyond the Score

Teachers use rubrics, scoring guides that define expectations at various performance levels, to guide their reading of student work. When any group of teachers meets to assess student writing, their first step is often to examine the rubric. Rubrics are meant to make the scoring of writing less subjective, but although this is a laudable goal, I have seen teachers in many scoring sessions wrestle to reach agreement on a particular score.

In my school district, which is heavily involved in using rubrics to examine student work, teachers often spend many hours scoring and cross-scoring samples of writing, determining which pieces best reflect various performance levels. Some good comes from this: We have raised our expectations for student writing, and we are more transparent about what we expect. But when our thinking doesn't move beyond reaching a score in these meetings, we are not taking advantage of what the writing can teach us.

Last spring, I worked with a group of about 20 teachers from grades K–12 in my district. We were meeting to align our district's benchmarks document with actual student writing samples. During one particular session, we decided to discuss one piece in a large group to clarify our own thinking. We chose the following 4th grade piece:

> *My favorite place to play is my bedroom. My bedroom is painted extremely light pink. Also I have a peanut-colored carpet. It is full of meowing. It never stops! Most of the time I play by myself. My friend Megan comes over sometimes. When Megan is in my room we play Pokemon Stadium. Another thing we do is play with my multicolored cat. Her name is Maxie. We throw a lime green toy mouse for Maxie and she sprints after it. Megan and I also throw a ball for Maxie to get. We also play Conga sometimes. I play in my room at 3:30 pm with Megan. I like to play in my room because it is very fun and it is mine. I love to play in my room!*

We spent about 15 minutes debating whether the student scored a *4, 3,* or *2* based on our state-designed writing rubric (see Table 7.3-1). Several teachers scored the paper a *2,* eight teachers scored it a *3,* and the rest gave it a *4.* That means this student could either be marked as an advanced, proficient, or partially proficient writer. The inconsistency concerned me because if a student consistently scores below proficient on standardized assessments in my district, then the school must develop a learning plan, hold a parent conference, and discuss interventions for the student. So if we intend for rubrics to clarify, how did this group of teachers end up in a potentially high-stakes debate on this student? And why did we spend 15 minutes talking about a score without thinking about how this piece might inform our instruction for this writer? If rubrics are to be used successfully for formative assessment, we must look beyond the search for a score.

Score Level	Content and Organization	Style and Fluency
4	• Supporting details are relevant and provide important information about the topic. • The writing has balance; the main idea stands out from the details. • The writer seems in control and develops the topic in a logical, organized way. • The writer connects ideas to the specified purpose.	• The writer selects words that are accurate, specific, and appropriate for the specified purpose. • The writer may experiment with words and/or use figurative language and/or imagery. • The writer uses a variety of sentence structures. • The writing is readable, neat, and nearly error-free.
3	• The writer has defined but not thoroughly developed the topic, idea, or story line. • Some supporting details are relevant but limited or overly general or less important. • The writer makes general observations without using specific details or does not delineate the main idea from the details. • The writer attempts to develop the topic in an organized way but may falter in either logic or organization. • The writer connects ideas with the specified topic implicitly rather than explicitly.	• The writer mostly selects words that are accurate, specific, and appropriate for the purpose of the writing. • The writer uses age-appropriate words that are accurate but may lack precision. • The writer uses simple but accurate sentence structures. • Errors in language usage, spelling, and mechanics do not impede communication.
2	• The writer has defined but not thoroughly developed the topic, idea, or story line; response may be unclear or sketchy or may read like a collection of thoughts from which no central idea emerges. • Supporting details are minimal or irrelevant or no distinction is made between main ideas and details. • The writer does not develop the topic in an organized way; response may be a list rather than a developed paragraph. • Ideas are not connected to the specified purpose.	• The writer sometimes selects words that are not accurate, specific, or appropriate for the purpose of the writing. • Writing may be choppy or repetitive. • Portions of the writing are unreadable or messy; errors may impede communication in some portions of the response.
1	• The writer has not defined the topic, idea, or story line. • Supporting details are absent. • Organization is not evident; may be a brief list. • Ideas are fragmented and unconnected with the specified purpose.	• Much of the writing is unreadable or messy. • Word choice is inaccurate or there are many repetitions. • Vocabulary is age-inappropriate. • The writer uses simple, repetitive sentence structures or many sentence fragments. • Errors severely impede communication.
0	• The response is off-topic or unreadable.	• The response is off-topic or unreadable.

TABLE 7.3-1. Holistic Writing Rubric for the Short Constructed-Response Task—Grades 4-10.

Courtesy of Unit of Assessment, Colorado Department of Education. This material also appeared in *When Writing Workshop Isn't Working*, by Mark Overmeyer, 2005, Portland, ME: Stenhouse. Used with permission.

Using Rubrics Formatively

Holistic rubrics that give only one score—which evaluators often use for state and national testing—are particularly difficult to use for informing instruction because the assessor cannot separate out individual qualities of the writing. Each piece can only receive one score. Trait-based rubrics lend themselves better to differentiated comments, but assessors still must give a single score for each trait. So even if a piece has strengths, readers can't highlight strengths fairly in the push to give the entire paper one mark. But teachers can, and should, adapt rubrics to serve the purposes of guiding our instruction as well as the purposes of testing.

When the teacher group I lead in finding exemplars for our district finally moved the conversation away from scoring the 4th grader's paragraph, we engaged in discussion about what this writer did well and how she could improve. We all agreed that the student clearly stayed on the topic, provided sufficient supporting details, and showed some strong word choice. We soon began discussing instructional strategies, which is a crucial step in assessing student writing. Everyone agreed that although specificity and rich vocabulary were the writer's strong suit, she could benefit from thinking about how to organize details within a piece of writing. This experience helped us realize as a group that the goal of looking at student writing must be to develop strategies to help students write better.

Signaling Strengths and Weaknesses

Because our group began focusing more on how to help teachers see our thinking about each piece of writing, we had to devise a format that would show teachers that deeper thinking and give them a model for using a rubric to inform instruction. Our goal was to provide a more helpful document than a tidy, completed rubric. We created a chart on writing strengths and weaknesses (shown in Table 7.3-2). This format draws from the state-created rubric (Table 7.3-1) but shows how a teacher can annotate student work in such a way as to discover what to teach a student next—in other words, to hear what the writing has to teach.

Table 7.3-2 shows how we pinpointed strengths and weaknesses for the 4th grader's piece on her room. It indicates which benchmarks from the rubric this writer meets (such as including relevant details), which benchmarks need more work (such as organization), and a few suggested next steps (such as creating a bulleted list). Comments on a chart like this can

Meets or Exceeds These Benchmarks	Does Not Meet These Benchmarks	Suggested Next Instructional Strategies
• Supporting details are relevant. • The writer connects ideas to the specified purpose. • The writer selects words that are accurate and specific. • The writer uses a variety of sentence structures. • The writing is nearly error-free.	• The writer seems in control and develops the topic in an organized way.	• This student may benefit from creating a bulleted list or a graphic organizer prior to writing. • The teacher can ask the student to read through the piece aloud to clarify any confusing details.

Sample chart annotating a piece of writing's strengths and weaknesses in terms of benchmarks on a standardized rubric. Benchmarks are drawn from the Colorado Department of Education's rubric for student writing.

Source: Overmeyer, M. (2007/2008). What Student Writing Can Teach Us. *Educational Leadership*, 65(4) [Online].

TABLE 7.3-2. Strengths and Weaknesses Found in a 4th Grader's Essay.

be directly aligned to the rubric, as shown here, or be based on teacher discussion. Either way, the goal is to read more deeply and go for teaching points.

We explained to administrators and curriculum leaders in language arts departments throughout the district our thinking about how student writing samples can be used to inform instruction and made this annotated format accessible on our district Web site. Teachers at all grade levels have used the format to work with student writing.

Like a well-written poem, each piece of student writing can teach us how to read it—and how to read the author's needs. Every piece of writing we collect from students can become part of formative assessment.

CPSIA information can be obtained
at www.ICGtesting.com
Printed in the USA
LVOW09s2309241016

510084LV00001B/1/P